THE PRESIDENT ON CAPITOL HILL

JEFFREY E. COHEN

THE PRESIDENT ON CAPITOL HILL

A Theory of Institutional Influence

Columbia University Press / New York

Columbia University Press
Publishers Since 1893
New York   Chichester, West Sussex
cup.columbia.edu

Library of Congress Cataloging-in-Publication Data
Names: Cohen, Jeffrey E., author.
Title: The president on Capitol Hill : a theory of institutional influence /
Jeffrey E. Cohen.
Description: New York : Columbia University Press, [2019] |
Includes bibliographical references and index.
Identifiers: LCCN 2018040235 (print) | LCCN 2018046015 (ebook) |
ISBN 9780231548199 (electronic) | ISBN 9780231189149 (cloth : acid-free paper) |
ISBN 9780231189156 (pbk.)-Subjects: LCSH: Presidents—United States. |
Executive-legislative relations—United States. | Executive power—
United States. | United States. Congress—Voting.
Classification: LCC JK585 (ebook) | LCC JK585 .C557 2019 (print) |
DDC 328.73/07456—dc23
LC record available at https://lccn.loc.gov/2018040235

Columbia University Press books are printed on permanent
and durable acid-free paper.

Printed in the United States of America

Cover design: Milenda Nan Ok Lee
Cover art: © Shutterstock

CONTENTS

CONTENTS

ACKNOWLEDGMENTS

THIS BOOK WAS a long time in the making, the seeds planted when I was a graduate student, more than forty years ago. Over the years, I have benefited immensely from having a large number of colleagues who generously offered their time to listen to my ideas and projects, offering advice, support, and inspiration. Three stand out for the numerous conversations about the presidency and about doing research on the presidency, and for their collegiality and friendship—Richard Fleisher, Jon Bond, and George Edwards. Although at times I take on some of their important work, this book would not have been possible without their prior research. I also want to thank one of my erstwhile coauthors, Brandon Rottinghaus, who patiently listened to me prattle on about this project.

The readers for Columbia University Press, Sharece Thrower of Vanderbilt University and Douglas Kriner of Cornell University, deserve a thank you. Their suggestions greatly improved this book. Stephen Wesley, the political science editor, also merits singling out for his enthusiasm and patience. Unlike many presses these days, Columbia University Press not only makes quality research a top priority but also pours generous resources into book preparation and production. It has been a joy to work with the press and its staff.

Finally, this book is dedicated to PJ. With all my love.

1

ON PRESIDENTIAL INFLUENCE
IN CONGRESS

I N THEIR SEMINAL study *The President in the Legislative Arena*, Jon R. Bond and Richard Fleisher make the important conceptual distinction between presidential success and influence in Congress. Prior to their work, scholars often used the terms "influence" and "success" interchangeably.[1] As Bond and Fleisher (1990) define it, "success" is whether the president wins or loses on a roll call, whether "the president's positions prevail" (ix). In contrast, "influence" is the ability of the president to change a member's roll call vote from opposing to voting with the executive. Influence may lead to success if the president can shift enough members on their roll call votes to transform the outcome from defeat to victory.[2]

Bond and Fleisher (1990) argue that "the question of success is broader and thus more important than the question of influence" (ix).[3] Success, they argue, ultimately relates to the production of public policies and thus has important implications for democratic theory as well as for representation, responsiveness, and accountability. Much research on presidential–congressional relations has followed Bond and Fleisher's lead, focusing on success rather than influence. *The President in the Legislative Arena* has made a seminal contribution to and produced a lasting legacy for the study of presidential–congressional relations.

Bond and Fleisher are undeniably correct that it is important to study success. But just as an exclusive focus on presidential influence may be too narrow, as Bond and Fleisher argue, because it neglects the question of success and policy production, an exclusive focus on success to the neglect of influence may also be too narrow, to the detriment of a fuller understanding of presidential–congressional relations, especially the linkage between influence and success.

Consider, for instance, some implications of studying only presidential success. First, studies tend to find that important factors accounting for a president's success generally are beyond the executive's ability to affect in a measurable way. For instance, considerable research identifies party control and polarization in Congress, and to a lesser extent presidential approval, as affecting presidential success in Congress (Bond, Fleisher, and Cohen 2015; Cohen, Bond, and Fleisher 2013, 2014). When the president's party controls Congress, presidents will be more successful than when the opposition party controls the legislature.[4] But presidents are unable to do much about these factors. As Bert Rockman (1981) has noted, success is "frequently inextricable from dumb luck" (211). That is, presidents are either successful or they are not, not because of anything they do or because of who they are but because they happen to be in office when, for instance, their party controls the chambers of Congress.

Furthermore, an exclusive focus on success renders presidents relatively uninteresting to study. If presidents have little if any impact on what Congress does when making policy, why study the presidency and its role in the legislative policy-making process? To push this line of argument further, instead of studying presidential success in Congress, we should be studying the legislative production of policy, some of which the president just happens to support or oppose. In other words, this type of focus on success, which argues that presidents can do little to improve the likelihood of success and are captives of political structures, alignments, and forces during their time in office, denies the president *human agency*, at least for legislating, with "agency" here conceived as the ability of the president to influence or affect others, such as legislators.[5]

Lawrence R. Jacobs and Desmond S. King make a similar argument, that agency is important for understanding presidential behavior, and they are careful not to reduce theories of presidential behavior and agency to personality.[6] Rather, the actions of presidents, their agency, is best understood in the context of the circumstances they face, such as political structures and conditions, or what Jacobs and King (2010) call the "structured agency" approach: "Presidents have opportunities to lead, but not under the circumstances they choose or control. These circumstances both restrict the parameters of presidential impact and highlight the significance of presidential skill in accurately identifying and exploiting opportunities" (794). The theory developed in the present book has much in common with Jacobs and King's structured agency perspective.

Similarly, if presidential actions are ineffective, if they have no impact, at least in the halls of Congress, why do presidents work so hard trying to get members to vote on their side of an issue so that their policy proposal will prevail? Why don't presidents spend their time doing other things, at which they might be more effective, which will derive greater net benefits, or which just may be more fun? Maybe it is the case, as some argue (e.g., Edwards 1990), that presidents are misguided and/or overconfident in assessing their ability to influence members of Congress. Perhaps presidential engagement in the legislative process is defensive, aimed at blocking Congress from enacting unacceptable policies (Godwin and Ilderton 2014).[7] Yet a growing body of research is finding that the strategic behaviors of presidents can influence both the voting behavior of members on roll calls and legislative outcomes (Beckmann 2010; Cameron 2000; Cameron and Park 2011; Canes-Wrone 2006; Cohen 2012; Hassell and Kernell 2016; Howell, Jackman, and Rogowski 2013; Marshall and Prins 2007; Sullivan 1990a).

The portrait of presidents as ineffectual, the argument that dumb luck accounts for success, also runs counter to another influential theory of the presidency, the modern presidency. Although it is not explicit in the literature on the modern presidency, there is an underlying assumption that modern presidents are more consequential, that is, more influential, in politics and policy making than premodern executives. In his important and seminal definition of the modern presidency, Fred I. Greenstein (1978, 1988) identifies four differences between modern and premodern presidents:

1. Modern presidents have far greater formal and informal power to make decisions on their own initiative . . .

2. Modern presidents have come to be the chief agenda setters in federal-level policy-making . . .

3. Modern presidents have been provided with a major staff and advisory capacity . . .

4. Modern presidents have become by far the most visible actors in the political system . . . (Greenstein 1988, 4)

Several important implications flow from Greenstein's definition of the modern presidency. Modern presidents will be more active in policy making, including the legislative policy-making process. And they are likely to be more influential than premodern executives in policy making. This is not to argue that modern presidents get everything they want from Congress. Obstacles stand in the way of complete presidential dominance of Congress, perhaps most importantly the inability of presidents to command Congress to follow their lead. But both the public and Congress expect modern presidents to play an active leadership role in forging policy and moving it toward enactment (Mervin 1987, 84). Those expectations, as well as the enhanced institutional resources that Greenstein identifies, should provide modern presidents with some advantages over premodern executives in dealing with Congress. The theory of the modern president is thus to some extent about presidential influence and how that influence grew, from the premodern to the modern era. A full understanding of the evolution of the office must assess the relative influence of premodern and modern presidents in their interactions with Congress.[8]

Lindsay and Steger (1993) make a similar point in their critique of the literature on the "two presidencies," the idea that presidents have more influence over foreign policy making than over domestic policy. As they state, "The question of presidential *influence* in Congress forms the core of the two presidencies literature." (108, emphasis mine).

Finally, it is important to address the question of whether presidents have enough influence to affect congressional outcomes—that is, does influence lead to higher success levels? Bond and Fleisher (1990) suggest the possibility that "presidential influence may increase success" (2). But the more commonly held view is that presidents have little influence (e.g., Edwards

1980, 1990, 2009b, 2012, 2016). Influence, therefore, is not likely to contribute in any meaningful or systematic way to success.

I argue that much past research has underestimated the amount of or potential for presidential influence.[9] This underestimation results from the way past research has conceptualized influence and the data used to assess how much influence presidents possess. This is not to argue that presidents are so influential as to get everything they want from Congress, that they can dominate the legislative policy-making process. They cannot. But presidential influence may be the deciding factor in winning some roll call votes that the president's side would otherwise have lost. Simply put, influence leads to higher success rates.

To make the claim that presidents have more influence than was previously thought, we need to think of influence as coming from the resources that presidents possess and the strategies that they employ, rather than viewing influence as a personal attribute of the individuals who occupy the office. This way of thinking about the institutional and strategic foundations of presidential influence leads to a new measurement approach. Before discussing this institutional-strategic conceptualization of presidential influence and the measurement strategy in detail, we will first discuss the reasons why past research has underestimated the amount of presidential influence in Congress.

THE UNDERESTIMATION OF PRESIDENTIAL INFLUENCE IN CONGRESS

In contrast to the view of much existing research, the argument here is that presidents have more influence in Congress than was previously recognized and that influence leads to increased success. Due to the president's influence, which I will define as the president's ability to move members of Congress to vote with him on roll calls, the president's side will win on a measurable number of roll calls that it would lose absent that influence. This represents a different understanding of presidential influence than is found in much of the literature, which contends that presidents have little if any ability to influence members to change their roll call behavior (e.g., Edwards 1980, 1990, 2009b, 2012, 2016; Bond and Fleisher 1990).

According to the perspective advanced in the present study, much past research has underestimated the amount of influence presidents have in Congress. To be sure, presidential influence is not so great that it can determine the outcome on any roll call on which the president decides to take a public stance. But for a substantively significant number of roll calls, the president's influence is important enough to turn a loss into a victory. Influence thus has implications for success, as Bond and Fleisher (1990) speculated may be the case.

One reason for the underestimation of presidential influence derives from the way it has been conceptualized. Past research has tended to view influence primarily as a personal attribute or trait of presidents (Wayne 2009; Beckmann 2010, 14–16). Rather than conceptualizing influence in personal terms, such as a president's skill or personality, this study views presidential influence as emerging from strategic decision making, in which presidents leverage institutional resources, including aspects of the political context, to their advantage.[10] Here, therefore, I develop a theory of the president's *institutional influence* with Congress, to differentiate my study from those that view presidential influence as primarily personal in nature.

A second reason for past underestimation of the amount of presidential influence is that previous studies have used only roll calls on which the president *has already taken a position*. The argument here is that presidents also accrue some influence merely by taking positions on roll calls. The reasons that presidents take such positions are many and varied. For instance, they may take positions to be associated with the winning side, to claim credit, because of prior commitments, to repay voters and groups for their support, and/or to attract new supporters.[11] But presidents also take positions to influence how members of Congress will vote on the roll call, to maximize the likelihood that the president's side will win the floor vote and thus to move the bill toward eventual enactment. There are times and conditions when it is useful to conceptualize presidential roll call position taking as *presidential lobbying* of Congress.

By taking a position, presidents transform for members of Congress the meaning of a roll call, from a roll call in which the president is not a very important consideration, what I will term a "nonpresidential" roll call, into a "presidential" roll call, in which members take into account the president's preferences when deciding how to vote. A president thus need not do anything other than announce a position on a roll call to influence (some) members of Congress. But presidents may do more than merely announce a position. For instance, they may work with leaders to structure the choices on which members will vote, what Beckmann (2010) calls earlygame agenda setting. They also may bargain with members or visit member districts to apply local political pressures on the member, among other things, to win a member's vote.

To measure the total amount of presidential influence, we need to take into account both the amount of influence that presidents receive from taking a position and the amount associated with their actions after taking a position. Figure 1.1 presents a schematic. Past research generally only looks at influence after the president has taken a position, the far-right box in the figure. The total amount of influence, however, should also include the influence that the president receives from position taking itself.

Ideally, to estimate the total amount of presidential influence, we want to know a member's vote intention both before and after the president has taken a position. The amount of presidential influence would compare the number of votes the president's side would receive both before and after the president takes a position. Thus, presidents will be influential if the number of votes on the president's side after the president has taken a position is larger than the number before taking the position. If there is no difference in the number of presidential votes before and after taking a position,

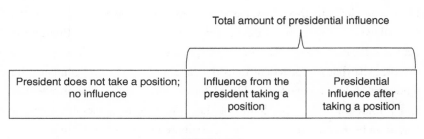

FIGURE 1.1

Components of presidential influence on congressional roll call voting then the president does not have any influence. And if the number of votes after the president takes a position is less than that before taking a position, then the president has negative influence. This perspective on influence is rooted in classical understandings of the concept (e.g., Dahl 1957). To a degree, it is an empirical question whether presidents are influential with members of Congress and, if so, whether they possess enough influence to convert losses into victories.

But, for a variety of reasons, we are unlikely to recover information on members' roll call preferences prior to the president taking a position. Members may stay silent about their vote intention to extract concessions from the administration, such as modifications to the bill or to some other bills. Members may even lie or dissemble about their vote intentions, perhaps for the same strategic reasons. Other members may not decide on a position on an issue until they see how the issue is defined, who lines up on which side, and which side is likely to win.[12] Moreover, inasmuch as presidents can set the congressional agenda, a member may not have a position on an issue until after the president *makes* it an issue—such as, for instance, by submitting legislation to Congress.

Absent the ability to identify members' roll call vote intentions prior to the president taking a position, I take a different tack in the present study by comparing the roll call behavior of members on *nonpresidential* and *presidential* roll calls. There are several complications in assessing the amount of presidential influence when making such comparisons. One is identifying the president's side of a vote when the executive does not take a roll call position. When the president takes a roll call position, it is relatively easy to determine whether the member voted on the same side as the president. Here, I develop a methodology, based on the work of Fowler and Hall (2013), that allows a comparison of member voting on presidential and nonpresidential roll calls. Thus, rather than trying to identify the president's position on roll calls that the president does not take a position on, I compare the tendency of a member to vote liberal (or conservative) on nonpresidential and presidential roll calls. Some of the difference in a member's voting record on both sets of roll calls may be attributed to presidential influence.

The second complication in comparing presidential with nonpresidential roll calls is that presidential roll calls are not a random sample of all roll calls, that is, there are systematic differences between presidential and nonpresidential roll calls. For instance, the two sets of votes may concern different types of issues (such as foreign versus domestic) and may differ in terms of political salience—the political salience of an issue may increase merely because the president enters the debate by taking a position. And, as Frances Lee (2008, 2009) has demonstrated, party polarization is higher on presidential than on nonpresidential roll calls.

Much of the empirical work here tries to control for these systematic differences between nonpresidential and presidential roll calls. I use several approaches to deal with these complications, including quasi-experimental treatment effects analysis in the presence of multiple treatments. All the analyses suggest differences in the voting patterns of members on presidential and nonpresidential roll calls, to the president's advantage, and suggests that this difference in roll call voting results in the president's side winning on some roll calls that it otherwise would have lost.[13]

The primary data for this study consists of all roll calls in the House of Representatives from 1953 to 2012, nearly 27,000 roll calls, with the president taking positions on approximately 20%. Another set of analyses pushes the data back to 1877 to 1952 inclusive, adding nearly 9,000 more roll calls, with the president taking positions on approximately 14% of those roll calls. This more historically expansive data set is used to test propositions about the relative influence of modern and premodern presidents.

PLAN OF THIS BOOK

Chapter 2 presents the theory of presidential influence in Congress. Presidential influence requires a member's preference or position on a roll call to change as a result of a presidential action. Presidential action to influence a member's vote is called presidential lobbying. Presidents lobby members either directly or indirectly. Direct lobbying entails presidents targeting specific members for their votes, while indirect lobbying is when the president activates aspects of the political environment, such as party loyalty or constituent preferences, to put pressure on members. Presidential influence, however, is only interesting if enough members change their votes to alter the outcome of a roll call so that the president's side wins, that is, if presidents have enough influence to affect the production of public policy.

Two elements of the theory are rarely observed: changes in member votes in response to presidential lobbying and presidential lobbying itself. Chapter 3 deals with these concerns to enable empirical tests of the theory. First, I conceptualize presidential position taking on roll calls as a generic form of presidential lobbying. Position taking thus encompasses the variety of ways in which a president lobbies Congress publicly. Then, roll calls may be classified as those on which the president takes positions and those on which the president does *not* take positions, or presidential and nonpresidential roll calls. My argument is that some of the difference in member votes on presidential and nonpresidential roll calls is a result of presidential lobbying.

There are two major issues with simply comparing member voting on presidential and nonpresidential roll calls as a way of estimating the amount of presidential influence. First, the two sets may differ systematically. Presidential roll calls are not a random subset of all roll calls. Second, presidents may have motivations to take a position besides lobbying members for their votes. Chapter 4 deals with these concerns, employing a variety of techniques on all House roll calls from 1953 through 2012. Results of these efforts suggest that presidents have a measurable amount of influence on enough members to affect the outcome of the roll call. Presidents' influence, therefore, can affect the production of public policy.

The next several chapters empirically test other implications of the theory. Chapters 5 through 7 investigate several indirect pathways of presidential influence: party (chapter 5), policy type (chapter 6), and public opinion (chapter 7). Analysis finds that each of these pathways affects member roll call voting.

Chapter 5 finds that presidents are more influential when their party is in control of the House and among co-partisans than when the president's party is in the minority and among opposition members. Importantly, presidents appear to have considerable influence on co-partisans but essentially no influence over opposition members.

Chapter 6 asks whether presidents have more influence on foreign than on domestic policy, the venerable *two presidencies* question. Overall, presidents do not appear to be more influential on foreign than on domestic policy, countering much of the research on the two presidencies thesis. But they appear more influential on opposition members than on co-partisans. The chapter also investigates the breakdown of the Cold War consensus, which was the basis for foreign policy making from 1953 until the Vietnam War era. As bipartisanship in foreign policy making gave way, presidential influence on foreign policy also fell. Opposition members in the post–Cold War era are more resistant to presidential influence than they were during the earlier era, when bipartisanship was an important element of foreign policy making.

Chapter 7 looks at the effect of public opinion on presidential influence. Most research on public opinion as a presidential resource focuses on approval. This chapter looks at approval but also at issue salience, or the importance of an issue to voters. Both aspects of public opinion provide the president with a resource to influence member roll call voting, but salience appears to have stronger and more substantively meaningful impacts than does approval.

Chapter 8 turns to the direct pathway of presidential influence, introducing the concept of *presidential lobbying effort*. Lobbying effort refers to the amount of work and resources that presidents deploy to convince members to support them. There is considerable debate over whether lobbying effort is effective. The chapter integrates the several strands of existing literature, offering a conditional lobbying effects theory. Low to medium levels of presidential lobbying efforts will have a positive effect on member voting, but high effort levels are not as effective. This curvilinear pattern is due to the reactive nature of the presidential lobbying effort decision. Presidents tend to exert only enough effort to win. When they are faced with a weak opposition, presidents do not have to lobby hard to win. When they face a stronger opposition, greater presidential lobbying effort is required, but it will not always result in victory. Analysis finds support for this conditional, curvilinear idea. Furthermore, co-partisans respond with increasing support as presidential lobbying effort intensifies but opposition members exhibit a curvilinear pattern, recoiling from the president at high lobbying effort levels, probably an indication of the counterlobbying by opponents to the president.

Chapters 9 and 10 turn to premodern presidents, especially those serving from 1877 to 1952. The theory of the modern presidency is a theory of presidential influence—that modern presidents wield more influence than do premodern executives. This theory is rarely empirically examined. Chapter 9 reviews the historical record on the legislative activity and influence of premodern presidents serving in the late nineteenth century, the supposed nadir of presidential influence and a crucial comparison point with modern presidents. There is important revisionist scholarship concerning presidents from 1877 to 1900. Although this revisionism does not claim that these presidents are as active and influential as modern presidents, it does argue that the late nineteenth-century presidents were not complete patsies either.

Chapter 10 offers an empirical comparison between presidents from 1877 to 1952 and those serving from 1953 to 2012, using the techniques developed here. Testing the modern presidency hypothesis requires comparable data on modern and premodern presidents. Presidents serving from 1877 to 1932 were categorized as "premodern," those serving from 1932 to 1952 as "early modern," and those serving from 1953 to 2012 as "later modern." Analysis finds that premodern presidents were less influential than both early and later modern presidents but also that the early moderns, Franklin Roosevelt and Harry Truman, were not as influential as the later moderns. This finding has implications for dating the development and onset of the modern presidency.

The concluding chapter summarizes the basic argument and findings. Then it critiques the study itself, outlining its major limitations, and makes suggestions for future research. The message of the study is that presidents can influence some members some of the time, and they can influence enough member to alter the outcome of a roll call frequently enough to affect the production of public policy. Presidential influence has consequences not only for relations between the president and Congress but for government policies as well. Presidential influence is therefore a topic worthy of study.

2

A THEORY OF PRESIDENTIAL
INFLUENCE IN CONGRESS

T HIS CHAPTER PRESENTS the theory of *presidential institutional influence* in Congress. Although the theory offered here grows out of existing research on presidential influence, it differs from that research in several ways. First, it views presidential position taking as sometimes an attempt to influence how members of Congress will vote on roll calls. In other words, position taking is a generic form of presidential lobbying and subsumes all forms of public presidential lobbying of members of Congress for their support.[1]

Second, the theory assumes that presidents are rational actors when it comes to taking positions on roll calls. Since position taking (and lobbying more broadly) also has costs, presidents will take positions for lobbying purposes when they think that the payoff from position taking is greater than its costs. The theory also recognizes that presidents take positions on roll calls for purposes other than lobbying members on roll calls, such as to claim credit and/or to repay voters and interest groups for their electoral support, among other reasons. An empirical complication, dealt with in succeeding chapters, is distinguishing position taking as lobbying of Congress from presidential position taking for other reasons.[2]

Finally, the theory identifies several mechanisms through which position taking influences members' roll call behavior. Presidents may couple position taking with additional, directed activities to secure the support of specific members. This may include bargaining, offering inducements, going public, and so forth, which we commonly think of as lobbying but which is useful to think of as *overt presidential lobbying*. But position taking may influence member roll call behavior without the president engaging in any overt lobbying activities. When a president takes a roll call position, the association between the president and the contextual factors that may also affect the member's vote, such as partisanship, type of issue, and presidential approval, is tightened because the roll call has been converted from a nonpresidential to a presidential one and members, in deciding how to cast their roll call votes, will begin to consider the president's preferences. In other words, presidential position taking interacts with other factors that may affect member roll call voting, such as partisanship, constituent opinion, and policy type. For nonpresidential roll calls, the president plays little or no role in the member's roll call calculus.

Before turning to the theory of *institutional presidential influence*, I will review several perspectives on how presidential influence has been treated in past research. Then I will define presidential influence as used in this study and present the theory.

PERSPECTIVES ON PRESIDENTIAL INFLUENCE

There are three prominent perspectives on the nature of presidential influence: personal influence, as exemplified in the work of Richard Neustadt; George Edwards's argument that presidents are not particularly influential; and strategic actor models that argue that, under some conditions, presidents can be influential. These approaches to understanding the nature of presidential influence serve as an important foundation and backdrop for this study.

The first perspective on presidential influence traces to Neustadt's book *Presidential Power*, first published in 1960 and updated in several editions. (The discussion here uses the 1991 edition.) Neustadt somewhat interchangeably uses the terms "power," "influence," and "persuasion." (In this study, I am going to use the term "influence" instead of "power," for the sake of clarity, noting that "power" and "influence" are often used interchangeably.)[3] Neustadt (1991) defines presidential power as the president's ability to *persuade*: "The essence of a President's persuasive task is to convince such men that what the White House wants of them is what they ought to do for their sake and on their authority" (30). Further, the president's "strength or weakness, then, turns on his personal capacity to influence the men who make up government" (4).

According to Neustadt, presidents must resort to persuasion because of the inherent institutional weakness of the office, which restricts the president's command authority. Since the chief executive cannot command others to follow, except under certain circumstances, the president must use other means, primarily persuasion, to get others to go along. Presidents are persuasive, in Neustadt's framework, when they change the preferences and/ or self-interest calculations of others such that those others will support the president even though they previously had opposed the executive. In this sense, Neustadt's understanding of persuasion closely resembles Robert Dahl's (1957) famous definition of power: the ability of X to get Y to do something Y would otherwise not do. Importantly, Neustadt does not argue that presidents always are influential but only that they have potential influence and can influence others if they are persuasive.

George Edwards (1990, 2009b, 2012, 2016) has refined our understanding of presidential influence. He argues that many commentators misunderstand the nature of presidential leadership, persuasion, and influence. Those commentators lay the blame for presidential defeats at the feet of the president, as due to, for example, the unwillingness or ineptitude of presidents in pressing their case with the people and/or with Congress. Edwards rightly argues that presidents are highly limited in creating opportunities to influence Congress. Instead, the context in which presidents govern is generally fixed, and presidents can do little to fundamentally alter that context. For instance, the president's strategic context may have these properties: congressional perceptions about whether the president has a mandate, whether the president's party controls Congress, and the degree of polarization between the congressional parties (Edwards 2016, 8). Presidents cannot do much, if anything, about these contextual factors. Rather, to understand presidential leadership, according to Edwards, we should focus on how presidents exploit those opportunities that are presented, and at the same time we must be cognizant of how the context constrains the president.[4]

The third perspective on presidential influence utilizes game theory and spatial modeling. This approach views presidents as strategic actors, with the context (political and otherwise) structuring their strategic decisions.[5] For example, Beckmann's (2010) model argues that presidents will be more influential if they follow an earlygame rather than an endgame approach to moving legislation through Congress. The earlygame approach derives from work on agenda setting, in which the agenda setter can structure the choices presented for members of Congress to vote on. Presidents, for example, may be able to keep "killer amendments" from reaching the floor, increasing the odds that the president's alternative will only be matched against less popular alternatives and thus increasing the prospects that the president's alternative will be passed and enacted. Endgame strategies are employed once the agenda has been set, and according to Beckmann, are less efficient for the president because massive effort and resources must be expended to secure votes compared to the earlygame strategy. Importantly, Beckmann also specifies different earlygame strategies for the president depending upon whether the president's party is in the majority or the minority, a recognition of how context structures presidential strategies.

There is considerable similarity between the strategic perspective and Edwards's exploiting-of-opportunities orientation. Both emphasize the importance of the surrounding context for understanding presidential behavior and accomplishment. Yet the strategic approach seems to suggest that sometimes presidents will possess a significant degree of influence, based upon existing strategic options.

DEFINING PRESIDENTIAL INFLUENCE IN CONGRESS

Presidential influence with a member of Congress on a roll call in this study is defined as when the president gets the member to vote differently from how the member would have voted had the president not tried to change the member's vote. We would observe presidential influence if, for instance, a member changes her vote from an expected nay to a yea, or from yea to nay, because the president acted on or targeted the member and tried to alter the member's expected vote. This is a conventional definition of influence, with roots in Dahl's (1957) definition of power.[6] It is also consistent with Neustadt (1960, 1991), with Edwards (1976), and with other studies' understanding of presidential influence in Congress.[7]

I define presidential lobbying as any action that the president takes to try to change a member's expected vote. Lobbying can take many forms or modes, including going public, threatening vetoes, election campaigning, personal appeals to members, bargaining with members, arm-twisting, providing services to members, and the like. The discussion here is less concerned with any particular lobbying mode than with presidential lobbying in general. Furthermore, we need to distinguish between lobbying mode and lobbying effort. Lobbying effort concerns the amount of time, resources, and so forth that the president deploys when lobbying Congress. Lobbying effort is dealt with in detail in chapter 8.

Figure 2.1 illustrates presidential influence on a member of Congress. In the figure, C represents the member's expected roll call vote prior to the president taking a position and/or lobbying the member, C' is the member's roll call vote after the president has lobbied the member, and P is the president's preferred policy outcome on the roll call. The figure identifies two regions: the region to the left is a nay vote, that is, a vote opposed to the president's preferred outcome, while the region to the right is a yea vote, a vote in agreement with the president's preference.[8] The figure shows that after the president lobbies the member, denoted by the white arrow, the member's position on the issue changes from C to C', and thus the member's vote switches from a nay to a yea, from against the president to with the president.

Figure 2.1 is useful for illustrating other possibilities as well. For instance, if after the president lobbies the member, the member's expected vote remains at C, then the president has not influenced the member's vote. A third possibility is that the member's expected vote is C', that is, that the member's expected vote already aligns with the president, and the

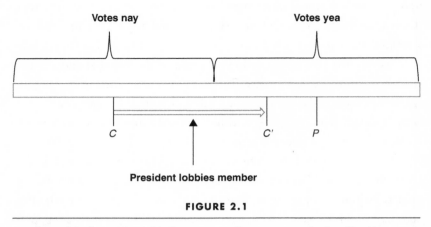

FIGURE 2.1

A model of presidential influence on a Congress member's roll call vote

C = Member's expected vote prior to a presidential influence attempt.
C' = Member's vote after a presidential influence attempt.
P = President's preferred policy outcome.

member will vote in agreement with the president with or without the president lobbying the member. In this situation, if the president lobbies the member, we cannot say that the president has influenced the member because the member's vote remains at C'; presidential lobbying has not affected the member's vote, as in the previous scenario, in which the member's vote remains at C, despite presidential lobbying.

It is unlikely, however, that a president will lobby a member located at C'. There is always a cost associated with lobbying. For instance, lobbying expends resources, and those resources could be more effectively used to lobby a different member, who is located at C. By lobbying a member at C', the president may be wasting lobbying resources that could be put to better use lobbying a member who does not already agree with the president. In addition, there are opportunity costs to lobbying. Presidents could be doing other things, like working on other issues or trying to burnish their image among voters. Spending time on lobbying when the member will already support the president curtails or reduces the time the president can spend on other potentially beneficial activities. Still, presidents may lobby a member at C' to ensure that the member remains a supporter of the president. They may do so to reinforce the member's support and/or to signal to the member that the president is watching and may take action against the member if the member's support for the president wavers (Leech and Baumgartner 1998). Or a president may lobby a member because of uncertainty about the member's likely vote.[9]

The difference between the second possibility (no change, member opposed) and the third (no change, member supports the president) is that the president does not receive the member's vote in the second possibility but does so in the third, even though the president did not change the member's vote in either situation. Thus, presidents do not have to be influential to receive a member's vote. And presidents may win on the roll call without influencing any members if enough members are already located at C'. This third possibility illustrates one of the key insights of the presidential success literature: presidents may win on a roll call vote not because of anything they did or did not do but because a majority of members already agreed with them.

Further, we cannot speak about presidential influence if the president does not hold a preference or does not take a public stand on the roll call. We can only speak about presidential influence if the president announces a public position and attempts to change the expected vote of at least some members from opposition to support. (We leave aside for the moment that presidents may take positions for reasons other than trying to influence the votes of members of Congress.) Presidential influence is thus both relational and requires presidential action, an attempt at influence. This raises an important question: What if a member's position changes from C to C' but the president did not take a position on the roll call? Moreover, how can we even speak of a presidential policy preference if the president does not take a position?

Conceptually, it is useful to distinguish between a privately held preference and those the executive publicly expresses. Covington (1987) and Canes-Wrone (2006) argue that it is sometimes in the president's interest to stay private rather than to go public on an issue or roll call. For example, by going public a president may activate opponents, leading them to work harder against the president. Also, by going public a president may raise the salience of the issue to voters, which would be detrimental to the president if the public prefers a policy option that differs from the president's (Canes-Wrone 2006). As Clinton et al. (2004, 5) argue,

> It seems likely that presidents simultaneously use both public and private means of influence to achieve their policy objectives. Disentangling the independent effects of public and private presidential activity is both challenging and consequential. Without accounting for presidential private activities, we are likely to overestimate and misunderstand the influence of the president's public influence both formally in empirical models (due to omitted variable bias) and informally in our impressionistic analysis.

Members of Congress may have a good sense of the president's views on an issue, even if the president does not take a public stance. Presidents may communicate privately held positions to (some) members of Congress, perhaps requiring that the information be kept private as a condition for striking a deal. And as experienced watchers of Washington politics, members may be able to estimate the president's preferences on a policy with some degree of accuracy, even when the president keeps those preferences private.

Based on the distinction between the president's public and privately held preferences, a member may change from C to C' based on expectations of what the president *might* do if the member voted C or C'. In other words, anticipated reactions may account for members changing their roll call votes even when the president stays on the sidelines and fails either to take a public position or to communicate (individually and/or privately) with the member.[10] A member may anticipate either a reward for shifting to support the president or a punishment for not changing to support the president and thus may change their vote in anticipation of a presidential response.[11]

To summarize, presidents may have preferences on policies on which they do not take a public stance. Keeping their preferences on issues private makes it difficult, if not impossible, to detect presidential influence over member roll call voting, because we do not observe a presidential influence attempt and/or because members may change their positions in anticipation of expected presidential reactions to a member's vote.

Finally, presidential lobbying (position taking) may be counterproductive, that is, a member's vote may move from C' to C, from being supportive of the president to opposed. From a rational actor perspective (e.g., Canes-Wrone 2006), we would not expect presidents to lobby Congress (to take a position) if they think that doing so will weaken or undermine the likelihood of receiving what they want from Congress. But Cameron and Park (2011), for instance, find a negative relationship between presidents going public in support of their Supreme Court nominees and Senate voting on those nominations. Their negative finding is consistent with the counterproductive perspective on presidential lobbying. Cameron and Park argue not that presidential going public (a form of lobbying) is counterproductive but that presidents are more likely to work harder in support of a nominee when that nominee is in trouble in Congress and/or when conditions in Congress are not favorable to the president, that is, when there is potent counteractive lobbying (Austen-Smith and Wright 1994; Baumgartner and Leech 1996).[12]

Another possibility is that, by lobbying Congress, presidents activate and mobilize opposition to their position. Sometimes the opposition may have greater influence and sway with Congress than does the president, which could account for member reversal from support to opposition to the president. For example, the 1993–1994 Bill Clinton administration efforts at health care reform stimulated a strong opposition that effectively and successfully countered the president's reform goals (Skocpol 1997; Hacker 2001). Similarly, the 2009–2010 emergence of the Tea Party movement can be viewed as a reaction to Barack Obama's policies, including increased government intervention in the economy, the growth of the federal government, and especially the passage of the Affordable Care Act ("Obamacare") in 2010 (Boykoff and Laschever 2011; Skocpol and Williamson 2012). Both anticipated reactions and counterproductive lobbying effects have implications for the empirical assessment of presidential influence in Congress. Chapter 8 specifically deals with the issue of counterproductive lobbying effects.

VARIETIES OF PRESIDENTIAL LOBBYING TACTICS

Ideally, to estimate presidential influence on members' roll call votes, we want data on presidential lobbying activity, a comparison of member roll call voting before and after the president lobbies, and an indication that, if vote change occurs, it does so after the president has lobbied. As I have noted, it is difficult if not impossible to observe all of these elements. Let us call the member's position prior to a presidential lobbying attempt the member's *expected vote*, since at this point the roll call vote has not been held. Generally, we do not know how a member will vote prior to the actual roll call, although, as will be discussed, we may be able to estimate a member's expected vote. For present purposes, presidential influence will be based on a comparison of the members' expected vote (before the president lobbies) with their actual vote (after the president has lobbied). To make this comparison requires a strategy for measuring a member's expected vote. One such measurement strategy will be discussed and is used in the present study.

There are other limitations of this behavioral definition of presidential influence. First, we never take into account presidential influence acquired through nonpublic lobbying, that is, when the president privately lobbies a member. Second, we do not take into account influence obtained through anticipated reactions processes. Empirically, then, this study only gives an assessment of the influence that presidents receive through public lobbying efforts. This leads to two questions: What forms does public presidential lobbying take, and how does this study measure public presidential lobbying?

EXISTING RESEARCH ON PRESIDENTIAL LOBBYING

There is considerable research on presidential lobbying of Congress. Some of the earliest research details the institutional development of formal liaison offices in the White House and its departments (Pipe 1966; Holtzman 1970; Heaphy 1975). Another research strand aims to assess the impact of liaison and executive lobbying activities, relying primarily on interviews with Congress and the executive and/or on documentary evidence to assess the effectiveness of such activities. Such documentary evidence is often culled from presidential libraries and other relevant archives (Davis 1979; Hart 1981, 1983; Mullen 1982; Covington 1986; Collier 1997).

These research strands, while important, are of limited value for this study and its focus on measuring the effects of presidential lobbying. The first strand, the institutional development of lobbying offices, does not deal with the effects of those offices and their practices. The second strand, although it may provide information on lobbying activities and effect, may not be systematic in the sense of including similar information across presidents, and even within presidencies such information may be available for only a subset of presidential/administration lobbying efforts.

There is a third strand that uses behavioral measures, such as success and support, to assess the impact of presidential lobbying activities and that is thus more directly relevant to the questions at hand (Manley 1978; Covington 1988; Kerbel 1991, 1993; Uslaner 1988; Beckmann 2010). One of the hurdles in assessing the effectiveness of lobbying is the myriad ways in which a president may lobby members of Congress. For instance, there are studies of these types of presidential lobbying activities: doing favors and providing services to members (Kerbel 1993); providing grants and projects in members' districts (Hamman and Cohen 1997; Berry, Burden, and Howell 2010; Kriner and Reeves 2014, 2015a, 2015b; Dynes and Huber 2015); inviting members to White House occasions such as state dinners (Covington 1988); campaigning for or against members in their reelection runs (Cohen, Krassa, and Hamman 1991; Hoddie and Routh 2004; Jacobson, Kernell, and Lazarus 2004; Sellers and Denton 2006; Herrnson and Morris 2007; Eshbaugh-Soha and Nicholson-Crotty 2009; Herrnson, Morris, and McTague 2011; Lang, Rottinghaus, and Peters 2011; Mellen and Searles 2013a, 2013b); going public (Kernell 1997; Canes-Wrone 2006); veto bargaining and threats (Cameron 2000; Hassell and Kernell 2016); contacting members (Uslaner 1998; Beckmann 2016); persuasion and bargaining (Neustadt 1960, 1991; Kerbel 1991, 1993; Sullivan 1990a); and other activities.[13]

Each of these activities may be viewed as a lobbying tactic as opposed to a lobbying strategy. A presidential lobbying strategy is "the general prescriptions for how a White House can best use their resources to pass the president's preferred policy without regard to a particular legislative context" (Beckmann 2004, 8). A tactic, in contrast, is a particular action by the president. The lobbying strategy dictates the tactics that presidents employ, and presidents may utilize several tactics simultaneously, in various combinations, depending on their legislative strategy.

For instance, strategically, presidents may decide to lobby publicly, to lobby privately, or to not engage the legislative process. In developing their strategy, presidents and their aides may decide on how much lobbying effort to expend and which members to lobby (for instance, all members, co-partisans, leaders of both parties, and so on). Based on the strategic plan, presidents may decide on relevant tactics, such as going public to lobby the entire Congress or offering inducements to select members. On some issues, the strategic plan will lead a president to employ several of these lobbying tactics, a multitactic lobbying strategy.

What can we say substantively about presidential lobbying effectiveness, based on these studies? A lobbying strategy and/or tactic is effective if it results in members switching from opposition to support for the president's position. Lobbying effectiveness can be assessed at both the micro and the macro level. Micro lobbying effectiveness asks whether the president influenced members whom the president targeted. Macro effectiveness looks at whether the president influenced enough members to win on the roll call.

Studies of the effectiveness of various lobbying tactics differ widely in their findings. Some studies find little or no impact from presidential lobbying, whereas others report significant impacts—the movement of a large number of targeted members and/or floor victories for the president. The large number of possible tactics and the complexity of the legislative process make it difficult to offer generalizations regarding the effectiveness of presidential lobbying on Congress. The influence that presidents derive from lobbying probably varies with factors such as the characteristics of a targeted member, the issue, the degree of presidential involvement, and the larger political context, as well as with the employed tactic.

LIMITATIONS OF EXISTING RESEARCH ON PRESIDENTIAL LOBBYING

There are two major limitations of the extant research on presidential lobbying. First, most studies only consider one lobbying activity or tactic at a

time (see Beckmann 2010, who compares earlygame and endgame lobbying, for one exception). Focusing on only one tactic may lead to omitted
variable bias, a form of model misspecification, if presidents employ and
coordinate multiple tactics. We might ascribe effects to tactic X when it is
tactic Y and/or the combination of tactics X and Y that leads to presidential
influence on targeted members. Furthermore, by focusing on only one tactic instead of the full complement of tactics that the president uses on a bill,
we may find that the tactic studied does not affect the votes of many members yet the president's side wins on the roll call. This might lead us to
emphasize the importance of the context, such as party control, but to
downplay the contribution of presidential lobbying in accounting for the
presidential success on the roll call.

Rather than focusing on one discrete presidential lobbying tactic, this
study aims for a more general conceptualization and measurement of presidential lobbying. Specifically, presidential position taking on roll calls can
be viewed as a generalized form of presidential lobbying. Position taking
subsumes and combines all the discrete lobbying tactics I have mentioned.
For instance, when presidents go public, their position on the roll call
becomes common and public knowledge. When presidents travel to some
members' districts, the executive is taking a public stand on an issue.
Although presidential travel may be meant to target legislators who represent
the visited district, legislators from unvisited districts also learn of the president's preferences on the issue. Public lobbying of a subset of members signals
to other members the president's preferences and the lengths to which the
president will go to win the floor vote. Thus, there may be spillover effects of
presidential lobbying from targeted to nontargeted members of Congress, as
long as the lobbying tactic and effort are public.[14]

Admittedly, there are limitations to this conceptualization of presidential lobbying, which does not capture the effects of private lobbying of a
member by the president. For instance, presidential position taking does
not account for instances of a president offering favors to a member to secure
the member's vote, with the details of the deal kept private between them.
Nor can this conceptualization distinguish the comparative effectiveness
of lobbying tactics or combinations of lobbying tactics. Moreover, this
conceptualization cannot distinguish the effects of focused presidential

targeting of members from generalized lobbying effects, as in Beckmann (2016), who distinguishes between presidential contacting of congressional leaders and the contacting of rank-and-file members. Still, as will be empirically demonstrated here, we can distinguish the effects of generalized lobbying on subsets of members, such as those from the president's party and those from the opposition party.[15]

Another limitation of viewing position taking as presidential lobbying is that it does not account for the effects of lobbying effort, the idea that the more effort the president expends in lobbying Congress, the greater the benefits, such as the number of members influenced. Beckmann (2010, 49–50) contends that increased presidential effort results in greater support for the president, albeit with diminishing returns. In chapter 8, I take into account the effects of presidential lobbying effort. The present study only looks at the effects of a generalized form of public presidential lobbying, position taking.[16]

A final limitation of conceptualizing position taking as presidential lobbying is that presidents may take positions for reasons other than trying to influence member roll call voting. For instance, presidents may take positions to claim credit (Mayhew 1974), to honor a pledge in their election campaign, to be associated with the winning side (Marshall and Prins 2007), to repay voters and interest groups for their electoral support, or to attract new voters and groups to the president's support coalition, among other reasons. One of the empirical tasks here, dealt with later, is to distinguish presidential position taking as lobbying from position taking for other motivations. It is necessary to distinguish among and control for the effects of different types of (or motivations for) position taking to be able to estimate with any degree of accuracy the amount of influence presidents derive from lobbying-based position taking. Although it is not possible to discern the motivations behind all of a president's positions, we can identify situations when the president takes a position but is not trying to lobby members for their votes.

A second major limitation of the existing research on presidential lobbying of Congress is that it tends to focus only on the direct effects of presidential lobbying, that is, whether the contact, inducement, or presidential campaigning for the member led to the member supporting the president. This study argues that presidential lobbying can also affect members by changing how members *interpret* the roll call. When a president takes a position, the roll call is transformed from a nonpresidential to a presidential roll call, which leads members of Congress to reinterpret their understanding of the roll call. In other words, by taking a position, the roll call to some degree becomes *associated* with the president, when there was little or no association between the president and a roll call when the president did not take a position. The next section distinguishes between direct and associational (or indirect) effects of presidential lobbying within a more general model of member roll call voting decisions.

FROM THE PRESIDENT'S POSITION TO THE MEMBER'S ROLL CALL VOTE

Presidential influence is one factor that may affect how members of Congress vote on roll calls. Any theory of presidential influence, therefore, must be rooted in a general theory of member roll call behavior. Research has identified numerous factors that appear to affect member roll call behavior, in addition to the influence of presidents. For example, studies indicate that the preferences of constituents and interest groups, partisan considerations, the member's own policy preferences, and their ideological orientations are at times strong influences on roll call behavior (e.g., Carroll and Poole 2014; Clausen 1973; Kingdon 1973; Roberts, Smith, and Haptonstahl 2016; for a review of the roll call literature, see Theriault, Hickey, and Blass 2011). These factors affect members' roll call behavior by making it easier or harder for members to achieve their goals, such as securing reelection, making good policy, increasing influence inside Washington, helping the party, and so on (Beckmann 2004, 22).

Let us assume a general model of member roll call voting without any presidential influence, as in equation (2.1):

$$\text{Roll call vote} = f(NP) \tag{2.1}$$

Equation (2.1) suggests that the member's roll call vote is a function of nonpresidential considerations (*NP*), such as constituency preferences, partisanship, interest group preferences, member preferences and ideology, and the like. The assumption of equation (2.1), that presidents have no influence on member voting when they do not take a position, may be overly restrictive and unrealistic. Presidents may have some influence on member voting on these roll calls because members may be able to infer the president's preferences, even if those preferences are not expressed publicly, and/or because presidents may communicate their preferences to some members privately.

Next, let us distinguish between presidential and nonpresidential roll calls. As before, presidential roll calls are those on which the president has taken a position, while nonpresidential roll calls are those on which the president has *not* expressed a public position. Members may take the president into account to a much greater extent in deciding how to vote on presidential than on nonpresidential roll calls, as in equation (2.2):

$$\text{Roll call vote} = f(NP, P) \qquad (2.2)$$

In equation (2.2), the member's roll call vote is a function of nonpresidential (*NP*) and presidential (*P*) considerations. Theoretically, the weight members assign to the president may range from zero, indicating no presidential influence despite presidential lobbying, to 1, which indicates that presidents determine the member's vote.[17] For nonpresidential roll calls, let us say that the member assigns a weight to presidential considerations such that the weight is greater on presidential than on nonpresidential roll calls. Equation (2.2) reduces to equation (2.1) when the weight assigned to the president is the same for presidential and nonpresidential roll calls and when the weight for presidential considerations is zero.

The weight that members assign to presidential and nonpresidential factors is based on their assessment of how the factor will affect the attainment of desired goals. When a member thinks that the factor will be important in attaining a desired goal, that factor will be weighted more heavily.

There are several important complications in building a general theory of member roll call behavior. First, the predominant member goal may change from vote to vote. For example, on issues lacking salience to voters, the reelection goal may not be of much concern to the member. No matter how they vote on the roll call, it will not affect their chances for reelection because their constituents do not care about the issue. Second, since members have multiple goals, there may be instances of goal conflict on a roll call; for instance, a member may have preferences for a policy solution that their constituents oppose. When there is goal conflict on a single roll call, members have to decide which goal is more important. Over numerous roll calls, members have the ability to balance conflicting goals, such as by sometimes voting their preferences and sometimes their constituents' preferences.[18] This enables the member, when running for reelection, to point to those votes when they sided with their constituents as evidence of the good job they are doing representing their district in Congress. The influence of the president on a member's roll call must be situated within this type of general framework on roll call voting behavior.[19]

PATHWAYS OF PRESIDENTIAL EFFECTS ON MEMBER ROLL CALL VOTING

Presidential roll call position taking can affect a member's vote directly and/or indirectly (Beckmann 2004, 16–17). Figure 2.2 diagrams the direct and indirect pathways from presidential position taking to the member's roll call vote. The arrow connecting the box "President takes a position on a roll call" to "Member's roll call vote" maps the direct pathway. The indirect pathway flows from the box "President takes a position on a roll call" through "Contextual factors: Partisanship, policy type, presidential approval" and then to "Member's roll call vote." Much existing research on presidential lobbying focuses only on the direct path, whereas the literature on presidential success often focuses on the impact of contextual factors on the member's roll call vote. The presidential success literature, however, rarely details the connection between presidential position taking (or lobbying) and contextual factors.

The direct effect of position taking on a member's roll call follows from this discussion. Members will take into account the president's preferences inasmuch as the president can affect member goal attainment. For instance,

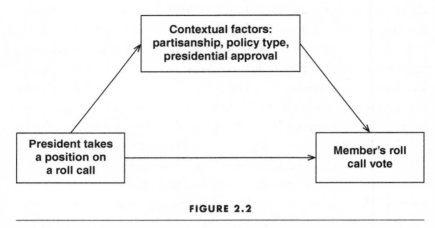

FIGURE 2.2

Pathways from the president's roll call position to the member's roll call vote

a member concerned about reelection may vote with the president because the president will then help their reelection campaign. The president might attend a fund-raiser for the candidate or, if the president is popular in the constituency, may appear at a campaign event designed to rally voters behind the member. Due to the president's (expected or negotiated) assistance in the campaign, the member will vote with the president. Similarly, a president might offer an inducement such as speeding up or supporting projects in the member's district—what we might think of as presidential "vote buying."[20] As a result of these presidential actions targeted at the member, the member increases his or her support for the president on floor votes. In these examples, there is a direct connection between the president's action and the member's roll call vote.

The indirect pathway from the president's position taking to the member's vote has not been discussed much in the existing literature. There are two ways that presidential position taking indirectly affects member voting. First, when a president takes a position, the vote is transformed from a nonpresidential to a presidential one. The member thus reinterprets or redefines the roll call into one in which the president weighs (more heavily) on the member's vote.

There is a second type of indirect effect of presidential position taking on member roll call voting. Aspects of the political context become more salient when the president takes a position. For example, partisanship often affects member voting. When the president takes a position and partisanship is an important influence on the member's vote, members come to view the roll call as one that involves *the president as party leader*, not merely as a contest between the parties. The empirical analysis that follows focuses on several contextual factors—partisanship, type of issue (for instance, domestic versus foreign), presidential approval, and issue salience—because of their importance in the presidential–congressional relations literature. Based on this line of thought, these factors should hypothetically affect member voting more strongly on presidential than on nonpresidential roll calls.

By taking a position, the president activates, triggers, and/or mobilizes aspects of the political context to his advantage (or disadvantage). The political context becomes a resource that the president may use to influence member roll call votes. But sometimes this process works to the president's disadvantage. For example, if the president is not popular, the president may harm his chances of securing legislation by linking his unpopularity to the bill (Canes-Wrone 2006).[21] In addition, the president may not be consciously aware that, by taking a roll call position, he is activating some contextual factors to his advantage or disadvantage. Yet there may be occasions when the president is aware of the implications of position taking and thus may work to turn the roll call into a matter of partisanship through his rhetoric and definition of the issue (Coleman and Manna 2007; Rhodes 2014).

This process has important conceptual similarities to George C. Edwards's (1990, 1991a, 2009b, 2012, 2016) view of presidents as *facilitators* rather than *directors* (also see Jacobs and King 2016). In Edwards's formulation, a president as director is one who is hypothesized to create opportunities by, for instance, restructuring the larger political context and environment, such as public preferences on issues, the president's approval, the degree of party polarization, and so on. As Edwards shows, presidents have at best a weak to modest ability to restructure the political context and environment in their favor. More likely, presidents are unable to restructure these contextual and environmental factors.

Presidents as facilitators, in contrast, exploit existing opportunities. The idea of exploiting opportunities is similar to my notion of a president activating or mobilizing a contextual factor through position taking. As in Edwards's view, these contextual factors become resources that presidents may use or exploit to influence members of Congress. Moreover, presidents may increase the salience of the roll call by taking a position (Cohen 1997; Canes-Wrone 2006). If, however, we consider salience to be a structural or contextual factor, then by taking a roll call position, presidents have some ability to restructure the environment or context surrounding a roll call. Compared to public preferences on issues and the partisan makeup of Congress, perhaps the best opportunity the president has to restructure the political context and environment is by increasing the salience of an issue.[22]

This perspective on indirect presidential influence has implications for the empirical estimation of presidential influence, one of the tasks of the present research. The indirect pathway suggests that contextual factors can magnify or diminish the effect of presidential position taking on member voting, in other words, that the contextual factors mediate the effect of presidential position taking on member voting. We can model statistically the effect of presidential position taking, controlling for the effects of nonpresidential factors, as expressed in equation (2.2), this way:

$$Y(\text{Presidential influence}) = \alpha + \beta_1(NP) + \beta_2(P) + \varepsilon; \qquad (2.3)$$

where α is the intercept to the regression equation, β_x are regression coefficients, and ε is a stochastic error term. Now assume that NP stands for only one contextual factor, party. This simplification makes it easier to explain the process and estimation strategy. To test for the indirect effects of position taking through party on voting, we use an interaction term that multiplies the contextual factor (such as party) and presidential position taking:[23]

$$Y(\text{Presidential influence}) = \alpha + \beta_1(NP) + \beta_2(P) + \beta_3(NP \times P) + \varepsilon; \quad (2.4)$$

If president position taking has an indirect effect on member voting, then the interaction term, $\beta_3(NP \times P)$, should affect member voting above and beyond the direct effect of position taking, $\beta_2(P)$, and party, $\beta_1(NP)$. This formulation also suggests that the indirect effect of position taking through contextual factors can theoretically undermine presidential influence on member voting, which would be the case if the sign on the interaction term were negative. For example, assume that presidents activate or intensify partisan considerations when taking roll call positions and that the opposition party controls the chambers. Presidential position taking may lead opposition members to vote against the president, and co-partisans to vote with the president. But since opposition members outnumber co-partisans, the president's side may lose votes when the president enters the legislative debate.

CONCLUSION

This chapter has defined presidential influence and presented a theory to account for the amount of influence presidents have in Congress. Presidents are influential when they can alter the votes of a member of Congress from opposing to supporting the president's position. According to the theory, presidents may be lobbying members for their support merely by taking a public position on a roll call. Furthermore, not only may position taking, a generic form of presidential lobbying, directly affect members' roll call votes but also position taking may affect member votes indirectly, by associating the roll call with the president and by activating aspects of the political context/environment for or against the president.

Several implications follow from this definition and theory. First, past research, by focusing only on what transpires once the president has taken a position, may have underestimated the amount of influence presidents have in Congress. The argument here is that presidents accrue some influence merely by taking a position. Second, influence requires a change in member voting from opposition to support, but rarely do we have systematic and clear data on such voting change.

The next chapter presents a methodology to allow us to estimate such change in member voting. Rather than comparing member preferences before and after a president has taken a position, which is not possible for the vast majority of roll calls, the methodology compares member voting patterns on presidential roll calls with those on nonpresidential roll calls. However, there are several complications in making such comparisons. First, how do we determine the president's position on a roll call when the president has not taken a position? Second, how do we compare presidential and nonpresidential roll calls when presidential roll calls are not a random subset of all roll calls?

3

ESTIMATING PRESIDENTIAL
INFLUENCE IN CONGRESS

T HE THEORY DEVELOPED in chapter 2 conceptualizes position taking on roll calls as a generic form of presidential lobbying of Congress, noting that presidents may take positions for reasons besides trying to lobby Congress. As a generic form of lobbying, position taking subsumes numerous discrete types of presidential lobbying activities, such as doing favors, going public, threatening vetoes, and others. Further, the previous chapter defined presidential influence as existing when a member's vote changes from opposition to support because of a presidential lobbying activity.[1] Thus, presidential influence requires both a presidential action to alter a member's roll call and a change in the member's vote.

This theory and definition of influence has implications for studying presidential influence in Congress and differs from much past research. Existing research looks at member voting on presidential roll calls, ignoring nonpresidential roll calls, when assessing member support/opposition to the president. Typically, existing research investigates whether members vote for or against the president on presidential roll calls, or whether the president's side won or lost, again only for presidential roll calls. Research that uses only presidential roll calls ignores the influence that presidents may obtain from position taking itself, as is argued in chapter 2.

Examining only patterns of support/opposition on presidential roll calls has two important consequences for the study of presidential influence in

Congress. First, limiting analysis to presidential roll calls may underestimate the amount of presidential influence because presidents may derive some influence merely from position taking, which converts a nonpresidential roll call into a presidential one. Second, such a restricted analysis leads to an incomplete understanding of the processes and factors that lead to or frustrate presidential influence with Congress.

With regard to underestimating the amount of presidential influence, we have noted that when presidents take a position on a roll call, the roll call is transformed from a nonpresidential into a presidential vote. This process alters the member's roll call vote calculus, adding a presidential factor or consideration into that calculus (Lee 2008, 2009; Lebo and O'Geen 2011).[2] As long as that presidential factor has an effect greater than zero, presidential position taking may influence how members vote. If the presidential factor is large enough, it may alter the member's expected vote from against to for the president. Studies that use only presidential roll calls miss the influence of presidents on members of Congress through the act of position taking.

This study emphasizes two points in the legislative process at which presidents may influence members' roll calls: first, when presidents decide to take a position; and second, when presidents decide to do something beyond mere position taking, such as targeting members for other lobbying efforts— bargaining, doing favors, helping in reelection campaigns, and the like. It is important to mention that there are other points in the legislative process, not considered explicitly or empirically in this study, at which presidents may influence the legislative process and member voting, such as working with the leadership to set the agenda, floor debate, and voting rules; keeping some alternatives or bills from reaching the floor; and influencing committees, where many of the substantive details of legislation are hammered out.

Past research generally has investigated presidential influence only for the post-position-taking phase of the process, not the position-taking stage, and rarely for the other stages of the legislative process, like agenda setting (but see Beckmann 2010; Krutz 2005).[3] If influence accrues to the president from position taking, then past research has underestimated the amount of presidential influence over congressional roll call voting, assuming that presidents receive some influence from taking a position.

Turning to the second point, understanding the processes and factors associated with presidential influence, studies that use only presidential roll calls can say nothing about how position taking influences the support/opposition of members of Congress. The processes and mechanisms of influence from position taking may differ from those associated with lobbying activities that presidents employ after having taken a position. For example, presidential position taking may have an agenda-setting effect, leading members to think of or interpret a roll call in presidential terms. When presidents take a roll call position, and members redefine the roll call from a nonpresidential to a presidential roll call, the president has affected the interpretation and composition of the legislative agenda, associating with the president's agenda some issues that previously were not part of it.[4]

Conceptualizing position taking as presidential lobbying has implications for estimating the amount of presidential influence in Congress, as well as for understanding the processes and mechanisms associated with that influence. There are at least two key issues with conceptualizing position taking as lobbying and thus with assessing whether presidential position taking influences members' roll call votes. First, presidents may take a position on a roll call for reasons other than trying to alter how members vote. For instance, they may take positions to claim credit, to represent the concerns of constituents, to repay those who supported the president during the election campaign, or for other reasons. One of the challenges in studying the effect of position taking on member voting is distinguishing lobbying-motivated position taking from other types of position taking.

Second, and ideally, we would like to know the member's expected vote before the president took a position and compare that expected vote with the member's actual vote after the president has taken a position. The difference between the member's expected vote (pre-presidential position taking) and his or her actual vote (post-presidential position taking) would tell us whether presidential position taking or other types and aspects of presidential lobbying influence the roll call behavior of legislators.

Unfortunately, we lack systematic and reliable information on members' expected roll call votes prior to presidential position taking.

Bond and Fleisher (1990) raise this point in their critique of Kiewiet and McCubbins's (1988) examination of presidential influence in the appropriations process. Kiewiet and McCubbins build a formal model that predicts that the congressional appropriation level will be closer to the president's proposed appropriation when the president asks for less rather than more, because he can veto appropriations that exceed what he is willing to spend. Although they find such a result, Bond and Fleisher (1990) rightly argue that, since Kiewiet and McCubbins "do not have an estimate of congressional preferences independent of the president's request, they do not know whether the actual appropriation levels reflect true congressional preferences or presidential influence" (3). Edwards (1980) generalizes this observation, but uses the term "power" as opposed to "influence," "To attribute power to the president, it is necessary to see whether members of Congress give him more support under some conditions than others" (49).

There is a small amount of literature on the timing of legislators' announcements of a position on an issue (Boehmke 2006; Box-Steffensmeier, Arnold, and Zorn 1997; Caldeira and Zorn 2004; Huang and Theriault 2012; Krehbiel 1991). That literature views announcement timing as strategic, arguing that some members use early announcements to affect the votes of other legislators. These studies are limited for our purposes because they look at only one issue at a time and do not incorporate the timing of the president's position, which would be a constant across members on any single vote anyway.

Lacking data on whether members' vote intentions shift due to presidential position taking, we can get a handle on the *potential* for presidential influence by comparing member voting on presidential and nonpresidential roll calls. There are two complications, however, in making such a comparison. First, we need to establish a basis for comparison—how do we identify the president's position when the president has not taken a position? Second, the two sets of roll calls differ systematically in ways besides being a presidential versus a nonpresidential vote; presidents' roll calls are not a random subset of all roll calls.

For presidential roll calls, the standard approach is to examine whether a member voted with or against the president. To compare member voting on presidential and nonpresidential roll calls requires a different comparison, because we cannot define the president's position on a nonpresidential roll call. Voting with or against the president is not a meaningful basis for comparing presidential with nonpresidential roll calls. This chapter introduces a method for comparing member roll call voting across these two types of roll calls, enabling us to estimate how "liberal" or "conservative" a member votes on presidential and on nonpresidential roll calls. Some of the difference in member "liberalism" on the two sets of roll calls may be attributed to the president influencing the member.

Yet we must be careful in comparing the liberal/conservative voting of members on presidential and nonpresidential roll calls because the two sets differ in systematic ways besides being classified as a presidential or nonpresidential vote. Roll calls on which presidents have taken a position are not a random subset of roll calls that reach the floors of the House and Senate. For example, presidential and nonpresidential roll calls may vary by policy substance. Due to presidential responsibilities, presidents may be more inclined to take positions on foreign policy than on non–foreign policy issues. Public opinion pressures may lead presidents to take positions more frequently on salient than on less salient issues, leading to a salience difference between the two types of roll calls. Plus, presidents may take positions to claim credit or to be on the winning side (Mayhew 1974), motivations that have little to do with influencing member votes.[5] Thus, there may be a greater representation of lopsided, "hurrah" votes—votes with overwhelming majorities on one side—on presidential than on nonpresidential roll calls.

To a degree, we can deal with these concerns by controlling for them in the analysis that follows. In addition, we can use quasi-experimental analysis techniques for comparing member voting on presidential and nonpresidential roll calls to assess how differently they vote on the two types of roll calls, as I also will do. These analyses all point to the same conclusion: there are differences in member voting patterns on nonpresidential and presidential roll calls. This difference is consistent with the idea that presidents influence member voting. Moreover, the estimated amount of presidential influence is much larger than previous research would lead us to expect, and, due to this influence, presidents win on a measurable and meaningful number of roll calls that they would have lost had they not taken a position. Before presenting this new method for measuring this difference, which I call *potential presidential influence*, I will review and critique the existing research that has tried to measure presidential influence in Congress.

PAST APPROACHES TO MEASURING PRESIDENTIAL INFLUENCE

There is much conceptual and language confusion in the literature on presidential relations with Congress. Studies interchangeably use terms like "influence," "power," "persuasion," "success," and "support." There are important differences in the meaning of these terms with regard to presidential–congressional relations, especially between the two overarching concepts of influence and success. Influence (and power and persuasion) is concerned with the president's ability to change a member's roll call vote.[6] In contrast, success (and the related concept of support) is concerned with the outcome of the vote, with whether the president's side prevailed and whether the member voted with the president (see Bond and Fleisher 1990).[7]

Past research has employed several methods of measuring presidential influence: comparing variation in success (or support) on presidential roll calls, comparing headcounts with later roll calls ("sway"), and comparing presidential with nonpresidential roll calls. Each approach has added to our understanding of presidential influence, but each also has its limitations.

USING VARIATION IN SUCCESS OR SUPPORT TO ESTIMATE INFLUENCE

The most common approach in the literature on presidential–congressional relations looks at presidential success or support levels on roll calls on which *the president has already taken a position*. Success is defined as whether the president's side won or lost the roll call, across roll calls, while support looks at whether individual members of Congress voted on the president's side or with the opposition. This approach assumes that nonpresidential roll calls are irrelevant for estimating presidential influence.

As was discussed in the chapter 2, it is not clear that success reflects well on presidential influence. Success rates under varying conditions may be viewed as being due to the influence of the president, among other factors that affect member voting, such as ideology, party, and so forth. For example, we could compare the success rates of presidents across policy types within a Congress, or across Congresses.[8] Tests of the two presidencies hypothesis—that presidents will be more successful on foreign than on domestic policy—often make such a comparison, and these usually find presidential success rates are higher for foreign than for domestic policy.[9]

One might interpret presidents as being more influential in foreign than in domestic policy, based on such results, but a simple comparison of success rates may mask the impact of nonpresidential factors on members' votes. For example, if members and the president are more likely to agree on foreign than on domestic policy a priori, then higher presidential success on foreign than on domestic policy may be merely a function of pre-existing policy agreement, not of presidential influence. Recall that the definition of "influence" used here requires a change in member behavior from opposition to support of the president's position. If members and the president already agree on a policy, then there will be no change in member roll call behavior and thus no influence.

As a large body of literature demonstrates, presidents can be highly successful in Congress merely because the political environment advantages them. Majority presidents win more frequently than minority presidents because congressional co-partisans share the president's policy preferences and the majority will use its numerical superiority and control over institutional levers to enact its preferred policies. This political environment perspective suggests that majority presidents do not have to do much to obtain legislative results and do not need to be influential in order to get the policies from Congress that they want.

The political environment perspective argues that presidential attempts to influence members are secondary in importance in explaining presidential success and support, and that, at most, presidents can only influence Congress "at the margins" (Edwards 1990). In contrast, the *strategic president perspective* contends that, under certain circumstances, presidential attempts to influence Congress—for instance, through veto bargaining and threats, doing favors, campaigning for members seeking reelection, going public, earlygame lobbying, and so forth—may significantly enhance presidential success because of the influence that results from the strategic use of these techniques and tactics.

The political environment and strategic perspectives differ over the amount of presidential influence, with the strategic perspective suggesting a greater degree of presidential influence than does the environmental perspective. But even the strategic perspective may underestimate the amount of presidential influence, because those studies generally only compare voting on presidential roll calls. As I argue here, however, comparing only the voting on presidential roll calls neglects the increment of influence that presidents receive from position taking. We need to include this increment of presidential influence to estimate the total amount of influence presidents exert on roll calls.

An important implication of the perspective proposed here is that we cannot simply compare voting on presidential roll calls if we are to estimate presidential influence fully. Ideally, we need to compare member voting *on the same roll call* before and after the president takes a position. Only such a comparison allows us to determine whether the member moves from opposition to support for the president's position *as a consequence of presidential position taking*. If we only compare member voting across presidential roll calls, we ignore a potential increment of presidential influence and thus will underestimate presidential influence. Ignoring the influence that presidents derive from position taking also limits our theoretical understanding of the nature of presidential influence in Congress.

COMPARING HEADCOUNTS WITH FINAL ROLL CALLS

One issue with using roll calls for measuring influence is that we only observe the final vote tally and not the process that led to the outcome. The aspect of influence we are concerned with in this study is whether presidents can *change* the roll call behavior of members, whether by position taking or by other, more discrete, targeted forms of lobbying, such as veto threats, campaigning for members, doing favors, and the like.

In several intriguing studies, Terry Sullivan (1988, 1990, 1991) has attempted to uncover something about the process of building a presidential coalition on the final roll call by comparing the final vote tally with headcounts of member positions taken sometime before the floor vote. The difference between the headcount tally and the final roll call gives us some information about the effectiveness of the president in securing support from members who profess to being either undecided or opposed to the president at the headcount stage. Sullivan terms this difference "presidential sway."[10]

There are several issues with such headcount data (Edwards 1991b). First, as Edwards argues, the headcount may come too late in the process of coalition building, thereby "missing much of the [president's] influence" (726). For example, the headcount may come after the president has staked out a public position; I have noted why presidential position taking itself may influence members. Second, the headcount may be an unreliable guide to expected member roll call behavior. Members may appear to be uncommitted to extract concessions from and/or to bargain with the president. If so, headcounts may understate the number of members who will eventually vote with the president even if the president does not target them for influence attempts. If, due to strategic posturing,[11] the headcount underestimates the number of members who will eventually vote with the president—that is, if the headcount finds lots of "uncommitted" or "nonsupportive" members who would have voted with the president anyway—the difference between the headcount and the final vote may *overestimate* the amount of presidential influence. As Edwards (1991b, 727) remarks, "headcounts are often not very reliable." Sullivan (1990) attempts to address this issue and finds that a limited number of members are hesitant to take a support/oppose posture at the headcount stage and that such hesitancy or bluffing is more common among core presidential supporters.

A third issue with headcount data is their lack of availability. The various Sullivan and Conley-Yon studies use headcount data from the Eisenhower through Nixon presidencies. To my knowledge, there is no published study using headcounts for any presidency after Ford's. Collecting headcount data is a painstaking process that requires locating the data in presidential libraries. Some of these collections are not yet open for public or scholarly use.

Finally, various presidents may not count heads on the same types of issues. We know very little about why presidents decide to count heads on some bills but not on others, other than that presidents appear to be more likely to take a headcount on bills that are important to the administration. Presidents also may decide not to count heads when it appears they will lose on the vote.[12] Headcounts may be more likely on close votes, to efficiently and effectively target members open to presidential persuasion efforts, and even on votes that the administration thinks it can easily win, perhaps ensuring that supporters remain in the fold.

MAKING COMPARISONS ACROSS PRESIDENTIAL AND NONPRESIDENTIAL ROLL CALLS

Rather than using only presidential roll calls, several studies use all roll calls, presidential and nonpresidential, to gain a handle on presidential influence. But presidents cannot win or lose on a roll call when they do not take a public position, even though they might have a privately held preference. To compare voting on presidential and nonpresidential roll calls requires a measurement other than simply victory/defeat in order to compare voting across the two types of votes.

William G. Howell and his colleagues have developed an intriguing method for addressing the question of whether presidential influence in Congress is higher in wartime than in peacetime (see Howell, Jackman, and Rogowski 2013; Howell and Rogowski 2013). Their theoretical argument is that presidents have more influence on member voting when an issue is viewed as national rather than local in scope, which is similar to the theory proposed here, that once a president takes a position on an issue the issue is transformed from a nonpresidential to a presidential issue.

Howell and colleagues compare member voting patterns during peacetime and wartime within comparable time periods, such as for the same Congress and/or president. They compare a member's ideal point placement on a liberal/conservative continuum for the two periods (for example, for wartime and peacetime) and then ask, Does the member's ideal point shift in the president's direction from peacetime to wartime? For most of the wars they study, there is a discernible shift in voting patterns toward the president from peacetime to wartime.[13]

Importantly, they find that voting shifts are not restricted to foreign policy/national security issues but also are detected for domestic issues, that is, presidents are more influential on domestic issues during wartime than during peacetime. War's effects, it seems, spill over into domestic politics and policy making. Inasmuch as war mutes party differences and enhances presidential influence in Congress, presidents and their parties may see war as an opportunity to move their domestic agenda to fruition. They also may see domestic policies as necessary for building public and political support for the administration's policies, both foreign and domestic. For instance, during the Civil War, Congress implemented an expansive Republican Party domestic agenda, which included the building of the transcontinental railroad; the land grant college system, through the Morrill Land-Grant Acts of 1862; and the Homestead Act of 1862, which encouraged western migration and settlement.[14] These domestic policies were designed in part to build and strengthen the Republican Party in Congress and among voters. A stronger Republican Party also would provide a foundation of support for prosecuting the Civil War.

Still, there are limitations of the Howell et al. method for our purposes here. While their method provides a way to assess presidential influence in two periods, it does not allow us to assess whether presidents gain influence in Congress through lobbying itself. The Howell et al. method, in essence, inspects how an environmental or contextual factor (peacetime versus wartime) affects presidential influence, and not whether specific presidential activities have an effect on member voting, which is the concern of this research. Still, it points in an important direction for this research, suggesting that it may be useful and possible to compare member voting on more than just presidential roll calls to assess presidential influence in Congress.[15]

Milner and Tingley (2015) also are interested in the influence of presidents but restrict their attention to foreign policy matters. In their analysis of presidential influence on foreign policy roll calls, they use the yea–nay distribution as their dependent variable, and whether the president took a position, to test for presidential influence. Although they are mostly concerned with foreign policy and whether presidents have more influence in Congress on subtypes of foreign policies and policy instruments, Milner and Tingley also test the more basic hypothesis that there will be a greater number of yea or nay votes depending on whether the president took a yea or nay position versus the president not taking a roll call position in the House.[16]

Variously, their analysis includes only foreign policy votes or all roll call votes from 1953 to 2008 on two dependent variables: the yea–nay split for members of the president's party or for all members. They find strong support for their hypothesis that the president's position has a direct effect on the vote split within the executive's party and for all members, an effect that increases if the roll call concerns national security. Moreover, presidents appear to have more influence on the roll call voting of co-partisans than among opposition members in the House. These are important findings and reveal the value of comparing presidential with nonpresidential votes and of categorizing votes by policy area.

Milner and Tingley (2015) justify the yea–nay dependent variable because presidents almost never oppose increased international engagement. Thus, through the position that a president takes, one can identify whether a yea or a nay vote means support for increased international engagement. But when the president does not take a position and/or when the vote does not concern foreign policy, the meaning of a yea versus a nay vote is unclear. On domestic issues, a yea position can be either liberal or conservative, depending upon the president's preferences and how the roll call options are presented to members. A yea option may be conservative, such as on a vote to overturn a preexisting liberal domestic program. But a yea vote also may be the liberal option, as in an increase or expansion of a preexisting liberal program.

The method developed in the next section deals with these concerns about the Howell et. al. and the Milner and Tingley methods for measuring presidential influence across time and across roll calls. Moreover, the method developed here can easily be applied to all Congresses and to other voting bodies. Yet, as will be pointed out, it is not without its limitations and issues.

A METHOD FOR IDENTIFYING PRESIDENTIAL INFLUENCE ON ROLL CALLS

Each of the reviewed methods for estimating presidential influence on congressional roll calls, however appealing and important, has limitations. Using only presidential roll calls may underestimate the potential influence that presidents have by not accounting for the influence that presidents wield in the act of taking a position. Headcount data may be unreliable, are available for only a limited number of presidents, and may not be comparable across presidents. The approach taken by Howell and his colleagues (Howell, Jackman, and Rogowski 2013; Howell and Rogowski 2013) does not isolate presidential activities but looks only at the effect of one contextual factor—peace versus war—on voting in Congress. Finally, there are ambiguities in substantively interpreting the meaning of yea–nay vote splits on roll calls for non–foreign policy votes and when presidents do not take positions, as in the Milner and Tingley (2015) approach. The method developed here aims to overcome these issues for the focus of my research, though these other approaches may be useful for their theoretical concerns.

The method developed here is rooted in extensive literature on member roll call voting and on common assumptions about member roll call voting. A great deal of literature shows that most roll calls can be arrayed on a single dimension, which has been labeled "liberal versus conservative." The most famous such technique is the DW-NOMINATE procedure developed by Keith Poole and Howard Rosenthal (1997).

The method here builds on this idea that we can identify whether *members and presidents* vote (or take) liberal or conservative positions on roll calls. With such information, we can compare the liberal/conservative voting of members on presidential and nonpresidential roll calls. Thus, instead of comparing whether a member voted with or against the president on presidential roll calls, this method compares voting *patterns* on roll calls.

Simply put, the method compares the difference in members' liberalism/conservatism on presidential and nonpresidential roll calls. Some of that difference *may* be due to presidential influence, but other factors also may account for the difference. One possibility is that presidential and nonpresidential roll calls may cover different types of issues, or agenda composition effects. There may, for instance, be a higher proportion of foreign policy votes on presidential than on nonpresidential roll calls. The empirical work here tries to take into account the various factors that affect the difference in member voting in an attempt to isolate, as much as possible, presidential influence from other sources of difference in member voting. The total difference in member voting across presidential and nonpresidential roll calls is termed "potential presidential influence" to reflect the multiplicity of factors other than presidential influence that may affect member voting patterns.

To anticipate the results of the analysis, presidents appear able to influence a larger number of members than previous research indicates. Due to this influence, presidents win on a measurable number of roll calls that they would not have won had they not taken a position. Presidential influence thus has public policy implications, allowing the president to put his stamp on a significant amount of legislation. Presidential influence varies in systematic ways, consistent with existing research and with the theory presented in chapter 2. That is, presidents have greater influence under some conditions, for some types of roll calls, and for some types of members. Yet, consistent with existing literature, presidential influence is not omnipresent; presidents do not determine how each and every member votes on all the roll calls on which they take a position.

IDENTIFYING MEMBER LIBERALISM/CONSERVATISM ON ROLL CALLS

There are numerous approaches to identifying member liberalism/conservatism on roll calls.[17] Although the DW-NOMINATE approach is the most famous and widely used measure for identifying member and roll call liberalism or conservatism, DW-NOMINATE is not well suited for the present purposes. First, DW-NOMINATE estimates a single score, which is constant for each member (and president) across their entire congressional (or presidential) career, and assumes no change in member and presidential policy preferences and roll call voting over the course of their careers. To estimate presidential influence, however, we need to know about differences in voting behavior across presidential and nonpresidential roll calls, across presidents, and under differing political contexts. This research requires a more dynamic measure of member and presidential roll call voting.[18] Second, the DW-NOMINATE score is not intuitively or easily interpretable. What, for instance, does an increase in X-units on the DW-NOMINATE scale mean? It would be useful to have a measure of presidential influence that resulted in an intuitive and easily understood quantity.

One alternative to DW-NOMINATE are interest group–based roll call scores, like the Americans for Democratic Action (ADA) scores. Although ADA scores are expressed in proportional or percentage terms that are easily understood (e.g., the percentage of times a member and the president voted with the ADA on roll calls that the ADA identifies as tests of liberalism), there are two major problems with ADA scores. First, the simple ADA percentage support scores are not comparable across years because, across years, the roll call votes used may vary in how strongly they test liberal/conservative divisions. In some years it may be easy for members to take the ADA's position on the selected set of votes, but in other years it may be harder for members to vote with the ADA. Several factors may account for such variability across years, including party control (which affects the set of roll calls that members are asked to vote on) and the public mood (it may be easier to vote with the ADA when the public is in a liberal mood). The Groseclose, Levitt, and Snyder (1999) adjusted ADA scores correct for this lack of comparability over time, but as with DW-NOMINATE, adjusted ADA scores do not have an easy or intuitive interpretation (see also Anderson and Habel 2009).

Second, the sample of ADA votes is quite small, around twenty per year. There may be too few ADA roll calls on which presidents take positions to enable reliable analysis. In addition, ADA only began scoring members in 1947, but chapter 10 of the present study tests for presidential influence effects dating to 1877. Using the ADA scores would preclude such a historical analysis of presidential influence in Congress. For these reasons, none of these popular methods of identifying member voting tendencies is useful for this study.

USING CONSERVATIVE VOTE PROBABILITIES FOR IDENTIFYING MEMBER IDEOLOGY

Owing to the problems just identified, I turn to a very recent approach to identifying member liberal/conservative voting patterns, Fowler and Hall's (2013) conservative vote probability (CVP) estimation technique.[19] The CVP technique is flexible, uses all roll calls that we care to include, and provides quantities of interest that have an intuitive interpretation. Caution, however, must be taken in using the actual CVP estimates for each member and for the president. Since they are measured as member and presidential liberalism (or conservatism) differences from the median member (or from any other baseline), one cannot use the CVP estimates across time for time series analysis.[20]

As explained in Fowler and Hall (2013), CVPs are estimated with this ordinary least squares (OLS) regression:

$$Y_{ib} = \alpha + \beta_{ib} + \delta_{ib} + \varepsilon_{ib};$$ (3.1)

where Y is the vote (liberal or conservative), the subscripts ib refer to each individual member (i) and each bill (b), β is a dummy variable for each member, and δ is a dummy variable for each bill, while ε is the stochastic error term. The dependent variable, then, is the individual member's vote on each bill, arrayed in a "long" data file. For each Congress (or any other time unit), a member's vote on a roll call is a function of the member and the bill. The member coefficient informs us as to the probability that the member will vote more or less conservatively than the median member (or any other anchor), controlling for the specific effects of each bill. One value of the CVP estimate is the ease of interpretation. The coefficient β can be viewed as the probability on a scale from zero to 1 for how much more or less conservative a member is compared to the median member.[21]

For this analysis, I score the dependent variable 1 when a member casts a liberal vote and zero for a conservative vote.[22] The president is included as if he were a voting member of the House. Earlier I critiqued the Milner and Tingley (2015) yea–nay vote split analysis, arguing that the yea–nay division is often substantively ambiguous, at least for domestic issues. The procedure here, in contrast, scales each member's vote as liberal or conservative, which is substantively more meaningful than yea–nay when comparing all roll calls and not just foreign policy votes, as in Milner and Tingley.

Fowler and Hall (2013) offer a method for automatically scoring each bill as being liberal or conservative without having to rely on expert judgments on each bill, which would be daunting for the 55,000 or so roll calls in the House and Senate from 1953 to 2012. They propose an iterative process, which "guesses" whether a vote is liberal or conservative by running equation (3.1): "The resulting coefficients on the legislator fixed effects are the proposed CVPs after this first iteration. Next, we check to see whether the estimates are positively or negatively correlated with the coded votes for each bill. If the correlation is negative for a given bill, we flip the coding for that bill, recoding liberal votes as conservative, and vice versa" (5).

Since Fowler and Hall did not include the president in their CVP estimates, I use their automatic scoring process, but in two stages, which is necessary to determine the president's position on the roll call. First, I ran equation (3.1) but added the president as another legislator.[23] This recovers the liberal/conservative position of the president for each roll call on which the president took a position. Presidents are scored 1 when they take a liberal position, –1 when they take a conservative position, and zero when they do not take a position. This allows us to distinguish roll call voting when presidents take and do not take positions, as well as the direction of the president's position on presidential roll calls.

Thus, this procedure identifies the liberal/conservative voting of each member and of the president. Having identified the president's position, the data are reconfigured, such that the president's position (liberal, conservative, or no position) is added as an independent variable, P, in equation (3.1), producing equation (3.2):[24]

$$Y_{ib} = \alpha + \beta_{ib} + \delta_{ib} + P_{ib} + \varepsilon_{ib};$$

(3.2)

Recall that equation (3.1) is estimated separately for each year from 1953 to 2012, a total of sixty separate regressions, and the dependent variable is each member's vote on each roll call. It is possible to combine these data across all years. But there are at least two issues with analysis conducted at this level of member roll call vote. First, it produces a cumbersome and extremely massive data set—10,763,665 individual member roll call votes. A data set this large will tax many statistical analyses. Second, and perhaps more important, the individual member roll call vote data is one step removed from the theoretical interest of this study, which is presidential influence and whether that influence provides the margin of victory on presidential roll calls. Presidential influence is most interesting to study when it affects the production of public policy, that is, when it leads to higher success rates.

To investigate the influence and success implications of presidential position taking, I aggregated the individual member votes to the roll call level. The dependent variable is now the number of members voting liberal and conservative on each roll call. As we will see later, we can aggregate by subsets of members, for instance by Democrats and Republicans, to obtain the number of Democrats (or Republicans) who voted liberal versus those voting conservative. Plus, for each roll call we have data on whether the president took the liberal, the conservative, or no position. We can then compare whether there are more liberal/conservative votes when the president takes a liberal/conservative position than when the president does not take a position. With the data configured this way, we also can test whether factors such as characteristics of members (e.g., party affiliation), the roll call (e.g., policy type), the president, presidential lobbying effort (see chapter 8), or the political environment affect the amount of presidential influence.

It is possible that presidential position taking (and other lobbying efforts) may be endogenous to expectations about the final outcome of the roll call, that attributes of the congressional environment may affect presidential behavior. In other words, *Congress may exert influence over the president*. Presidents may refrain from taking a roll call position because of their expectations about congressional reactions, such as the likelihood of being defeated (Canes-Wrone, Howell, and Lewis 2008; Cohen 2010; Marshall and Prins 2007). But presidents may also moderate their positions, moving toward what Congress wants and away from their most preferred position, depending on congressional factors, such as opposition party control (Cohen 2010).

Another complication in comparing member voting on presidential and nonpresidential roll calls is that presidential roll calls are not a random subset of all roll calls. Presidents take positions on roll calls for particular reasons, such as to try to influence members, to claim credit, to be on the winning side, and/or to maintain and attract electoral supporters. Moreover, when trying to influence members, presidents may be more likely to take positions on roll calls on which they think they can influence members than on those for which they are not so optimistic about having any discernible impact. These considerations have to be taken into account when using this technique of comparing member voting on presidential and nonpresidential roll calls to estimate the amount and consequences of presidential influence. Chapter 4 presents a variety of approaches for dealing with these complications. All produce highly similar results, suggesting that presidents have more influence in Congress than previous research has indicated.

4

PRESIDENTIAL INFLUENCE IN THE HOUSE IN THE MODERN ERA

T HIS CHAPTER FIRST presents the results of applying the Fowler and Hall (2013) conservative vote probability (CVP) method to compare member voting on presidential and nonpresidential roll calls. Second, it assesses whether the difference in voting across the two types of roll calls can be attributed to presidential influence, taking into account other factors that might affect how members vote on roll calls.

The theory developed in chapter 2 suggests that presidents sometimes take positions on roll calls to lobby members for their support. Presidents lobby to alter how members vote on roll calls, especially to move them from opposing to supporting the president's position. The lobbying effect of presidential position taking comes about through a process of transformation, in which the vote becomes more closely associated with the president. On nonpresidential roll calls, the president does not factor as heavily into the member's roll call voting calculus as on presidential roll calls. But once the president takes a position, the roll call becomes more closely and tightly associated with the president. This presidential consideration thus has a greater weight in members' voting on presidential than on nonpresidential roll calls.

Presidential position taking sometimes links the president more tightly with important aspects of the larger political environment and/or the context surrounding the vote, such as party loyalty, constituent preferences, and type of issue. For example, when the president takes a position on an issue that normally divides the parties, the roll call becomes a presidential party vote. These environmental or contextual factors can work to either the president's advantage or disadvantage, depending on how they are arrayed. Under some conditions, the strength of the presidential consideration will affect whether a member changes from opposing to supporting the president's position.[1]

One complication of conceptualizing position taking as lobbying is that, as we have noted, presidents may have other reasons for taking a position, such as to claim credit, to be associated with the winning side, to maintain and attract electoral support, and so on. To isolate how much of the difference in voting on presidential and nonpresidential roll calls derives from presidential influence requires distinguishing the motivations for presidential position taking on a roll call. The empirical analysis here aims to distinguish between lobbying to gain support and other reasons for presidential position taking.

The theory also outlines two pathways through which presidential position taking may influence a member's vote: direct and indirect. The direct pathway involves such traditionally understood lobbying tactics as doing favors, helping members in reelection campaigns, vote trading, and the like. In the case of the indirect pathway, the linkage between the president and aspects of the political environment and/or the context surrounding the vote, to the president's advantage (or disadvantage), is tightened. For example, partisan loyalty of members may intensify because the president takes a position. Or constituent opinion may become more important to the member because, through the president taking a position, the issue's importance or salience to voters has risen (Canes-Wrone 2006). The empirical analyses in the following chapters try to distinguish the relative importance of these two pathways of presidential influence on member roll call voting.

This theoretical perspective on presidential position taking, lobbying, and influence differs from that found in much of the extant literature, which views presidential influence as deriving from the personal characteristics of presidents. For instance, Neustadt (1960, 1991) suggests that presidents increase or preserve their power (influence) by being sensitive to the prospective implications of their actions, whether they will succeed or not, and how that success or failure will affect their future power situation in the eyes of Washington insiders (reputation) or with the public (prestige). A related strand of research tries to assess the president's skill and examine whether traits, personality, background, or other elements are associated with the president's skill level (Greenstein 2004, 2009; Kellerman 1984; Wayne 2009). Another, smaller set of studies has attempted to test whether presidents reputed to be effective and influential in their dealings with Congress are in fact so (Fleisher, Bond, and Wood 2008; Teodoro and Bond 2017).

One aim of this chapter is to assess the individualistic perspective on presidential influence, using the new measure of presidential influence developed here, and to make an initial attempt to compare the usefulness of the personal-based perspective with the more strategic and institutionally based conceptualization of influence.[2] The first task of this chapter, however, is to apply the Fowler and Hall CVP method to the data, which is all House roll calls from 1953 to 2012.

PRESIDENTIAL INFLUENCE AT THE ROLL CALL LEVEL

There are several complications in estimating presidential influence from position taking. Presidential influence might be inflated if presidents take positions on popular roll calls, that is, on votes with large proportions of members voting on the same side, no matter the member's party. Bond and Fleisher (1984, 1990) and Bond, Fleisher, and Wood (2003) recommend and routinely drop such "hurrah" or lopsided votes from their analyses, arguing that such votes do not provide good tests of the factors that affect presidential success.[3] On hurrah votes, presidents may be doing nothing more than jumping on the congressional bandwagon. It may be the case that the popularity of a vote in Congress *influences the president* to take a position on that roll call, with the president aligning with the popular side rather than trying to influence the voting behavior of members. In estimating presidential influence, we need to distinguish instances of presidents influencing member voting from instances of members influencing the president.

Second, the composition of the agenda may change from year to year (or from Congress to Congress). Presidents may have an easier time influencing member voting on some types of issues and on some conditions than on others. For instance, assume that presidents have more influence on foreign than on domestic policy, the two presidencies thesis (Canes-Wrone, Howell, and Lewis 2008; Howell, Jackman, and Rogowski 2013; Lindsay and Steger 1993; Shull 1991; Wildavsky 1966). If there are proportionately more foreign policy roll calls in one year than in another, this agenda composition difference may make presidents *appear* to be more influential.

Third, the most important reason to study presidential influence is to find out whether influence leads to winning on some roll calls that the president's side would otherwise have lost. To do this requires estimating how many additional votes the president's side acquired due to the executive's influence. The ultimate question with regard to presidential influence is not whether the executive influenced members to vote on his side but whether the president influenced enough members to convert a likely defeat into a presidential victory. Influence without consequences for the production of public policy is much less interesting to study than influence that leads to policy outcomes the president desires.

The analysis in this and subsequent chapters is based on combining all the roll calls from 1953 to 2012, after establishing whether the member and the president took a liberal or a conservative position, or whether the president did not take a position, using the CVP procedure described in chapter 3. For each roll call, characteristics of the roll call, such as policy type (e.g., foreign versus domestic), the president, and the political context, can be identified. These characteristics can be used either as controls or to test whether these characteristics condition presidential influence, that is, whether presidential influence on a roll call varies with these bill and contextual characteristics. Later chapters present such analyses. For this chapter, the key question concerns the amount of influence presidents derive from position taking and whether that influence can convert defeats into victories on enough roll calls to be substantively meaningful.

This roll call–level data set also allows one to test whether presidents are highly likely to take positions on hurrah votes. It is quite easy, using the roll call–level data, to separate hurrah or lopsided from contested votes. Finally, the roll call–level data set allows one to employ quasi-experimental methods to assess the causal impact of presidential position taking on member roll call voting. Selection effects and endogeneity in presidential position taking have plagued studies attempting to assess the amount of impact or influence presidents have in Congress (e.g., Howell and Rogowski 2013, 150). Quasi-experimental analysis is one method of establishing causality in observational data.

OVERALL PRESIDENTIAL INFLUENCE
AT THE ROLL CALL LEVEL

From 1953 to 2012, the House of Representative held 26,921 recorded roll call votes. During those years, presidents took liberal positions on 2,039 (7.6%) roll calls and conservative positions on 2,356 (8.8%). Overall, presidents took positions on slightly more than 16% of all roll calls. By comparing the vote splits on nonpresidential and presidential roll calls, we can begin to estimate whether presidents influence member voting. Presidents can be said to be influential if members are more likely to vote liberal (or conservative) when the president takes a liberal (or conservative) position than when the president does not take a position.

These roll call–level data suggest the possibility of presidential influence on member voting. Table 4.1 presents regression results of presidential position taking on the liberal/conservative vote proportion, pooling all the roll calls from 1953 to 2012 but not distinguishing across presidents. This analysis only controls for year, using dummy indicators for each year. The dependent variable is the proportion (zero to 1) voting on the liberal side. Since the dependent variable is a proportion, I also use fractional regression.[4]

Since fractional regression results use the logistic distribution, they are not intuitively interpretable. To make the results across the two estimations comparable and to render the fractional regression results more easily understandable, table 4.2 presents the marginal effects of presidential position taking, in this case, the proportion of liberal votes by type of presidential

TABLE 4.1 IMPACT OF PRESIDENTIAL POSITION TAKING ON MEMBER VOTING (PROPORTION LIBERAL), HOUSE OF REPRESENTATIVES, 1953–2012

VARIABLE	ALL ROLL CALLS		LOPSIDED ROLL CALLS EXCLUDED	
	REGRESSION[a]	FRACTIONAL REGRESSION[b]	REGRESSION[a]	BETA REGRESSION[a]
President's position	0.0523***	0.315***	0.0151**	0.0605**
	(0.00993)	(0.0161)	(0.00716)	(0.0278)
Constant	0.603***	0.04	0.525***	0.0973***
	0.012	(0.123)	0.009	0.036
/ln_phi	—	—	—	2.546***
	—	—	—	(0.0326)
phi	—	—	—	12.755
	—	—	—	0.415
Observations	26,909	26,909	16,457	16,457
R^2	0.006	—	0.002	—
Pseudo R^2	—	0.02	—	—
Wald chi-square	—	2,592.81	—	4.74
F	27.79	—	4.469	—
Regression sum of squares	2,139	—	301.6	—
Log likelihood	—	–17,712	—	9,728

Note: Dependent variable is the proportion (zero to 1) liberal. Presidential position is scored 1 = Liberal position; 0 = No position; –1 = Conservative position. Robust standard errors in parentheses.

[a] Clustered on year.

[b] Yearly dummies, 2012 set as the criterion.

* $p < 0.1$, ** $p < 0.05$, *** $p < 0.01$.

position. Each cell in the table presents the proportion of members voting liberal. The difference in these proportions tells us what proportion of members voted liberal on presidential roll calls compared to voting liberal on nonpresidential roll calls. Although this simple analysis is far from definitive with regard to the amount of presidential influence, the hypothesis of presidential influence would predict the highest liberal proportion when

TABLE 4.2 MARGINAL EFFECT OF PRESIDENTIAL POSITION TAKING ON MEMBER VOTING, HOUSE OF REPRESENTATIVES, 1953–2012 (PROPORTION VOTING LIBERAL)

	ALL ROLL CALLS		LOPSIDED ROLL CALLS EXCLUDED	
	REGRESSION	FRACTIONAL REGRESSION	REGRESSION	BETA REGRESSION
President's Position				
Conservative	.55	.53	.51	.51
No position	.60	.60	.52	.52
Liberal	.65	.67	.54	.54
n	26,909	26,909	16,457	16,457

Note: Each cell represents the proportion voting liberal. Based on analysis from table 4.1.

presidents take a liberal position and the smallest liberal proportion when the president takes a conservative position.[5]

The regression and fractional regression produce similar findings, although the fractional regression slightly suggests a stronger impact of presidential position taking than the ordinary least squares (OLS) estimates (table 4.2). Depending on the statistical technique, presidents move approximately 5% to 7% of members to their side by taking a position, either liberal or conservative, compared to not taking a position. In other words, the regression results indicate that presidents can move about twenty-two members (out of 435) to their side just by taking a position, while the fractional regression estimates indicate about thirty to thirty-one members. Depending on the closeness of the roll call vote, movements of twenty-two to thirty-one members can easily turn an expected loss into a victory.

DO PRESIDENTS INFLATE THEIR INFLUENCE SCORES BY TAKING POSITIONS ON LOPSIDED VOTES?

The estimates of presidential influence introduced earlier may be inflated if presidents take a relatively large number of positions on lopsided roll calls. When a president takes a position on a roll call that receives overwhelming support in Congress, the percentage of members on the president's side will by definition be higher, with a higher average proportion of members voting on the president's side. When there is strong support for a roll call in Congress, the popularity of the issue among members may influence the president to take a position on the popular side, rather than the president influencing enough members to produce such high levels of congressional support for their position. Under such circumstances, presidents may want to be associated with the winning side and thus are motivated to take a public position. In estimating presidential influence, therefore, we do not want to conflate roll calls where the president influences members with roll calls where popularity among members of Congress influences the president to take a position. Moreover, even if the president influences members on lopsided votes, it is unlikely that the president would influence enough members to convert a defeat into a lopsided victory. Presidential influence is most interesting to study if the influence is great enough to convert an expected defeat into a victory.

This section addresses this question. How would we know whether the president's motivations to take positions differ between lopsided and closely contested roll calls? And how would we know whether, by taking a position, the president influenced enough members to convert a defeat into a victory? Ideally, we would like information on the expected vote division before the president decides to announce a position, but such information is rare. As a second-best alternative, we can use the actual vote split on the roll call. It is highly unlikely that a vote expected to have a narrow outcome will turn out to be lopsided once the vote is taken.[6] The objective here is not to be precise about the expected vote split but rather to distinguish the easy, lopsided, and/or popular roll calls from more contested ones and to estimate presidential influence and its consequences for the more contested set of roll calls.

Admittedly, the dividing line between lopsided and close roll calls is arbitrarily drawn. Various studies use either a 90% versus 10% or an 80% versus 20% criterion, with the president siding with the majority, in classifying lopsided or hurrah votes (Bond and Fleisher 1990; Cohen, Bond, and Fleisher 2013, 2014; Edwards 1985, 1990). When the president takes the minority position on lopsided votes, the executive is "rolled" (Jenkins and

Monroe 2016).[7] Rolls may be useful for studying both presidential influence and success. Since the 80% versus 20% split will categorize more votes as lopsided than the 90% versus 10% split, I use that line to distinguish lopsided from closer roll calls.

First, let's define lopsided roll calls as any vote that received 80% or more members voting on the same side. By this definition, about 39% of roll calls are lopsided.[8] Presidents are more likely to take positions on non-lopsided, conflictual roll calls (19.9%) than on lopsided roll calls (10.7%), a difference that is statistically significant ($X^2 = 396.4, p = 0.000$). Presidents sometimes take positions on the losing side of lopsided votes, or *rolls*. In these data, there are 325 rolls, about 1.2% of all roll calls. Presidents are rarely rolled. Combining rolls with non-lopsided votes for presidential position taking does not alter the story of presidential position taking very much. Using this revised definition of lopsided versus non-lopsided votes, which includes both easy wins and rolls, presidents take positions on only 7.8% of lopsided but on 21.5% of non-lopsided roll calls.

From another perspective, the bulk of presidential positions are on contested as opposed to lopsided votes. Of the 4,393 roll calls in these data, 25.5% (1,118) of presidential positions are on lopsided votes, compared to 74.5% (3,275) on contested votes. Distinguishing rolls from lopsided victories, presidents take 18.1% of their positions (793) on lopsided winning roll calls, 7.4% on lopsided losses (rolls), and 74.5% on contested roll calls.

Presidents do not seem to take positions frequently or primarily on roll calls merely to be associated with the winning side, as a credit-claiming model would predict (e.g., Mayhew 1974), although they take positions on a nontrivial number of such votes. Instead, most of the time, presidents take positions when the vote split is narrower, and thus we may assume that presidents frequently take positions for policy-related reasons and/or to try to influence Congress to enact their preferred legislation. They may take positions on contested votes because they feel strongly about the issue (that is, it is a high presidential priority); because of party, interest group, or voter pressure on the president to become involved in the issue; or perhaps because they believe that they can swing enough members to their side to convert a defeat into a victory.

Of these three types of roll call positions—lopsided wins, rolls, and contested votes—two are not theoretically interesting from an influence perspective. Even if presidents move members to their side on lopsided votes, any such movement probably would not alter the outcome. And it may be the case that both the president and some members decide to join the herd on lopsided winning votes to claim credit, to be associated with the winning side, and/or to be linked with popular issues (Balla et al. 2002; Weaver 1986).

Rolls are not particularly interesting from a presidential influence perspective, either. Recall that rolls are defined here as 80% or more members voting against the president. Even if the president could move some members to his column on such votes, the outcome probably would not be altered—the president in all likelihood could not influence enough members to convert a defeat into a victory when 80% or more of members already oppose the president. Most critically, rolls indicate an extreme lack of influence by the president. By this definition, rolling a president requires a large segment of the president's party to defect and vote against the president. Moreover, presidential rolls are very rare. It is unclear why presidents get rolled. It may be that they committed to a course of action previously and thus felt bound by that public commitment.[9] Presidential influence is of most theoretical interest on contested votes, where presidential influence may affect the outcome.

Tables 4.1 and 4.2 also present results of estimations that exclude all lopsided votes, including rolls. Presidential influence is markedly reduced when considering only contested roll calls compared to all roll calls. Both the OLS and beta regressions indicate an average effect of 1.5%, or a movement of about six to seven members to the president's column.[10] This is a considerably weaker effect of presidential position taking than was noted earlier. The addition of six or seven members to the president's column might not be consequential enough to convert defeats into victories very often. Rather, this meager magnitude of effect is in line with Edwards's (1990) marginal effects perspective (see also Bond and Fleisher 1990). Perhaps there is not all that much to presidential influence, even using the more expansive definition applied here.

Finally, the marginal effects from table 4.2 suggest an asymmetry in presidential influence, with liberal position taking being more potent in influencing members than conservative position taking. When a president takes a liberal position, the effect is 2% (eight to nine members), compared to 1% (four members) when taking a conservative position. Again, however, neither liberal nor conservative position taking appears to move very many members.

PRESIDENTIAL INFLUENCE AND CROSS-PARTY POSITION TAKING

Subsequent chapters will investigate in detail the factors that may condition presidential influence, such as party control, public opinion, policy type, and presidential lobbying effort. For now, let us entertain only one possibility: that influence may be conditional on the party of the president and on whether presidents take positions that align with their party's ideological leanings. Generally, Democrats take liberal positions and Republicans take conservative ones. But sometimes Democratic and Republican presidents take positions opposite from these general tendencies, which I will call "cross-party position taking." In the presidential position data, Democrats took conservative positions 10% of the time and Republicans took liberal positions 19% of the time.[11] Thus, while presidents tend to line up ideologically with their parties for the vast majority of their positions, for a significant fraction of their positions, presidents take the opposing party's typical position.

Do presidents undercut or enhance their influence when taking cross-party positions? For instance, taking a cross-party position may do nothing to ingratiate the president with the opposition party, but it may alienate co-partisans. Some co-partisans might be inclined to support the president's position, even voting against district interests and personal reelection needs. But they might balk at supporting the president when the president cooperates with the opposition in making policy, that is, when the president takes the position usually associated with the opposition. Conversely, cross-party position taking may suggest successful

TABLE 4.3 MARGINAL EFFECT OF PRESIDENTIAL POSITION TAKING BY PRESIDENT'S PARTY AND HOUSE PARTY, 1953–2012, PROPORTION VOTING LIBERAL, LOPSIDED VOTES EXCLUDED

PRESIDENT'S POSITION	DEMOCRATIC PRESIDENTS	REPUBLICAN PRESIDENTS
Conservative	.46	.52
No position	.50	.54
Liberal	.54	.57

Note: Based on an ordinary least squares estimation, as used in tables 4.1 and 4.2, but with the addition of an interaction term between president's party and whether the president took a liberal or a conservative position.

negotiation between the president and the opposition, with the opposition deciding to support the president's position despite partisan and other reasons not to do so. Cross-party position taking may mobilize support for the president from the opposition without alienating support among co-partisans. Table 4.3 presents marginal effects based on a regression equation that interacts presidential position taking with the president's party.[12]

Democratic presidents are more influential than Republicans on average, but there does not appear to be much asymmetry associated with cross-party position taking. Whether Democrats take liberal or conservative positions, they move about 4% of members (seventeen) to their side. Republicans are a bit less influential overall than Democrats. When taking a conservative position, Republicans add about 2% (eight or nine) to their column, but 3% (thirteen) when taking a liberal position. Clearly, these simple models do not take into account all the conditions that may affect presidential influence. Moreover, it is not clear why Democrats are slightly more influential than Republicans. Chapter 5 explores in more detail the factors that condition presidential influence.

WHO ARE THE MOST INFLUENTIAL PRESIDENTS?

The roll call–level estimates suggest much less presidential influence once we exclude lopsided votes from consideration. We can use these data to assess the individualistic perspective on presidential influence—whether some presidents, due to their personal characteristics or skill, are more influential than other presidents. For instance, Genovese, Belt, and Lammers (2016, 2) argue, "What determines whether presidents achieve the political results their opportunity levels permit? *Skill*" (italics in original).[13] A typical observation from this perspective is that Lyndon Johnson and Ronald Reagan were effective and influential with Congress, whereas Jimmy Carter is a prime example of an ineffective president, without much influence in Congress. The many years that Johnson served in Congress honed his legislative skills, which supposedly served him well once he became president. Ronald Reagan, while he lacked Johnson's congressional experience, seemed to possess a keen strategic sense and flexibility in forging legislation. In contrast, Carter's moralizing and rigid personality undermined his relations with key members of Congress, such as Speaker of the House Thomas "Tip" O'Neill, undercutting his ability to leverage the massively large Democratic majorities in the House and Senate to his advantage.[14]

Table 4.4 presents summary statistics of roll call–level influence by president. These data are based on annual OLS regressions of presidential position taking on the percentage of members voting liberal, excluding the lopsided votes, whether hurrah or rolls. Then these annual roll call–level influence coefficients are averaged within presidencies.[15] Averaging across presidents is consistent with the individualistic perspective, which argues that personal traits and skills of presidents are important sources of their influence and that such personal attributes do not change much during a president's tenure.

Table 4.4 reports that Nixon and the elder Bush are the most influential presidents, at 0.06, with Eisenhower a close third at 0.05.[16] These coefficients convert into Nixon and Bush influencing twenty-six members to their side and Eisenhower twenty-two. A larger number of presidents, in contrast, appear to possess little if any pull with members of Congress, with coefficients ranging from zero to 0.2. Ford, Clinton, Obama, Kennedy, and G. W. Bush notably fall into this set of presidents, who seemingly lack any measurable influence with Congress. The two presidents historically rated as the most individually influential (or skilled), Johnson and Reagan, are only average here, with scores of 0.04 and 0.03 (the average across all

TABLE 4.4 COMPARING PRESIDENTIAL
INFLUENCE BY PRESIDENT

	ROLL CALL–LEVEL INFLUENCE		
PRESIDENT	MEAN	STD. DEV.	N
Eisenhower	0.05	0.05	8
Kennedy	0.02	0.02	3
Johnson	0.04	0.02	5
Nixon	0.06	0.03	6
Ford	0.00	0.01	2
Carter	0.03	0.01	4
Reagan	0.03	0.02	8
Bush, G. H. W.	0.06	0.01	4
Clinton	0.01	0.03	8
Bush, G. W.	0.02	0.03	8
Obama	0.01	0.02	4
Total	0.03	0.03	60

Note: Roll call–level influence is based on yearly ordinary least squares estimations, excluding lopsided roll calls and rolls, and averaged across years within presidencies, from the analysis of table 4.1.

presidents is 0.03). Moreover, Carter, usually depicted as the least influential and skillful in his relations with Congress, possesses an average rating of 0.03. Clearly, these roll call–level influence estimates hardly resemble the historical accounts of these modern presidents.

The personal president perspective also hypothesizes relatively invariant personal effects for each president, as the president's ability to influence members of Congress derives from a personal trait, such as personality, that the incumbent possesses before entering office and that is relatively stable. Thus, this hypothesis predicts standard deviations in influence across the years in office to be zero. But this is not the case. Even though the standard deviations all appear to be quite small, averaging 0.03 and ranging from 0.01 to 0.05, the roll call effects coefficients

(b) themselves only range from 0.00 to 0.06.[17] In other words, the standard deviation of influence within presidencies is comparable in size to the average level of influence across tenure in office. There appears to be much within-presidency variation in influence, which is contrary to the personalistic account of presidential influence.

THE CAUSAL IMPACT OF POSITION TAKING: A TREATMENT EFFECTS ANALYSIS

Analysis thus far suggests that presidents may possess a modest degree of influence on member voting when taking positions on roll calls. Across all contested roll calls, presidents do not appear to influence enough members to carry the day for any but the most narrowly decided roll calls. Nor would we have expected presidents to be so influential as to swing large numbers of members to their side on large numbers of roll calls. Still, results thus far indicate that presidents can influence only a small number of members to their column by taking a position, which calls into question the value of studying presidential influence in Congress, as this study intends.

Yet there are important limitations to the above regression analysis. The analysis did not take into account the possible increase or decrease in presidential influence with changes in presidential behavior and/or with the political context, as the theory outlined in chapter 2 suggests. Before attempting to understand those conditional effects on presidential influence, we need to determine whether position taking has a true causal effect on member voting. In other words, do presidents influence the roll call votes of members by taking a position or do presidents merely take positions when they think they will be successful, when there is already strong agreement between the president and members of Congress on the issue?

To a degree, the previous analysis attempted to deal with this endogeneity issue by excluding lopsided roll calls. Presidents, for instance, may take positions on highly popular roll calls to be associated with the winning side and/or to take credit for the floor victory (Mayhew 1974). Such presidential credit claiming behavior will inflate the apparent amount of influence presidents have on member roll call votes. When lopsided votes are excluded, presidential influence declined from about twenty to thirty-five votes across all roll calls to slightly less than ten. Still, presidents may take positions on contested votes for multiple reasons besides trying to influence how members vote. More importantly, excluding lopsided votes does not definitely correct for the fundamental problem of the methodology used to compare voting on nonpresidential and presidential roll calls. There still may be systematic differences between presidential and nonpresidential roll calls, even after excluding lopsided roll calls.

Howell and Rogowski (2013) aptly explain this concern (see also Canes-Wrone, Howell, and Lewis 2008; Howell, Jackman, and Rogowski 2013). According to Howell and Rogowski (2013), studies that use samples of roll calls, such as, for instance, only roll calls on which the president has taken a position,

> face a basic challenge: they focus exclusively on samples of legislative initiatives on which the president took public positions. Ascertaining presidential power on the basis of roll-call votes on presidential initiatives, however, is extraordinarily difficult. Presidents do not randomly select elements from their policy agenda to put before Congress. Rather, presidents choose those policies that they think stand a decent chance of passage and set aside the rest. If such selectivity is a function of war—and there are ample reasons to believe that it is—then systematic biases are introduced that, uncorrected, may obscure war's genuine effects on presidential power. (152)

Simply put, roll calls on which presidents take a position are not a random subset of the universe of roll calls. Presidents may take positions based on expectations of what Congress will do; the position-taking decision thus may be endogenous to presidential expectations about congressional behavior. Such selection effects may bias the estimation of presidential impacts on congressional roll calls.

Past research has used several methods to address this endogeneity–selection bias problem. For instance, in their test of the two presidencies thesis when using budgetary data, Canes-Wrone, Howell, and Lewis (2008, 9) use an instrumental variable solution (see also Kiewiet and McCubbins

1988, 1991). Marshall and Prins (2007), in their test of the effects of approval on roll call success, use a Heckman selection model, in which they first model the presidential decision to take a position and then, in the second stage, model the factors that affect success. They find that popular presidents are more likely to take positions, presumably because they think that their popularity will lead members to support them. Marshall and Prins also find stronger effects of approval on the vote result compared to that which is detailed in much existing research.[18] In a study of presidential legislative proposals, I argue, like Marshall and Prins, that presidents will censor their legislative agendas when they expect to be defeated—when, for instance, the opposition party controls Congress (Cohen 2012). Consistent with this hypothesis, the president's legislative agenda is smaller in the face of an opposition Congress than when his party controls the legislature.

In their study of the effects of war on presidential influence, Howell and Rogowski (2013) use all roll calls within a Congress, separating the Congress into two periods—prior to the war and after the war begins—to deal with this endogeneity issue. They argue that "by analyzing the universe of congressional roll calls within these time frames, rather than the subset of bills on which presidents have taken public positions, we substantially reduce the selection biases that confront previous research on war and congressional voting behavior" (153).

The Howell and Rogowski (and Howell, Jackman, and Rogowski 2013) approach is similar to that taken here by using all roll calls. To further deal with heterogeneity in presidential position taking, as well as to focus only on those instances when we expect presidential influence to be theoretically and substantively meaningful, the earlier analysis excluded all lopsided votes. Still, there is more that we can do to establish whether presidential position taking can affect member voting.

A QUASI-EXPERIMENTAL MATCHING APPROACH TO ESTIMATING PRESIDENTIAL INFLUENCE

It is notoriously difficult to establish causality with observational data. A large number of techniques have been developed, from instrumental variables, difference-in-differences estimation, and regression discontinuity to propensity scores and matching (Imbens and Wooldridge 2009). A matching-propensity quasi-experimental approach is appropriate for the data used here.

Let us conceptualize presidential position taking as a treatment on members of Congress. Matching designs organize treated and untreated cases into two sets, aiming to make the two resemble each other as closely as possible, based on observable characteristics, with the "only" difference being included in the treated or the untreated group (Rubin 1973). Matching designs, in effect, try to simulate the random assignment mechanism of experiments.

But effective matching may not always be possible. Cases in one group with no suitable match in the other group are excluded from the analysis, which may bias the estimate of the treatment effect (Morgan and Harding 2006; West, Biesanz, and Pitts 2000). For instance, if presidents took positions on every foreign policy roll call, these roll calls would have to be excluded from the matching procedure because there would be no suitable match among the nonpresidential roll calls. This would seriously distort our understanding of presidential influence, because it would not include the type of roll call on which much literature suggests presidential influence is at its greatest, foreign policy.

Moreover, matching and related propensity scoring techniques are most commonly used when there is only one treatment, that is, when there are only two groups of cases, the treated and the untreated. In this study, since presidents can take either a liberal or a conservative position, there are in effect two treatments, a liberal treatment and a conservative treatment. A roll call may be treated with either a liberal or a conservative presidential position, or it may not be treated because the president did not take a position. This requires that we use a multiple treatments technique. There are several multiple treatment effects techniques, including regression adjustment, inverse probability weights, inverse probability weights–regression adjustment (IPWRA), and augmented inverse probability weights (AIPW) (Austin 2011; Cattaneo 2010).

Regression adjustment uses a two-step process. First, regression adjustment statistically models the different treatments, using covariates in a multivariate regression framework. Essentially, regression adjustment reweights the sample across treatment levels by controlling for covariates that affect the treatment level (the category) to which the case is assigned. This process parallels propensity score matching techniques. Regression adjustment "corrects" for differences in covariates across outcome levels. In contrast, inverse probability weights statistically models the treatment based on a missing data problem, which is that each case can be assigned to only one potential outcome (e.g., liberal position, no position, or conservative position). Inverse probability weights "corrects" for nonrandom assignment to the treatment.

Inverse probability weights–regression adjustment combines both techniques, allowing one to model both the outcome and the treatment. When using any of these multiple treatment techniques, it is important that the resulting outcomes are balanced, that is, that the variance in the covariates are same for all treatment outcomes. When this condition holds, one can argue that cases were randomly assigned to the treatment(s). Like IPWRA, augmented inverse probability weights statistically models both the outcome and the treatment, but adds a bias correction to the outcome model. If there is any bias in the treatment equation, AIPW adds the correction to the treatment estimation, but if there is no bias in the treatment equation, the bias correction is set to zero.[19]

Since the IPWRA and AIPW allow one to model both the treatment and the outcome and thus to "correct" for bias associated with both the outcome and treatment, I employ these techniques. The outcome equation is modeled as a function six variables: whether there was a Democratic majority in the House (= 1), whether the vote was on foreign policy (= 1), presidential approval during the month of the vote, the level of party polarization in the House, whether the president's party was the majority in the House (= 1), and whether the president was a Democrat (= 1). The treatment equation employs two variables, whether the president was a Democrat (= 1) and the public mood. The appendix to this chapter provides the complete statistical results of these treatment effects analyses.[20]

Both treatment estimations suggest that presidents can influence congressional voting through position taking. The IPWRA finds a 4.9% (twenty-one-member) effect when presidents take a conservative position, while the AIPW estimates the effect at a similar magnitude, 4.4%

(nineteen members). When the president takes a liberal position, the effects are smaller—2.2% for IPWRA (nine members) and 2.3% for AIPW (ten members).[21]

These results are substantively important, showing that presidents can move a substantial, albeit not overwhelming, number of members to their side by taking a position, with conservative position taking being more potent than liberal position taking. The results are also theoretically important, as the treatment effects analysis helps establish causality from presidential position taking to member roll call voting. Finally, these estimated treatment effects are somewhat larger than that found for the regression models that excluded lopsided votes, even though lopsided roll calls were excluded from the treatment effects analysis. But the treatment effects results are somewhat smaller compared to the regression results that used all roll calls.

Comparing all of these analyses, there remains some degree of uncertainty over the number of members that presidents can influence when they take roll call positions, although all analyses suggest that presidents can influence member votes through position taking. Since the regression analysis that excluded lopsided votes produced the smallest influence effects, most of the analyses in this book use regression on contested votes. By doing so, the following analyses use the most conservative or smallest estimates of presidential influence. Being analytically conservative in this sense will bolster confidence in the meaningfulness of findings, assuming any of the findings are meaningful and substantively important.

INFLUENCE AND VICTORY MARGINS ON ROLL CALLS

Having established that presidents can influence a measurable number of members to vote on their side—from nine to twenty-one, depending on the analytical technique used—does this degree of influence have any practical implications for winning roll calls? Does the president's side win votes that they would otherwise have lost had the president not taken a position, and if so, how many?

TABLE 4.5 PRESIDENTIAL VICTORIES ON ROLL CALLS DUE TO
PRESIDENTIAL INFLUENCE, CONTESTED ROLL CALLS,
HOUSE OF REPRESENTATIVES, 1953–2012

OUTCOME	LIBERAL POSITIONS	CONSERVATIVE POSITIONS	ALL POSITIONS
Defeats	618 (36.2%)	848 (54.0%)	1,466 (44.7%)
Victories due to influence	122 (7.2%)	177 (11.3%)	299 (9.1%)
Victories without need for influence	965 (56.6%)	543 (34.6%)	1,508 (46.0%)

Note: Based on 4% treatment effect for conservative positions and 2% for liberal positions. Analysis excludes lopsided roll calls, defined as when 80% or more members voted liberal or when 20% or less voted liberal.

To estimate the number of roll call victories in the House that are due to presidential influence, I first use as a baseline the estimates from the treatment effects analysis. I define a presidential victory as more than 50% of members voting on the same side as the president.[22] Slightly rounding down from the treatment effects findings, I use 4% as the additional votes presidents receive from taking conservative positions, and 2% as the additional votes when they take liberal positions. Thus the question is, among conservative positions, how many roll calls fell into the range of 46% to 50% of members voting liberally, and among liberal positions, how many fell into the 50% to 52% range?[23]

Table 4.5 presents the breakdown of liberal and conservative positions, separately, and all positions combined. Presidents win an additional 7.2% of roll calls due to the influence from taking a liberal position and an additional 11.3% when taking a conservative position. Across all positions, presidents win an additional 9.1% of roll calls. With an average of fifty-four presidential positions per year from 1953 to 2012, presidents will win approximately an additional five roll call votes each year. These results suggest that presidents win a substantial number of additional floor votes as a result of their influence over member voting.

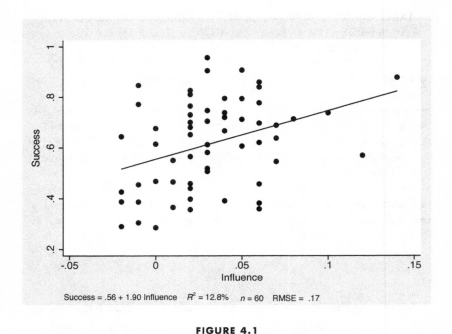

Success = .56 + 1.90 Influence R^2 = 12.8% n = 60   RMSE = .17

FIGURE 4.1

Scatter plot between annual influence on contested votes and success,
House of Representatives, 1953–2012

INFLUENCE AND SUCCESS

With these results in mind, it is useful to turn to the issue of the relationship between influence and success—does influence lead to higher
presidential success rates in the House? Annual influence on contested roll
calls and success correlate at 0.36 (Pearson's r, p = 0.005), a statistically
significant, if not overwhelmingly strong relationship.[24] Figure 4.1 presents the scatter plot between the two variables. As roll call–level influence
rises, so does success. The regression equation printed on the scatter plot
indicates that each 1.9% increase in influence leads to a 1% increase in
success.[25]

The figure also hints at three values that may be affecting the strength
of the relationship for 1953, 1954, and 1972. The influence coefficient topped

0.10 in each of those years, which is quite high compared to other years. Removing these years does not alter the relationship between contested roll call–level influence and annual success, as the two remain correlated at essentially the same magnitude (Pearson's $r = 0.34$, $p = 0.01$). Without these three data points, it takes a 2.25% shift in influence to increase success by 1.0%, a similar if slightly weaker impact than with all sixty data points. There appears to be a relationship between presidential influence at the roll call level and success, reinforcing the findings from the previous section that presidential influence leads to the president's side winning a meaningful number of additional roll calls because of presidential position taking.

Sorting out the causal impact of influence on contested votes, independent of other factors that affect success, is more difficult, because variables that affect success may also affect influence. Specifically, in a standard model of success (which includes majority status, House polarization, their interaction, and presidential approval), all but approval appear to account statistically for the annual roll call–level influence coefficient (see table 4.8 in the appendix to this chapter for details). Even with time series data, it can be difficult to sort out the causality between two variables that are measured contemporaneously, as is the case between success and influence here.[26]

But it makes sense that there should be a relationship between roll call influence and success, since earlier analysis in this chapter found evidence of measurable presidential influence. The analyses here support Bond and Fleisher's speculation that presidential influence should lead to higher success levels. Presidential influence is linked to success and has substantively consequential implications for policy production. Presidential influence is a theoretically and substantively meaningful part of presidential–congressional relations.

CONCLUSION

This chapter raised these questions: How much influence do presidents have with Congress, and do presidents have enough influence to convert expected defeats into victories? The analyses reported significant amounts of presidential influence, with presidents able to move from nine to twenty-one members to their side by taking a position. Additionally, the analysis failed to detect much support for the personal presidency perspective, which is that the personal and individual attributes of presidents account for this influence. Within presidencies, there was considerable variation in presidential influence, but the personalistic perspective predicts that influence within a presidency should not vary from year to year because the personal-based characteristics, which determine influence, are stable and do not fluctuate during a president's tenure.

As to the second question, presidents win on a good number of additional votes, approximately 10% more in the House, because of the influence that derives from position taking. Insofar as any of these additional victories concern important issues, the effects of presidential influence may have important public policy implications. Moreover, these results are theoretically meaningful, adding to our understanding of presidential relations with Congress. Presidential influence matters, to borrow a phrase from George Edwards (1990), "at the margins." But marginal effects can sometimes be consequential. For the vast bulk of roll calls on which presidents take a position, approximately 90%, the added votes that presidents receive will not affect the outcome. Either presidents cannot influence enough members to vote with them or the additional votes do not matter because the president's side already possessed enough support in the House to win. Still, the amount of influence reported here is wider than is portrayed in much of the existing research on the president in Congress.

Having established that presidents can influence members by taking positions on roll calls, we can now go on to the next question: What are the mechanisms through which presidential influence operates? Analysis in this chapter tested for the possibility that personal presidential skill, one mechanism to account for presidential influence and success, is wanting. The theory presented in chapter 2 suggests two other pathways by which presidential position taking might influence congressional voting, direct and indirect pathways. The next several chapters take up the question of distinguishing the direct and indirect pathways of presidential influence. Chapter 5 looks at the partisan pathway, chapter 6 the policy type pathway, and chapter 7 the public opinion pathway. Chapter 8 looks at presidential lobbying effort and presidential influence in Congress.

APPENDIX

TABLE 4.6 TREATMENT EFFECTS, INVERSE PROBABILITY–WEIGHTED REGRESSION ADJUSTMENT, HOUSE, 1953–2012, CONTESTED VOTES

VARIABLE	ATE	OUTCOME EQUATION– CONSERVATIVE	OUTCOME EQUATION– NO POSITION	OUTCOME EQUATION– LIBERAL	TREATMENT EQUATION– CONSERVATIVE POSITION	TREATMENT EQUATION– LIBERAL POSITION
Democratic House majority	—	0.098***	0.119***	0.076***	—	—
	—	(0.015)	(0.002)	(0.029)	—	—
Foreign policy roll call	—	-0.042***	-0.028***	0.009	—	—
	—	(0.012)	(0.003)	(0.009)	—	—
Presidential approval	—	0.00036	0.001***	0.008**	—	—
	—	(0.00047)	(0.0001)	(0.0004)	—	—
House polarization	—	0.095*	0.09***	0.007	—	—
	—	(0.047)	(0.008)	(0.037)	—	—
Democratic president (= 1)	—	-0.071***	-0.015***	-0.07**	-2.16***	1.79***
	—	(0.013)	(0.002)	(0.029)	(0.09)	(0.079)

President's party controls house	−0.023*	0.001	0.06*	—	—
	(0.012)	(0.002)	(0.028)	—	—
Conservative position	−0.049***	—	—	—	—
	(0.007)	—	—	—	—
Public mood	—	—	—	−0.026***	0.06***
	—	—	—	(0.007)	(0.009)
Liberal position	0.022***	—	—	—	—
	(0.008)	—	—	—	—
Potential outcome mean	0.526***	—	—	—	—
	(0.001)	—	—	—	—
Constant	0.39***	0.36***	0.47***	0.09	−6.94***
	(0.047)	(0.009)	(0.043)	(0.45)	(0.59)

Note: Observations = 16,447; robust standard errors in parentheses.

*$p < 0.05$, **$p < 0.01$, ***$p < 0.001$.

TABLE 4.7 TREATMENT EFFECTS, AUGMENTED INVERSE PROBABILITY–WEIGHTED REGRESSION ADJUSTMENT, HOUSE, 1953–2012, CONTESTED VOTES

VARIABLE	AVERAGE TREATMENT EFFECTS	OUTCOME EQUATION–CONSERVATIVE	OUTCOME EQUATION–NO POSITION	OUTCOME EQUATION–LIBERAL	TREATMENT EQUATION–CONSERVATIVE POSITION	TREATMENT EQUATION–LIBERAL POSITION
Democratic House majority	—	0.10***	0.12***	0.10***	—	—
	—	(0.01)	(0.002)	(0.03)	—	—
Foreign policy roll call	—	-0.06***	-0.03***	0.001	—	—
	—	(0.01)	(0.003)	(0.01)	—	—
Presidential approval	—	0.0004	0.001***	0.001***	—	—
	—	(0.0003)	(0.0001)	(0.0002)	—	—
House party polarization	—	0.18***	0.09***	0.07***	—	—
	—	(0.03)	(0.01)	(0.02)	—	—
Democratic president (= 1)	—	-0.07***	-0.02***	-0.07**	-2.16***	1.79***
	—	(0.01)	(0.002)	(0.03)	(0.09)	(0.08)

President's party controls House	—	−0.026**	0.0007	0.05*	—	—
	—	(0.013)	(0.002)	(0.03)	—	—
Conservative position	−0.044***	—	—	—	—	—
	(0.006)	—	—	—	—	—
Public mood	—	—	—	—	−0.03***	0.06***
	—	—	—	—	(0.007)	(0.01)
Liberal position	0.023**	—	—	—	—	—
	(0.08)	—	—	—	—	—
Potential outcome mean	0.526***	—	—	—	—	—
	(0.001)	—	—	—	—	—
Constant	—	0.34***	0.36***	0.40***	0.09	−6.94***
	—	(0.03)	(0.01)	(0.04)	(0.45)	(0.59)

Note: Observations = 16,447; robust standard errors in parentheses.

*$p < 0.05$, **$p < 0.01$, ***$p < 0.001$.

TABLE 4.8 RELATIONSHIP BETWEEN ANNUAL INFLUENCE ON CONTESTED VOTES AND SUCCESS, HOUSE OF REPRESENTATIVES, 1953–2012

VARIABLE	(1) SUCCESS	(2) SUCCESS	(3) INFLUENCE
Majority president	−0.09	−0.08	−0.03
	(0.10)	(0.10)	(0.03)
House party polarization	−0.59***	−0.55***	−0.11***
	(0.11)	(0.12)	(0.04)
Interaction (majority × polarization)	0.68***	0.66***	0.08
	(0.18)	(0.18)	(0.06)
Approval	0.002**	0.002*	0.0004
	(0.001)	(0.001)	(0.0003)
Influence	—	0.33	—
	—	(0.42)	—
Constant	0.68***	0.66***	0.06**
	(0.09)	(0.09)	(0.03)
Observations	60	60	60
R^2	0.74	0.74	0.22
df_m	4	5	4
F	39.18	31.25	3.92
Rss	0.48	0.48	0.051
Log likelihood	59.69	60.03	127.0

Note: Standard errors in parentheses.

$^*p < 0$, $^{**}p < 0.05$, $^{***}p < 0.01$.

5

POLITICAL PARTIES AS A SOURCE OF PRESIDENTIAL INFLUENCE

ACCORDING TO THE results detailed in chapter 4, presidents appear to influence enough members, merely by taking a position, to convert expected defeats into victories on approximately 10% of presidential roll calls. Winning an additional 10% of roll calls can have important implications for producing policy. Through position taking, presidents leave a larger and perhaps more substantively consequential stamp on public policy than if they stayed on the sidelines. The actions that presidents take in the legislative policy-making process appear to have consequences for roll call outcomes and thus for the production of public policy.

But what is it about position taking that influences members to shift their vote from opposition to support? The theory developed in chapter 2 identifies two pathways from presidential position taking to influence over members' votes on roll calls, one direct and the other indirect. The direct pathway relates most closely to common understandings of presidential lobbying, including, for instance, doing favors, going public, bargaining, threatening vetoes, and/or providing targeted members with inducements to secure their support on a roll call.

In contrast, the indirect pathway suggests that the roll call is transformed, for members of Congress, from a nonpresidential to a presidential roll call. The transformation helps to link the president to other factors that influence member voting, such as party, policy type, and/or public opinion. This presidential consideration thus flows through these other considerations to affect member voting so that, for example, a party consideration becomes simultaneously a *president and party* consideration. Sometimes this associational or linkage process works to the president's advantage, but other times it may disadvantage the president.

The primary task of this and the next two chapters is to test whether position taking influences member roll call voting through this indirect pathway. This chapter focuses on how presidential position taking flows through the party to increase (or decrease) member support for the president. The next two chapters look at policy type (such as foreign versus domestic) and at public opinion.

Specifically, this chapter tests these two conditional hypotheses:

1. Over and above the direct effects of position taking, presidential position taking will be more influential when the president's party controls the chamber than when the opposition is in control.
2. Over and above the direct effects of position taking, presidential position taking will have more influence on members of the president's party than on the opposition party.

Both of these hypotheses suggest an interaction between presidential position taking and party. Presidents will receive an additional increment of influence, over and above that received from position taking alone, when their party controls Congress, and more among co-partisans than among opposition members. The next section elaborates on why presidents receive an influence boost when their party controls the chamber, and among co-partisans compared to among opposition members.

PARTISAN SOURCES OF PRESIDENTIAL INFLUENCE

Political parties have a major impact on the behavior of legislators.[1] For a variety of reasons, discussed extensively in the literature on presidential relations with Congress, presidents should expect greater support from legislators of their party than from the opposition, and more when their party is in the majority (e.g., Bond and Fleisher 1990, 13–18; Edwards 1989). As Barrett and Eshbaugh-Soha (2007, 102) say in their pithy summary of the vast research linking party control to presidential success, "Party control in Congress is by far the most important factor affecting presidential success in the legislative arena."

The theory proposed here argues that party also provides a source of *influence* in Congress. When presidents take a position on a roll call, two processes occur. First, members link the president's position to their party. The president's position and the party's position are fused. This merging of president and party intensifies incentives (or pressures) for co-partisans to vote with the president and for opposition members to vote against the president, compared to roll calls on which the president has not taken a position. As Lee (2008, 2009) argues, presidential position taking increases polarization between the congressional parties.

Second, when the president takes a position, the party leadership works to ensure the passage of the president's policy when the party is in the majority, or its defeat if the opposition is in control. The president's position on an issue becomes the party's position. Inasmuch as presidential position taking heightens the salience of the issue to voters (Cohen 1997; Canes-Wrone 2006), whether the president's side wins or loses has consequences for the president and for the party. As Lebo and O'Geen (2011) show, presidential success in Congress affects the performance of the congressional parties in the next election; the president's party loses seats when success is low but may gain or retain seats when success is high.

Thus, the party leadership has incentives to use its institutional resources to help or to hinder the president. Control over the legislative agenda—which bills will come to the floor for consideration, the timing of floor consideration, and accompanying voting rules—provides congressional leadership with an institutional resource that can either benefit or undermine the president, depending upon which party controls the House (Bond and Fleisher 1990, 122–151; Cox and McCubbins 2005; Covington, Wrighton, and Kinney 1995; Beckmann 2008, 2010).

The polarization between the congressional parties may further inten-sify these processes. Party polarization has two dimensions or character-istics. First, the distance between the parties' positions on issues widens. Second, within the parties, members vote in blocs and party cohesion increases. Standard accounts identify four mechanisms to account for party cohesion in Congress—policy, electoral, loyalty, and organizational mechanisms. Presidential position taking links presidents to their party through these mechanisms, leading to presidential influence in Congress above and beyond the effect of these party-related factors in the absence of a presidential position. Consistent with this viewpoint, Lee (2008, 2009) finds that party polarization is greater on presidential than on nonpresi-dential roll calls across almost all issues (also see Fett 1994; Mak and Sid-man 2014).

Because voters view the president as the party's leader, when the presi-dent takes a position on a roll call, that position becomes the party's posi-tion in the eyes of voters. Voters do not discriminate between the president and the president's party when the president takes a position. This has important electoral implications for members, intensifying pressures on co-partisans to vote with the president and on the opposition party to vote against the president. Whether they like it or not, when running for reelection, members are to some degree running on the president's posi-tions, regardless of whether the president's side prevailed (Lebo and O'Geen 2011), whether they voted with or against the president (Canes-Wrone, Brady, and Cogan 2002; Hollibaugh, Rothenberg, and Rulison 2013), and whether voters in the member's district agree or disagree with the presi-dent (Gronke, Koch, and Wilson 2003).

This process parallels the one described in Howell, Jackman, and Rogowski (2013) on the implications of war for presidential influence. In their model, members weigh district and national factors in deciding how to vote on roll calls. During wartime, national factors weigh more heavily than they do during peacetime. Since national factors are associ-ated with the president and the administration's war policies, presidents are more influential in Congress during wartime than during peacetime. The point here is similar. When a president takes a roll call position, the president as a "national" force becomes more relevant to voters and to the parties' reputations, and thus to members roll call voting decisions.

Just as a presidential position will affect member roll call decisions, party leaders respond and exert their institutional resources in support of or in opposition to the president. They do so because of the effects of presidential performance in Congress on their parties and because of their desire to maintain or gain majority control. By keeping majority control, the party's leaders increase the likelihood that their party will realize necessary and favorable policy and that they will retain their institutional power.

Majority party leaders, through their control over the organization and rules of the chamber, can help the president on floor votes by deciding which roll calls come up for a vote, when they come up, under what rules, and so on. Beckmann (2010) argues that this type of agenda control is especially important and effective for presidents in securing passage of their legislative proposals. The minority party, although not possessing the institutional resources of the majority, is not without its ability to frustrate, embarrass, or harm the president and his party. For example, the minority may engage in obstructionist behavior (Egar 2016; Green 2015). In the Senate, filibuster threats have become a common device for minority parties in an age of heightened polarization to stymie the president's legislative initiatives (Bond, Fleisher, and Cohen 2015). But, in general, the majority party and its leaders have more power than does the minority.

This leads to our two party–based hypotheses. First, presidents will be more influential when their party controls the chamber than when the chamber is under opposition control. Second, presidents will be more influential with co-partisans than with opposition legislators. Although these hypotheses appear to be just standard hypotheses found in studies of presidential success in Congress, there is a notable difference between them and the presidential success hypotheses. As discussed earlier, the presidential success hypotheses look only at roll calls on which the president has taken a position. Coincidental factors, like shared policy preferences, may account for higher support on this restricted set of presidential roll calls. The hypotheses under investigation here, in contrast, compare member voting on presidential and on nonpresidential roll calls, which allows us to assess *the influence of the president*, not merely coincidental factors that lead to member-presidential agreement.

In addition, these hypotheses suggest that presidents receive an additional increment of influence from position taking, moderated through party. In other words, the hypotheses enable us to distinguish the direct effects of position taking from the indirect effects of position taking moderated through party.

This chapter tests these hypotheses, finding unequivocal support for both the majority status and member party hypotheses. The bulk of the findings point to enhanced presidential influence when the president is in the majority and among co-partisans. Moreover, presidents still directly affect member voting, controlling for the interactive effects of position taking and the party variables. Thus, consistent with the theory, presidential position taking has both direct and indirect impacts on member roll call voting.

MAJORITY STATUS AND INFLUENCE AT THE ROLL CALL LEVEL

As I argued in chapter 4, it makes the most sense to restrict the analysis to roll calls on which presidents may be able to affect the outcome, contested roll calls. Lopsided roll calls, even when the president is on the losing side, are ones on which a president will not be able to turn an expected defeat into a victory, no matter how many resources they deploy or how hard they work. And even if presidential influence brings additional votes to the winning side when the president decides to jump on the bandwagon of a vote that looks like it will pass easily, those additional votes are unnecessary and thus presidential involvement did not affect the outcome.

Table 5.1 presents the results of regressing presidential positions on the percentage of members voting liberal on non-lopsided roll calls. The estimations are clustered by year to hold constant the varying annual number of roll calls as well as any unmeasured factors associated with year, which may affect member roll call decisions. Repeating the analysis presented chapter 4, presidential position taking has a meager, albeit statistically

TABLE 5.1 CONDITIONAL EFFECTS OF MAJORITY STATUS AND
POLARIZATION ON PRESIDENTIAL INFLUENCE IN HOUSE,
1953–2012, CONTESTED VOTES

VARIABLE	(1) OVERALL LIBERAL (%)	(2) OVERALL LIBERAL (%)	(3) OVERALL LIBERAL (%)
Presidential position	0.015*	−0.01	0.14***
	(0.07)	(0.01)	(0.02)
Majority president	—	−0.001	−0.07
	—	(0.02)	(0.05)
Position × Majority	—	0.07***	−0.14***
	—	(0.01)	(0.03)
Polarization	—	—	−0.14**
	—	—	(0.07)
Position × Polarization	—	—	−0.27***
	—	—	(0.03)
Majority × Polarization	—	—	0.13
	—	—	(0.10)
Majority × Position × Polarization	—	—	0.40***
	—	—	(0.05)
Constant	0.52***	0.52***	0.61***
	(0.01)	(0.01)	(0.03)
Observations	16,457	16,457	16,457
R^2	0.003	0.016	0.041

Note: Robust standard errors in parentheses.
*$p < 0.1$, **$p < 0.05$, ***$p < 0.01$.

significant, impact on roll call voting (see table 5.1, model 1, which only
includes presidential position taking as an independent variable).[2] The
coefficient indicates an approximately 1.5% presidential effect, that is, presidents add about six or seven votes to their side. This is not very much, but
in very close votes it is enough to produce a victory.

To test the majority president hypothesis, model 2 adds a dummy variable for whether the president's party controls the House (= 1), interacting
that dummy with the presidential position-taking variable. The interaction term tells us the impact of presidential position taking when the
president's party is in the majority, while the position-taking variable

tells us the impact when the president's party is in the minority. Results indicate no significant impact from presidential position taking under minority control—in fact, the sign is negative, although it is close to zero, at -0.01. In contrast, majority party presidents have a statistically and substantively significant impact on House voting.[3]

The regression coefficient indicates a 7% effect on congressional roll call voting when majority presidents take a position, which translates into approximately thirty to thirty-one additional members voting with the president's side.[4] A beta regression produces somewhat smaller, albeit substantial effects of 5%, or twenty-two members. Majority presidents appear to move a relatively large number of members to their side by taking a position on a roll call.

But does this movement of additional members to the president's column have implications for floor success? Do majority presidents win additional votes due to the influence they receive from position taking? Based on the 5% to 7% range from the beta regression and ordinary least squares (OLS) results, from 29% to 40% of roll call victories *for majority presidents* are due to the influence derived from position taking. This is three to four times the percentage of roll calls than the 10% of victories found in chapter 4, which did not distinguish between majority and minority control of the House. Stated another way, when in the majority, presidents took an average of fifty-two roll call positions per year. Of these, presidents won from fifteen to twenty-one votes because of the influence they received from position taking. The effects of presidential position taking for majority presidents is substantial and consequential for producing public policies, at least in terms of winning floor votes in the House.

ROBUSTNESS TESTS

Some may question the magnitude of the results for the influence of presidential position taking when the executive's party controls the House. First, recall that "influence," as used here, does not refer to personal presidential influence, as is the case in so much of the literature on presidential influence. Rather, this study conceptualizes influence in institutional resource terms. By taking a position on a roll call, presidents set in motion a series of processes that may activate a political resource, to their benefit or to their detriment.

Position taking mobilizes the institutional resource of party, for example, in part by tightening the association between the president and his party. If the president's party controls the House, then the majority party leadership may set the roll call options to the president's benefit, and co-partisans may feel heightened incentives to support the president due to electoral considerations, party loyalty, or other reasons. The opposition will act to stop or defeat the president on roll calls. This combination provides net benefits to the president when his party controls the House.

Still, there are several threats to the analysis. First, presidential position taking may be endogenous to the vote. Dropping lopsided wins from the analysis partially helps with this endogeneity issue. Plus, the quasi-experimental treatment effects analysis in chapter 4 provided support for the idea that presidential position taking can influence member roll call voting. Second, agenda composition differences may pose a threat to the findings. The analysis in this chapter thus far assumes no systematic differences in the types of issues for presidential and nonpresidential roll calls. Inasmuch as there are differences, the sets of presidential and nonpresidential roll calls may not be comparable. This may affect the voting tendencies of members across the two sets of roll calls. Thus, rather than the president affecting member voting on the two sets of roll calls, it may be the difference in the composition of those roll calls that affects member voting. Finally, other variables may affect how members vote on a roll call. The effects of presidential position taking may be spurious.

To address the agenda composition critique, I entered dummy variables for issue type for each roll call, using the Policy Agendas Project issue categorization scheme. In all, there are twenty-one major issue areas, ranging from macroeconomics to domestic policies to foreign policies. To deal with the spuriousness critique, I added two variables that reflect the public opinion environment at the time of the roll call, "public mood" and "macropartisanship," both from James Stimson. The public mood variable registers how liberal to conservative voters are, in general, across issues of the day. We should expect that members will be more inclined to vote liberal (or conservative) when the public leans in a liberal (or conservative) direction. The macropartisanship variable measures the Democratic advantage/disadvantage compared to Republicans in terms of party identification in the mass public. When the public leans toward the Democrats, we should expect members to vote liberal more often than when the public leans toward the Republicans.[5]

I added these control variables to the analysis, using both OLS and beta regression, for the reasons discussed in chapter 4. Finally, because beta regression does not allow clustering, I entered annual dummy variables into that estimation. Full results are presented in the appendix to this chapter.

The results of both of these fuller estimations are exactly in line with the majority party effects from above.[6] Where the beta regression previously indicated a 5% effect for majority control, the effect increases slightly with these additional controls, to 6%. And where the previous OLS results indicated a 7% effect, with these additional controls the effect drops slightly, to 5%. Thus, even with these additional controls, the effects of presidential position taking when in the majority remains in the 5% to 7% range.

Finally, I conducted a treatment effects analysis, as done in chapter 4. Initially, I attempted a treatment effects analysis for the interaction between presidential position taking and majority control by creating a five-category treatment effects variable (conservative position–majority control, conservative position–minority control, no position taken, liberal position–majority control, and liberal position–minority control), but such an estimation would not converge to a solution. As a compromise, I ran the treatment effects analysis restricted to those roll calls when the president's party was in the majority.[7]

The treatment effects analysis finds very strong impacts for conservative position taking, but the inverse probability weights–regression adjustment (IPWRA) and augmented inverse probability weights (AIWP) estimations disagree somewhat on the impact of liberal position taking. Both treatment effects models report an 8.6% effect for conservative position taking. But where the IPWRA indicates a 1.8% effect for liberal position taking (which is not statistically significant), the AIPW finds a stronger 4.8% effect for liberal position taking. Other than the weak IPWRA effect for liberal position taking, these treatment effects results are in line with, if not a bit stronger than (at least when presidents take a conservative position) the effects using OLS and beta regression. Overall, it appears that presidents strongly influence member voting when their party controls the House. Party, it appears, provides an institutional resource that presidents activate when they take a position, but this benefits the president only if his party controls the House.

THE CONDITIONING EFFECTS OF POLARIZATION

Bond, Fleisher, and Cohen (2015), Bond, Fleisher, and Wood (2003), and Cohen, Bond, and Fleisher (2013, 2014) find that polarization conditions majority control. Presidential influence in the House rises when the president's party controls that legislative chamber. Does polarization further add to the influence of majority party presidents at the roll call level? We can test this hypothesis by adding the House polarization variable (see Cohen, Bond, and Fleisher 2013) and interacting it with the position taking–majority control interaction. This is, in other words, a three-variable interaction: majority control × presidential position taking × House polarization.

Table 5.1, model 3, presents unequivocal results: as polarization increases, so does the influence of being a majority party president.[8] All the more remarkable is the statistically significant effect of the three-way interaction variable, given the high multicollinearity that usually exists between such variables and the several constituent variables. When the president's party is in the majority, influence increases with polarization ($b = 0.13$, $p = 0.001$). In contrast, when the president's party is in the minority, influence declines as polarization rises ($b = -0.27$, $p < 0.0001$).

To facilitate substantive interpretation of the results, figure 5.1 plots the effect of presidential position taking conditional on majority–minority status and House polarization. The left panel presents results when presidents take a conservative position and the right panel when they take a liberal position. The solid line indicates the effect of position taking for majority presidents and the dashed line the effect for minority presidents. Whether presidents take a conservative or a liberal position, the percentage of members voting with the president increases when their party is in the majority and as polarization rises.

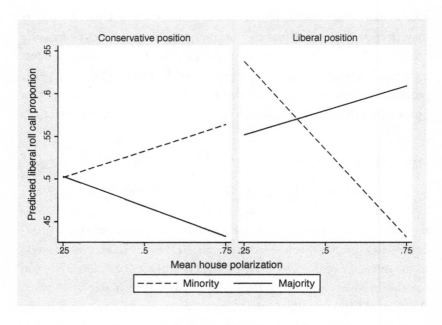

FIGURE 5.1

Conditional effect of majority status and polarization on presidential
influence in the House, 1953–2012, contested votes

Note: Based on results from table 5.1.

For instance, when polarization is low (0.25), presidents are in the majority, and they take a conservative position, the predicted percentage of liberal
votes hovers at 50%. But when polarization rises to a high level (0.75), the
liberal voting percentage drops to about 43%. A similar pattern exists when
majority presidents take a liberal position. When polarization is low (0.25),
about 55% of members vote on the liberal side, compared to 60% when
polarization rises to a high level (0.75). The pattern reverses for minority
presidents. When the president is in the minority, takes a conservative position, and polarization is low (0.25), about 50% of members vote liberally. But
about 56% vote liberally when polarization rises to a high level (0.75). The
effects of polarization on minority presidents who take a liberal position are

even more dramatic. When polarization is low (0.25), about 64% of members will vote on the liberal side, compared to 43% when polarization reaches a high level (0.75), a stunning 21% difference.

Results are quite clear and are consistent with the results from Bond and his colleagues. Presidents influence member roll call voting when their party controls the House. Polarization further conditions presidential influence when the president is in the majority. But when the president is in the minority, polarization *undermines* presidential influence from position taking.

MEMBER PARTY AND PRESIDENTIAL INFLUENCE

But whom do presidents influence when they take positions on roll calls—members of their party or the opposition? Just as we looked at the liberal/conservative voting tendencies across all members, we can compare the behavior of same party and opposition party members when the president takes a position. Are presidents similarly able to influence their co-partisans and the opposition? Do the factors already discussed, majority control and polarization, condition the responsiveness of the two sets of partisans to presidential position taking?

For this analysis, I constructed two new dependent variables, the percentage of co-partisans and opposition members voting liberal for each roll call.[9] Table 5.2, estimations 1 and 2, displays the comparative effect of presidential position taking on co-partisans and opposition members. Where presidents appear to influence members of their own party ($b = 0.25$, $p = 0.01$), opposition members tend to vote against the president, as the negative sign on the coefficient indicates ($b = -0.21$, $p = 0.001$), another demonstration of the polarizing effect of presidential position taking (Lee 2008, 2009).[10] Not only does presidential position taking push the parties further apart on roll calls but also the effect on both parties is of comparable magnitude. What the president gains by influencing co-partisans to vote on his side he loses as opposition members vote in dissent.

TABLE 5.2 CONDITIONAL EFFECTS OF MAJORITY PRESIDENTIAL STATUS AND MEMBER PARTY ON PRESIDENTIAL INFLUENCE IN THE HOUSE, 1953–2012, CONTESTED VOTES

VARIABLE	(1) SAME PARTY LIBERAL (%)	(2) OPPOSITION PARTY LIBERAL (%)	(3) SAME PARTY LIBERAL (%)	(4) OPPOSITION PARTY LIBERAL (%)	(5) SAME PARTY LIBERAL (%)	(6) OPPOSITION PARTY LIBERAL (%)
Presidential position	0.25***	−0.21***	0.23***	−0.20***	−0.08*	0.31***
	(0.01)	(0.01)	(0.02)	(0.03)	(0.04)	(0.05)
Majority president	—	—	0.07	−0.10	0.72**	−0.87***
			(0.10)	(0.10)	(0.29)	(0.30)
Majority × Position	—	—	0.03	0.01	−0.14	−0.05
			(0.06)	(0.06)	(0.10)	(0.08)
Polarization	—	—	—	—	0.62	−0.67
					(0.41)	(0.45)
Position × Polarization	—	—	—	—	0.53***	−0.91***
					(0.06)	(0.09)
Majority × Polarization	—	—	—	—	−1.09*	1.29**
					(0.62)	(0.64)
Majority × Position × Polarization	—	—	—	—	0.30**	0.15
					(0.14)	(0.13)
Constant	0.49***	0.51***	0.46***	0.55***	0.11	0.94***
	(0.05)	(0.05)	(0.06)	(0.07)	(0.18)	(0.21)
Observations	16,457	16,457	16,457	16,457	16,457	16,457
R^2	0.10	0.07	0.11	0.08	0.17	0.16

Note: Robust standard errors in parentheses. *$p < 0.1$, **$p < 0.05$, ***$p < 0.01$.

Whether the president derives a net advantage or disadvantage from this parallel but opposing movement depends upon the relative size of the parties. If the president's party is in the majority, such polarizing movement will be a net benefit for the president, but it becomes a net disadvantage when the opposition party controls the House, underscoring the importance of party control for the president.

The greatest difference in party size in the House occurred during the Johnson years, during the 89th Congress (1965 to 1966), when the Democrats held 295 seats to the Republicans' 140. The narrowest margin between the parties from 1953 to 2012 was the 221 to 213 Republican–Democrat split during the 83rd Congress (1953 to 1954). On average, during these sixty years, the Democrats held fifty-six more seats than the Republicans.

Assume the president's party is in the majority at historically average levels, a fifty-six-seat margin, 245 to 189.[11] Using the coefficients just outlined, the president will receive a net addition of twenty-one to twenty-two votes. In contrast, assuming the president's party is in the minority, with the same party ratio, the president now will lose four votes from position taking. (The asymmetry in effect is due to the slightly larger positive impact on co-partisans than on the opposition, 0.25 versus –0.21). When the division between the parties is narrow, at eight seats, as in 1953 to 1954, the president will gain ten or eleven votes when in the majority but lose seven when in the minority. Finally, the boost that Johnson received during the 89th Congress was massive, at forty-four. Gerald Ford was the most disadvantaged president, with only 144 Republicans compared to 291 Democrats, during the 94th Congress (1976 to 1977). Whenever he took a position, he would lose twenty-six votes, assuring that his side would be defeated frequently.

Majority–minority status, however, does not condition the effect of presidential position taking on same and opposition party members (see table 5.2, estimations 3 and 4). The coefficients for position taking hardly budge and the interaction terms fall well short of statistical significance. Insignificant interaction terms, however, do not provide a definitive test of the significance of an interaction. High levels of multicollinearity among the variables necessary to test for interactions may affect the significance level of an interaction term as well as the constituent variables that compose it. Plus, interactions can be important over a subset of values rather than the full range of both variables. Therefore, in another analysis (not shown), same party and opposition party voting is regressed on position taking for majority and minority presidents separately. The resulting coefficients are 0.25 (p < 0.0001) for co-partisans and 0.23 (p = 0.0001) for majority and minority presidents, nearly identical effects. For opposition legislators, the coefficients for majority and minority presidents are –0.19 (p < 0.001) and –0.20 (p < 0.001), again nearly identical.[12]

Finally, we turn to the conditioning effects of polarization on same party and opposition party members. As polarization between the parties grows, the incentives to support or oppose the president (depending on the member's party) also strengthen. To test this idea, I enter House party polarization into the estimation to test for its conditional effects on presidential influence. As above, this requires including a three-way interaction, composed of the president's position, majority versus minority status, and polarization. Three-way interactions can be especially difficult and complex to interpret. Results of this analysis are presented in table 5.2, models 5 and 6, for same and for opposition party members, respectively.

Despite the numerous correlated variables, the three-way interaction shows a statistically significant and positive impact for presidential co-partisans. In contrast, while the interaction for opposition legislators also is positive, it falls short of conventional levels of statistical significance. Yet, as already noted, significance tests may not always tell us whether an interaction is substantively and/or theoretically consequential. To help with that determination, figure 5.2 presents plots of the combined effects of the president's position, majority status, and polarization on the roll call behavior of same party and opposition party legislators.

The leftmost panel on the figure is for when the president takes a liberal position and is in the minority. The dashed line indicates the percentage of opposition members voting liberal and the solid line is for co-partisans. The predicted regression lines move in opposite directions, as expected. As polarization increases, co-partisans become increasing liberal, while opposition party members move in the reverse direction. Moreover, and notably, the slope is much steeper for opposition members than for co-partisans.[13] Minority party presidents who take a liberal position induce a stronger

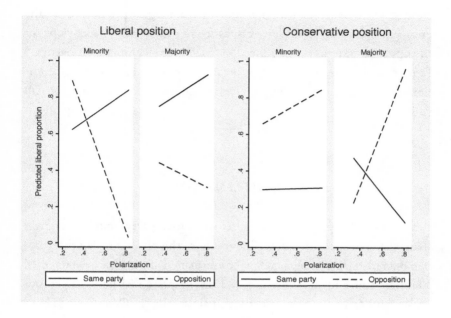

FIGURE 5.2

Conditional effect of majority status, member party, and polarization on presidential influence in the House, 1953–2012, contested votes

Note: Based on results from table 5.2.

counterreaction among the opposition than the support they breed among co-partisans. A similar story is told when looking at presidents who take a conservative position and are in the minority, which is presented in the third panel from the left. Again, opposition members become more liberal as polarization intensifies, but now presidents appear to have no discernible impact on their co-partisans, as the slope is essentially flat.[14]

The movement of co-partisans and opposition members is similar, but of differing magnitudes when the president's party controls the House. Again, as polarization increases, co-partisan liberalness increases when the president takes a liberal position, while the opposition moves in the other direction, but not as steeply as witnessed for minority party presidents who take a liberal position.[15] Conservative position taking appears to elicit a stronger reaction among the opposition than among co-partisans when the president's party controls Congress, as seen in the much steeper slope for the opposition, even though the slopes are very steep for both parties.[16] From this analysis, it is clear that polarization often has stunning conditional effects on the ability of presidents to influence congressional roll call voting.

CONCLUSION

It is a truism that presidents fair better when their party controls Congress than when the opposition does. The results of this chapter repeat that finding. But rather than being merely a reconfirmation of what has been reported countless times in the literature, the results presented here deepen our understanding of the linkage between partisanship in Congress and both presidential influence and success.

Party control is generally conceived as an environmental condition that affects presidential success with Congress, but party control is not something presidents can do much about. This "dumb luck" environmental perspective suggests that presidents are captive to the party configuration of Congress. The theory and analysis in this book tell a different story: party control is a resource that presidents can activate to their advantage, when their party controls the chamber, but it becomes a disadvantage when the opposition is in control. Presidents influence member voting through the association between their position taking and the member's party. We see this in the changes in members' liberal/conservative voting between nonpresidential and presidential roll calls.

Unlike most existing research, which looks only at partisan voting configurations on presidential roll calls, this study compares those configurations on both presidential and nonpresidential roll calls. This enables us to estimate the effects of presidential position taking on how members of the two parties vote. The theory developed here hypothesizes that, often, when presidents take positions on roll calls, they are lobbying members to vote on their side. In addition, when presidents take positions, they tighten the association between themselves and the roll calls. This association, in turn, triggers partisan reactions. Co-partisans rally behind the president, while opposition members distance themselves, increasing the likelihood that they will vote against the president. The results presented in this chapter support the theory's predictions about the response of co-partisan and opposition members to presidential position taking.

These results further our understanding of the forces that promote polarization in Congress. In her study of the Senate, Lee (2008, 2009) finds greater differentiation in party voting on presidential than on nonpresidential roll calls. I find the same for the House, while also revealing an element unnoticed in Lee's study. The influence in the House that presidents receive from position taking is isolated to co-partisans. There is virtually no ideological movement, when comparing presidential and nonpresidential roll calls, in the expected vote of opposition members. When presidents take a position, we see movement toward the president in the voting of co-partisans. By taking a position, presidents increase the degree of polarization in congressional voting by moving co-partisans toward their positions. Presidential influence on co-partisan voting is part of the story of why the congressional parties polarize. To fully understand polarization in the national legislature requires looking at presidential–congressional relations, something rarely discussed in the literature on Congress (but see Cameron 2002; Cohen 2011; Galvin 2012).

APPENDIX

TABLE 5.3 CONDITIONAL EFFECTS OF MAJORITY STATUS ON PRESIDENTIAL INFLUENCE IN THE HOUSE, CONTROLLING FOR POLICY TYPE AND THE PUBLIC OPINION CONTEXT, 1953–2012, CONTESTED VOTES

VARIABLE	(1) ORDINARY LEAST SQUARES	(2) BETA REGRESSION
Presidential position	−0.01	0.08***
	(0.01)	(0.01)
Majority control (= 1)	−0.01	0.12
	(0.01)	(0.18)
Position × Majority control	**0.05***	**0.06***
	(0.01)	**(0.02)**
Public mood	0.01***	0.03
	(0.00)	(0.03)
Macro partisanship	0.01***	0.02**
	(0.00)	(0.01)
Macroeconomics	−0.14***	−0.85**
	(0.03)	(0.36)
Civil rights	−0.15***	−0.91**
	(0.03)	(0.36)
Health	−0.13***	−0.77**
	(0.03)	(0.36)
Agriculture	−0.11***	−0.72**
	(0.03)	(0.36)
Labor	−0.11***	−0.75**
	(0.02)	(0.36)
Education	−0.11***	−0.72**
	(0.03)	(0.36)
Environment	−0.15***	−0.81**
	(0.02)	(0.36)
Energy	−0.15***	−0.82**
	(0.03)	(0.36)
Immigration	−0.14***	−0.89**
	(0.03)	(0.36)
Transportation	−0.10***	−0.72**
	(0.02)	(0.36)
Law and crime	−0.15***	−0.90**
	(0.02)	(0.36)

VARIABLE	(1) ORDINARY LEAST SQUARES	(2) BETA REGRESSION
Social welfare	−0.10***	−0.71**
	(0.03)	(0.36)
Community development	−0.11***	−0.75**
	(0.02)	(0.36)
Banking	−0.14***	−0.85**
	(0.03)	(0.36)
Defense	−0.17***	−0.99***
	(0.03)	(0.36)
Space and science	−0.12***	−0.82**
	(0.02)	(0.36)
Foreign trade	−0.12***	−0.76**
	(0.03)	(0.36)
International affairs	−0.12***	−0.80**
	(0.02)	(0.36)
Government operations	−0.10***	−0.73**
	(0.03)	(0.36)
Public lands	−0.09***	−0.67*
	(0.03)	(0.36)
1954	—	0.02
	—	(0.15)
1955	—	0.37***
	—	(0.08)
1956	—	0.38***
	—	(0.07)
1957	—	0.50***
	—	(0.11)
1958	—	0.34***
	—	(0.07)
1959	—	0.50***
	—	(0.10)
1960	—	0.42***
	—	(0.10)
1961	—	0.07
	—	(0.35)
1962	—	0.09
	—	(0.35)
1963	—	0.09
	—	(0.27)

(continued)

TABLE 5.3 CONDITIONAL EFFECTS OF MAJORITY STATUS ON
PRESIDENTIAL INFLUENCE IN THE HOUSE, CONTROLLING
FOR POLICY TYPE AND THE PUBLIC OPINION CONTEXT,
1953–2012, CONTESTED VOTES *(CONTINUED)*

VARIABLE	(1) ORDINARY LEAST SQUARES	(2) BETA REGRESSION
1964	—	0.20
	—	(0.21)
1965	—	0.36***
	—	(0.13)
1966	—	0.20
	—	(0.17)
1967	—	0.14
	—	(0.17)
1968	—	0.28**
	—	(0.11)
1969	—	0.46**
	—	(0.20)
1970	—	0.28***
	—	(0.06)
1971	—	0.12
	—	(0.07)
1972	—	0.17***
	—	(0.06)
1973	—	0.41***
	—	(0.09)
1974	—	0.36***
	—	(0.11)
1975	—	0.47***
	—	(0.12)
1976	—	0.47***
	—	(0.13)
1977	—	0.34***
	—	(0.09)
1978	—	0.27***
	—	(0.08)
1979	—	0.25***
	—	(0.09)
1980	—	0.39***
	—	(0.12)

VARIABLE	(1) ORDINARY LEAST SQUARES	(2) BETA REGRESSION
1981	—	0.42**
	—	(0.21)
1982	—	0.56***
	—	(0.20)
1983	—	0.54***
	—	(0.10)
1984	—	0.63***
	—	(0.08)
1985	—	0.65***
	—	(0.08)
1986	—	0.66***
	—	(0.05)
1987	—	0.61***
	—	(0.04)
1988	—	0.55***
	—	(0.08)
1989	—	0.58***
	—	(0.11)
1990	—	0.59***
	—	(0.08)
1991	—	0.57***
	—	(0.10)
1992	—	0.46***
	—	(0.09)
1993	—	0.34*
	—	(0.19)
1994	—	0.40***
	—	(0.11)
1995	—	0.12
	—	(0.14)
1996	—	0.15
	—	(0.13)
1997	—	0.09
	—	(0.08)
1998	—	0.18**
	—	(0.08)
1999	—	0.21***
	—	(0.05)

(*continued*)

TABLE 5.3 CONDITIONAL EFFECTS OF MAJORITY STATUS ON PRESIDENTIAL INFLUENCE IN THE HOUSE, CONTROLLING FOR POLICY TYPE AND THE PUBLIC OPINION CONTEXT, 1953–2012, CONTESTED VOTES *(CONTINUED)*

VARIABLE	(1) ORDINARY LEAST SQUARES	(2) BETA REGRESSION
2000	—	0.22***
	—	(0.05)
2001	—	0.05
	—	(0.13)
2002	—	0.03
	—	(0.23)
2003	—	−0.07
	—	(0.28)
2004	—	0.00
	—	(0.25)
2005	—	−0.07
	—	(0.29)
2006	—	−0.01
	—	(0.29)
2007	—	0.36***
	—	(0.12)
2008	—	0.32***
	—	(0.12)
2009	—	0.34
	—	(0.26)
2010	—	0.35**
	—	(0.17)
Constant	−0.11	−1.97
	(0.18)	(1.65)
Scale	—	2.76***
	—	(0.01)
Observations	16,448	16,448
R^2	0.09	—
df	25	82
F	33.84	—
rss	275.9	—
Log likelihood	10,280	11,493

Note: Robust standard errors in parentheses. *$p < 0.1$, **$p < 0.05$, ***$p < 0.01$.

6

THE TWO PRESIDENCIES AND PRESIDENTIAL INFLUENCE

THIS CHAPTER ASKS the venerable question, Are presidents more influential in foreign than domestic policy?[1] Most research on the question uses roll calls on which the president has taken a position and thus employs the traditional approach of comparing presidential success or support rates on foreign versus domestic policy.[2] Although such a perspective tells us whether the president's side prevailed more often on foreign than on domestic roll calls, it does not tell us whether presidents were more *influential* on foreign compared to domestic policy. Presidents may win more frequently on foreign policy because of coincidental factors.

For instance, Meernik (1993) argues that there was a bipartisan agreement on foreign policy from the late 1940s until the end of US intervention in Vietnam (1973), what he terms the "Cold War consensus." During this period, the parties were united in their opposition to the spread of Soviet-backed communism; containment of communist expansion was the core goal for US foreign policy in both parties. Due to this bipartisan consensus, presidents did not have to influence members of Congress to support their foreign policy initiatives—members of Congress and the president already agreed (Fleisher et al. 2000; Prins and Marshall 2001). According to this view, presidents won more on foreign than domestic policy because there was broad, bipartisan agreement on foreign policy.[3]

As I argue here, comparing voting on presidential and nonpresidential roll calls enables us to assess whether member voting patterns differ between the two types of votes. If such a difference exists, some of that difference may be due to the president influencing members to change how they vote. The underlying theory advanced here is that position taking can be conceptualized as a form of presidential lobbying of Congress. By virtue of the president taking a position, the roll call is converted from a nonpresidential into a presidential vote, which alters members' roll call voting calculus. The president weighs more heavily as a consideration on presidential than on nonpresidential roll calls. If the presidential consideration is large enough, it may shift member voting to the president's side.

Besides estimating presidential influence on foreign versus domestic policy, this chapter makes several additional contributions to the two presidencies literature. First, it extends analysis through 2012—for the most part, the last roll call studies on the two presidencies use data only through the late 1990s (Fleisher et al. 2000; Schraufnagel and Shellman 2001; but see Mack, DeRouen, and Lanoue 2013). Since the late 1990s, there have been important changes that may have affected the amount of presidential influence (and success) on foreign versus domestic policy, particularly the increased polarization between the congressional parties. Party polarization in Congress should make it harder for presidents to influence and win, no matter the policy area, unless the president's party commands large majorities.

Second, unlike past research on the two presidencies, which compares Democratic and Republican support for the president (e.g., Edwards 1986; Fleisher and Bond 1988; Fleisher et al. 2000), this chapter compares same party with opposition party members. The reason for making this comparison is to uncover the ability of presidents to influence members of their party versus their ability to sway the opposition. The previous chapter found that presidents influence only their co-partisans in the House. But presidential influence patterns may differ when we look at foreign policy, as presidents may be able to influence opposition legislators on foreign policy. Schraufnagel and Shellman (2001), however, report no consistent pattern of presidents receiving greater support from the opposition than from their own party. The heightened level of polarization in Congress in recent years may have erected a barrier to presidential influence over opposition legislators, as polarization has converted a once bipartisan policy area, foreign policy, into a partisan one. If so, this does not bode well for presidents if opposition party members are the most fertile ground for picking up additional support on foreign policy issues.

Third, most of the research on the two presidencies over time emphasizes the breakdown of the bipartisan Cold War consensus. The consensus breakdown thesis argues that ideas motivate members' positions on foreign policy, instead of other calculations, such as electoral implications. Moreover, failed policies, especially associated with Vietnam and extended to containment more generally, led many members to rethink their support for these foreign policies (McCormick and Wittkopf 1990; Meernik 1993; Milner and Tingley 2015).

But an alternative theory to account for the breakdown in the Cold War consensus stresses the importance of party competition and the increased polarization between the parties. This perspective suggests that competitive pressures between the parties, closely related to the intensified polarization in Congress, has altered the way members think about foreign policy (Trumbore and Dulio 2013). From this perspective, ideas, principles, and ideology play a smaller role in how members think about foreign policy. Rather, members of Congress view foreign policy in partisan terms, much as they do domestic issues, which might also affect presidential opportunities to influence member voting on foreign policy roll calls. This chapter compares these two explanations.

FOREIGN POLICY AND THE PRESIDENTIAL CONSIDERATION

Chapter 4 demonstrated statistically and substantively significant differences in the roll call voting behavior of members on presidential and non-presidential votes, suggesting that presidents have some influence over members' voting. Crucially, there are significant differences in member voting on contested roll calls, the subset of votes where presidential position taking may alter the outcome from defeat to victory (or vice versa). Does presidential influence vary across policy areas? Do presidents have more influence on foreign than on domestic policy roll calls?

There are several reasons to believe that presidents possess more influence on foreign than on domestic policy. Canes-Wrone, Howell, and Lewis (2008) argue that presidents possess at least three advantages in foreign policy that do not apply to domestic policy. First, presidents have information advantages on foreign policy. The executive branch has much tighter control over information about foreign than about domestic policy. Compared to the executive branch, Congress does not have the institutional means or external sources, such as interest groups, to collect information on foreign policy. This induces the legislature to rely on the executive for information. In contrast, Congress can easily acquire information about domestic policy from interest groups, think tanks, the news media, constituents, and other sources. This informational advantage allows the president to structure foreign policy issues and debates. Lacking the ability to challenge the administration on these grounds, and given the stakes of foreign policy, Congress will generally follow the administration's lead on foreign policy.

Second, presidents have a first-mover advantage in foreign policy (Canes-Wrone, Howell, and Lewis 2008). Presidents, especially in the modern era, begin the process of making foreign policy outside of the legislative process. Sometimes they employ unilateral devices, like national security directives and executive agreements, but they also may make policy less formally, through speeches, trips to foreign nations, moving troops, and so forth. Other times, foreign policy making is a reaction to unanticipated actions by other nations, requiring a swift presidential response. As Alexander Hamilton wrote in Federalist No. 70: "Energy in the executive is a leading character in the definition of good government. It is essential to the protection of the community against foreign attacks." The first-mover advantage also allows presidents to set the foreign policy agenda and to structure debate on foreign policy issues.

Third, constituent pressures on members are stronger for domestic than for foreign policy. To gain reelection, members must pay close attention to their constituents, and constituents are much more likely to be concerned with domestic issues such as the economy than with foreign policy, except during wartime or in reaction to momentous foreign policy crises such as the terror attacks on September 11, 2001. Members are thus freer to follow the president on foreign than on domestic policy.[4]

Hence, we should expect presidents to be more influential on foreign than on domestic policy. But there is considerable controversy in the literature on this point. While numerous studies find support for the two presidencies thesis,[5] others do not, arguing that the two presidencies notion is time bound and only pertains to minority party presidents during some time periods. Other studies argue that the two presidencies idea only applies to some foreign policy issues, such as defense.[6] There are also contentions over which roll call votes to use, such as all votes, key votes, conflictual votes, and so on (Lindsay and Steger 1993; Shull and LeLoup 1981; Sigelman 1979).

PRESIDENTIAL INFLUENCE AND THE TWO PRESIDENCIES

We can use the roll call data to test the two presidencies idea; doing so requires categorizing roll calls as either foreign or domestic policy. To categorize each roll call, I merged the roll call data with data from the Policy Agendas Project (PAP), which codes all roll calls during this period into one of twenty policy areas.[7] To create the foreign policy category, I combined roll calls in the PAP Defense (category 16), International Affairs and Foreign Aid (category 19), and Foreign Trade (category 18) major topic areas. For present purposes, the other major topic areas were classified as domestic policy. Thus, foreign policy is measured as a dummy variable (1 = foreign policy, zero = domestic policy). Among conflictual roll calls over the sixty-year period, 3,061 (18.6%) are foreign policy votes, compared to 13,387 (81.4%) votes on domestic policy.[8]

To test the two presidencies hypothesis, an interaction term is created between presidential position and foreign policy. Presidents are somewhat more inclined to take positions on foreign than on domestic policy votes. Among conflictual roll calls from 1953 to 2012, presidents took positions on 31.9% of foreign policy votes, compared to 17.2% for domestic policy.[9] The estimation includes the presidential position variable as above (–1 = conservative position, zero = no presidential position, 1 = liberal position), the foreign policy dummy, and the interaction term between presidential position and foreign policy (presidential position × foreign policy). As above, the estimation clusters on year and uses only the conflictual roll calls.

Table 6.1 presents the results of this initial analysis, which indicates support for the two presidencies thesis, although the two presidencies effect does not appear to be very strong. The coefficient for the interaction between presidential position and foreign policy is positive and statistically

TABLE 6.1 IMPACT OF FOREIGN POLICY ROLL CALLS ON PRESIDENTIAL INFLUENCE, HOUSE OF REPRESENTATIVES, 1953–2012

VARIABLE	(1) OVERALL LIBERAL (%)	(2) OVERALL LIBERAL (%)	(3) OVERALL LIBERAL (%)
Presidential position	0.02**	0.00	-0.03***
	(0.01)	(0.01)	(0.01)
Foreign policy roll call	—	-0.03***	-0.03***
	—	(0.00)	(0.01)
Interaction (Position × Foreign policy)	—	0.03***	0.05***
	—	(0.01)	(0.01)
Majority control	—	—	-0.00
	—	—	(0.02)
Interaction (Majority control × Position)	—	—	0.09***
	—	—	(0.01)
Interaction (Majority control × Foreign policy)	—	—	0.00
	—	—	(0.00)
Interaction (Foreign × Majority × Position)	—	—	-0.04***
	—	—	(0.01)
Constant	0.52***	0.53***	0.53***
	(0.01)	(0.01)	(0.01)
Observations	16,457	16,448	16,448
R^2	0.00	0.01	0.03
F	4.469	19.68	43.65

Note: Analyses clustered on year. Robust standard errors in parentheses.
*$p < 0.1$, **$p < 0.05$, ***$p < 0.01$.

significant, although, with so many cases, even substantively weak relationships may easily reach significance at the conventional 0.05 level.

In table 6.1, model 2, the interaction term indicates the impact of position taking for foreign policy roll calls. The analysis suggests that presidential position taking registers a modest effect on members' foreign policy
voting. Members also tend to vote more conservatively on foreign than on
domestic policy roll calls, although the effect is not very large, about 3%
($b = -0.03$). For domestic policy, the presidential coefficient is zero, with a
$b = 0.005$, suggesting no presidential influence on domestic policy votes
when the president takes a position. In contrast, the coefficient for foreign
policy roll calls is 0.033, that is, presidents will generate about a 3.3% effect,
or about fourteen additional votes, when taking a foreign policy roll call
position. Although this effect is far from powerful, it may make the difference between being on the winning or the losing side of relatively close
votes.

POLITICAL PARTY, THE TWO PRESIDENCIES, AND PRESIDENTIAL INFLUENCE

Chapter 5 demonstrated the importance of party as a mediating factor on
presidential influence through position taking. Presidents are more influential when they are in the majority, and they have more influence over
co-partisans. Does party have similar mediating effects on foreign policy
roll calls?

There are good reasons to think that party should mediate the impact of
position taking on foreign policy voting, but rather than co-partisans being
more likely to rally to the president, we should find opposition party members shifting their votes to the president on foreign policy votes but not on
domestic policy. For co-partisans, the presidential effect of position taking
may be similar for domestic and for foreign policy votes; presidents will have
similar levels of influence on co-partisans irrespective of issue type.

Presidents should not influence the voting of opposition members on
domestic issues, as the combination of constituency and party considerations

may lead them to resist presidential attempts at influence. In contrast, on foreign policy issues, constituency factors do not loom as large for opposition party members because voters do not care as much about foreign policy as domestic policy. Plus, when the president takes a position on foreign policy, the party consideration may not greatly affect member voting. By taking a position, the president converts the issue into one that primarily concerns the national interest. Viewing an issue through a national interest lens may mute or dampen the effect of partisan consideration on member voting.[10] Consequently, two factors that often greatly affect member voting—constituency pressures and partisan considerations—do not have a very strong effect on foreign policy votes. But the presidential consideration may be strong on foreign policy issues. The combination of these processes opens up the potential for presidential influence on the votes of opposition members on foreign policy roll calls.

This perspective leads to several hypotheses. First, in contrast to the results detailed in chapter 5, being a majority president should not interact with foreign policy. Majority and minority presidents will be equally influential (or uninfluential) on the foreign and domestic policy votes of members of Congress. But we should expect presidents to have greater influence on the voting of opposition members on foreign than on domestic policy roll calls. Moreover, presidents will not have much, if any, influence on the roll call votes of opposition legislators on domestic issues.

Table 6.1 includes results for the majority president–foreign policy interaction. To test this hypothesis requires a complex three-way interaction among the president's position, policy type (foreign or domestic), and majority status (see model 3). Contrary to expectations, minority presidents seem to exhibit greater influence than majority presidents on foreign policy votes. The effect is substantial, with minority presidents realizing nineteen to twenty more votes than majority presidents on foreign policy compared to domestic policy roll calls.[11]

Why this unexpected effect? One possibility is that minority presidents may take less controversial positions than majority presidents on foreign policy votes, a reflection of their weaker leadership in Congress.[12] Conversely, majority presidents may take more aggressive and controversial foreign policy stances, perhaps because of their partisan strength in

Congress. Another possibility is that foreign nations, assuming that minority presidents are weaker than majority ones, take more actions that either directly or indirectly challenge the United States, its allies, and/or its interests. In the United States, members of both parties view such actions as undermining US national security and thus coalesce to support the president's responses to those foreign threats. To test these and other possible reasons for this unexpected finding requires more than just the roll call data used here.

Table 6.2 presents results for the impact of foreign policy position taking on the roll call behavior of co-partisan and opposition party members. Presidents appear to have slightly more influence on domestic than on foreign policy votes among co-partisans (model 1). The coefficient shows a negative sign for the foreign policy position-taking interaction ($b = -0.03$), that is, the president moves 3% fewer co-partisans to his side on foreign than on domestic policy. When the parties are evenly split (for instance, at 218 seats), presidents acquire about six to seven more votes from co-partisans on domestic than on foreign issues. When the president's majority is at average levels, about 245 seats, he will receive about seven fewer co-partisans voting with him on foreign than on domestic votes. During years of massive presidential party dominance, such as during parts of the Johnson and the Carter years, with 290 seats, this amounts only to a loss of about nine votes.

But what the president loses from co-partisans on foreign policy votes (compared to domestic policy votes) is more than made up by gains from the opposition. The coefficient is positively signed and quite large, at 0.09, or 9%. Again, if the two parties are equally split, the president gains nineteen to twenty opposition members, which more than makes up for the loss of six or seven co-partisans on foreign versus domestic votes. (We must be careful with this comparison—presidents retain the loyalty of co-partisans on foreign policy votes, just at lower levels than on domestic policy votes.) When the president's party holds 245 seats and the opposition holds 190, the president still receives from the opposition seventeen additional votes on foreign policy votes, which is much more than the seven lost among co-partisans. Finally, in the worst-case scenario, when the opposition holds only 145 seats to the 290 of the president's party, the president still comes

TABLE 6.2 IMPACT OF FOREIGN POLICY ROLL CALLS ON PRESIDENTIAL INFLUENCE BY MEMBER PARTY, HOUSE OF REPRESENTATIVES, 1953–2012

VARIABLE	(1) LIBERAL, SAME PARTY (%)	(2) LIBERAL, OPPOSITION PARTY (%)	(3) LIBERAL, SAME PARTY (%)	(4) LIBERAL, OPPOSITION PARTY (%)
Presidential position	0.26***	−0.24***	0.23***	−0.23***
	(0.01)	(0.02)	(0.03)	(0.04)
Foreign policy roll call	−0.06***	0.01	−0.05***	0.00
	(0.01)	(0.02)	(0.02)	(0.02)
Interaction (Position × Foreign policy)	−0.03**	0.09***	−0.02	0.10***
	(0.01)	(0.02)	(0.02)	(0.03)
Majority control	—	—	0.07	−0.11
	—	—	(0.10)	(0.11)
Interaction (Position × Majority control)	—	—	0.04	0.02
	—	—	(0.06)	(0.07)
Interaction (Foreign policy × Majority control)	—	—	−0.01	0.03
	—	—	(0.03)	(0.03)
Interaction (Position × Foreign × Majority)	—	—	−0.03	−0.04
	—	—	(0.03)	(0.04)
Constant	0.50***	0.51***	0.47***	0.55***
	(0.05)	(0.05)	(0.06)	(0.07)
Observations	16,448	16,448	16,448	16,448
R^2	0.10	0.07	0.11	0.09
F	282.5	90.59	139.3	44.00
Regression sum squares	1,837	2,121	1,817	2,081

Note: Analyses clustered on year. Robust standard errors in parentheses. *$p < 0.1$, **$p < 0.05$, ***$p < 0.01$.

out on the positive side, gaining thirteen opposition votes while losing nine co-partisans. Part of the reason that presidents win so much more frequently on foreign than on domestic policy votes is their strong ability to influence members of the opposition party, an effect that more than compensates for the lesser ability of presidents to influence co-partisans on foreign than on domestic policy votes.

THE COLD WAR CONSENSUS, THE TWO PRESIDENCIES, AND PRESIDENTIAL INFLUENCE

According to some studies, presidential influence on foreign versus domestic policy was limited to a specific time period, from the late 1940s until the end of the Vietnam War (Krebs 2015; Marshall and Prins 2002). During these years, a Cold War consensus drove US foreign policy, with both parties agreeing on the major goal of foreign policy, the containment of communist expansion around the world. Moreover, the two parties agreed on the means of achieving this end, which included providing aid to countries perceived as being at risk of a communist takeover and committing US troops in foreign nations, even in large numbers, such as during the Korean and Vietnam wars.

Several factors ended the bipartisan Cold War consensus. These included the length of the Vietnam War, the unpopularity of that war among important domestic constituencies, the cost of the war in both financial and human terms, and the inability of the United States to prevail in Vietnam in spite of the massive commitment of troops and other resources. Furthermore, some US critics of the Vietnam War saw it more as a civil war than as a battle between the United States and its communist competitors and foes. These "civil war" critics, at times, also argued that local populations should decide on their form of government and that the United States should not impose a government on them, as was perceived to be the case in Vietnam. Others questioned the willingness and capacity of the United States to combat communism in all corners of the globe. Finally, critics also argued that détente and coexistence was a better policy toward the Soviet

Union and its communist allies than containment—the United States could still maintain its national security, even with many nations adopting a communist form of government, if tensions between the United States and the Soviet Union were eased and if diplomatic rather than military approaches were employed. Thus, the Vietnam War raised a number of issues and criticisms of the long-standing policy of containment.

This debate over US foreign policy raged within both parties, but the critics of containment took control of the Democratic Party. Although détente advocates such as Richard Nixon, Henry Kissinger, and Gerald Ford were powerful within the Republican Party, "cold warriors" remained influential in that party, and by 1980, with the nomination and election of Ronald Reagan, the anticommunist wing effectively controlled the foreign policy direction of the party. Détente advocates lost power in the Republican Party. With the Republicans maintaining a type of Cold War mentality and the Democrats taking a stance critical of the old Cold War policy orientation, the bipartisan consensus gave way to vigorous partisan debate on foreign policy.

Not only did the two parties debate the direction of foreign policy, as they historically did on many domestic issues, but the difference between the parties on foreign policy widened, polarizing during the post-Vietnam era, much as it did for domestic policy. Due to this polarization on domestic policy, no liberals and few moderates could be found in the ranks of Republican officeholders, while conservatives and moderates became a rare, if nonexistent, breed among Democrats. Similarly, few adherents to the old Cold War orientation could be found within the Democratic Party, while the Republican Party could claim few supporters of détente (Bond and Fleisher 2004; Han and Brady 2007; Layman, Carsey, and Horowitz 2006; Hetherington 2009; Sinclair 2014).

We can use these roll call–level data to illustrate trends in the two parties on foreign and domestic policy, and the comparative differences between the parties at any one point in time. Figure 6.1 shows the average annual percentage of Democratic and Republican liberal votes on all domestic and foreign policy votes; figure 6.2 does the same, but only for conflictual votes. (We need to be cautious in interpreting the trends. Due to composition effects, members are voting on a different set of domestic and foreign policy votes over time, the same critique that Anderson and Habel [2009] and

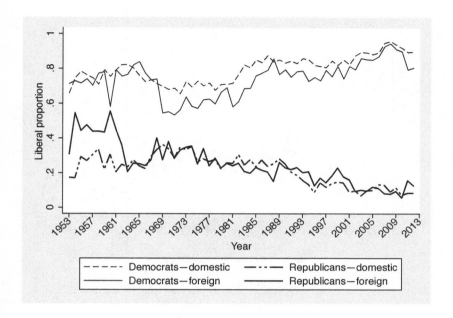

FIGURE 6.1

Annual average percentage of members casting liberal votes on all roll calls,
by party and policy type

Note: Based on roll call–level data, includes all nonpresidential and presidential roll calls.

Groseclose, Levitt, and Snyder [1999] make with regard to comparing Americans for Democratic Action scores over time.)

Both figures tell essentially the same story. In the 1950s there is a considerable gap in the percentage of Democrats and Republicans voting liberal on domestic policy roll calls, but the gap is much smaller on foreign policy, and at times there are no discernible partisan differences. The domestic policy gap narrows somewhat during the 1960s and 1970s, but whereas the Democrats appear to be moderating on foreign policy during those years, the Republicans drift to the right. Around the early 1980s, both parties begin to diverge on domestic policy, with the Democrats moving in a decidedly liberal direction and the Republicans becoming increasingly conservative. And the same pattern holds for foreign policy—in fact,

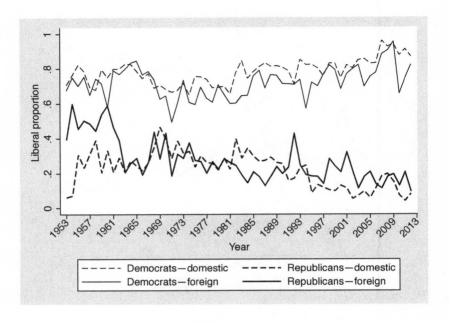

FIGURE 6.2

Annual average percentage of members casting liberal votes on non-lopsided, presidential roll calls, by party and policy type

Note: Based on roll call–level data, includes only presidential roll calls.

across all roll calls, there does not appear to be any difference in voting on domestic and on foreign policy for either party. Democrats are about as likely to take the liberal position on foreign as on domestic roll calls, and Republicans do the same in a conservative direction. The same general pattern of polarization on both types of policies is apparent for contested roll calls, although in both parties, members appear slightly more moderate on foreign than on domestic policy.

Whether one is looking at all roll calls or only contested ones, the differences between the parties on both domestic and foreign policy roll calls widens over time, and there is not much difference within the parties in the roll call behavior on either type of policy, especially after the 1950s to 1960s. Does this also mean that presidents have less influence in Congress on foreign than on domestic policy in the post–Cold War period? Has polarization between the parties across all types of issues overwhelmed the ability of presidents to receive additional support for their foreign policy initiatives from across the aisle?[13]

To test this hypothesis, I follow convention and define the Cold War consensus era as 1953 to 1973 (scored 1) and the post–Cold War era as 1974 to 2012 (scored zero). Then, this period dummy variable is interacted with presidential position and foreign policy, creating another three-way interaction: Presidential Position × Foreign Policy × Cold War Era. Table 6.3 presents results of this test on the overall percentage voting liberal as well as the liberal percentage for same party and opposition party members.

Table 6.3, model 1, presents results for the overall percentage of members casting liberal votes. The coefficient for the three-way interaction is properly signed but small, at $b = 0.02$. Again, since we have a complex three-way interaction, it is difficult to see the effects of the Cold War era on presidential influence from the regression results alone. To help with that, figure 6.3 illustrates graphically the impact of the Cold War era by presidential position and type of roll call (such as foreign versus domestic). On the figure, the solid line is for domestic policy, the dashed line is for foreign policy, while the vertical axis represents the predicted percentage of liberal votes based on table 6.3, model 1. There are separate panels for whether the president took a conservative or a liberal position.

During the Cold War era, presidents are more influential on foreign than on domestic policy votes. When presidents take a conservative position, the percentage voting liberal is nearly 8% lower for foreign than for domestic policy roll calls.[14] In other words, conservative-positioning presidents during the Cold War era will receive about thirty-five more votes on foreign than on domestic roll calls. Although the gap is smaller when presidents take a liberal position during the Cold War era, the percentage voting liberal is about 2% higher for foreign than for domestic policy votes, or about nine more votes. Much of the influence presidents receive on foreign policy during the Cold War era is concentrated when presidents take a conservative rather than a liberal position.

The pattern for domestic versus foreign policy roll calls is quite different during the post–Cold War era. Again, conservative position taking

TABLE 6.3 IMPACT OF THE COLD WAR CONSENSUS ON PRESIDENTIAL FOREIGN POLICY INFLUENCE, HOUSE OF REPRESENTATIVES, 1953–2012

VARIABLE	(1) OVERALL LIBERAL (%)	(2) SAME PARTY LIBERAL (%)	(3) OPPOSITION PARTY LIBERAL (%)
Presidential position	−0.01	0.27***	−0.27***
	(0.01)	(0.02)	(0.02)
Foreign policy roll call	−0.03***	−0.07***	0.01
	(0.01)	(0.02)	(0.02)
Interaction (Position × Foreign policy)	0.03***	−0.05**	0.10***
	(0.01)	(0.02)	(0.02)
Cold War–era dummy (1953–1973 = 1)	0.01	−0.06	0.07
	(0.01)	(0.06)	(0.07)
Interaction (Cold War × Position)	0.05***	−0.02	0.08***
	(0.01)	(0.02)	(0.03)
Interaction (Foreign × Cold War)	−0.00	0.05*	−0.03
	(0.01)	(0.02)	(0.03)
Interaction (Position × Foreign × Cold War)	0.02	0.05**	−0.01
	(0.02)	(0.02)	(0.04)
Constant	0.53***	0.51***	0.50***
	(0.01)	(0.05)	(0.06)
Observations	16,448	16,448	16,448
R^2	0.02	0.11	0.07
F	20.75	128.6	57.35
rss	296.4	1830	2107

Note: Analyses clustered on year, contested roll calls. Robust standard errors in parentheses.
*$p < 0.1$, **$p < 0.05$, ***$p < 0.01$.

produces some influence for presidents in foreign votes, compared to domestic votes, but the amount of influence is smaller than during the Cold War era, about 6% compared to 8%, or about twenty-six additional votes compared to the thirty-five during the Cold War era. But when presidents take a liberal posture during the post–Cold War era, there is no difference in the percentage voting liberal on foreign versus domestic policy votes.

Thus, while we still observe some influence advantage for presidents on foreign policy roll calls during the post–Cold War era, it is smaller than during the earlier, consensus era. Plus, during the post–Cold War era,

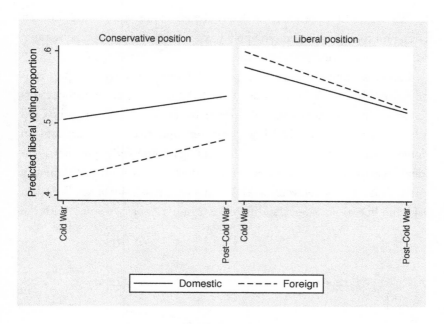

FIGURE 6.3

Impact of presidential position on domestic and foreign policy roll calls,
by Cold War era and Post–Cold War era, 1953–2012

Note: Overall liberal voting, presidential position: −1 = Conservative; 0 = No position;
1 = Liberal. Cold War era = 1953–1973; post–Cold War era = 1974–2012.
Based on results from table 6.3, model 1.

presidents have more influence on foreign than on domestic policy votes only when they take a conservative rather than a liberal position. As a more general point, in both eras presidents are more influential on foreign than on domestic policy when they take conservative rather than liberal positions, a pattern heretofore unnoted in the literature.

Earlier analyses in this chapter showed that presidential foreign policy influence is stronger among opposition party members than among co-partisans. The effect of the Cold War on opposition and same party members is presented in table 6.3, models 2 and 3. Again, due to the complex three-way interaction, is it hard to make sense of the impact of the Cold War era on voting merely by inspecting the regression results. Thus, figures 6.4 and 6.5 present graphically the effects of presidential position taking on foreign and domestic policy votes for the two eras among same party and opposition party members.

Earlier we found that presidents have less influence with co-partisans on foreign than on domestic issues (table 6.1). Figure 6.4 presents the results for presidential co-partisans, broken down by the two eras. During the Cold War era, presidents receive slightly greater support from co-partisans on domestic than on foreign policy. When taking a conservative position, presidents receive about 3% more support on domestic than on foreign policy votes, about six to seven votes when holding a slim majority of 218. But when taking a liberal position, the difference is only 1%, or two votes, with the

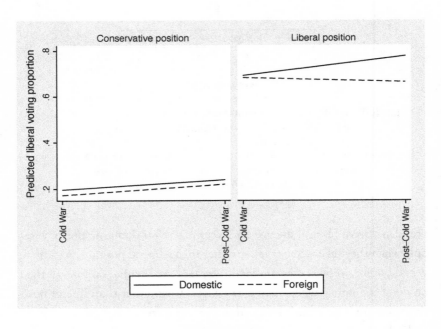

FIGURE 6.4

Impact on co-partisans of presidential position on domestic and foreign policy roll calls, by Cold War era and post–Cold War era, 1953–2012

Note: Same party liberal voting, presidential position: –1 = Conservative; 0 = No position; 1 = Liberal. Cold War era = 1953–1973; post–Cold War era = 1974–2012. Based on results from table 6.3, model 2.

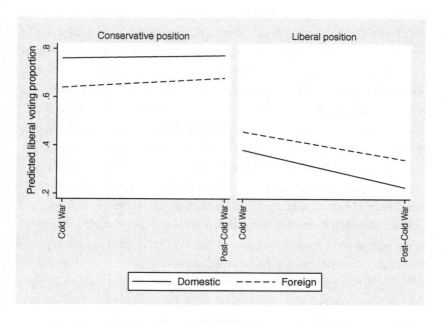

FIGURE 6.5

Impact of presidential position on domestic and foreign policy roll calls on opposition party members, by Cold War era and post–Cold War era, 1953–2012

Note: Opposition liberal voting, presidential position: –1 = Conservative; 0 = No position; 1 = Liberal. Cold War era = 1953–1973; post–Cold War Era = 1974–2012. Based on results from table 6.3, model 3.

same narrow majority. The increased support on domestic versus foreign policy votes grows during the post–Cold War era, however, jumping to 4% when the president takes a conservative position and 12% for a liberal position. This translates into about nine and twenty-six votes when the president's party commands the smallest majority, 218.

Matters differ greatly when one looks at opposition party members. During the Cold War era, presidents receive about 12% more support from the opposition on foreign than on domestic roll calls when taking a conservative position, and about 8% more support when taking a liberal position. Assuming the opposition has the largest minority possible (217 members), during the Cold War era, conservative and liberal positions will generate about twenty-six and sixteen additional votes. The greater influence that presidents have on foreign policy continues at roughly similar levels during the post–Cold War era, at about 9% and 11% when presidents take conservative and liberal positions, or nineteen and twenty-four more votes from the opposition on foreign than on domestic policy roll calls.

Although presidents possess a smaller influence advantage on foreign than on domestic roll calls during the post–Cold War era compared to the Cold War era, patterns are the same within the parties across the two eras. Presidents move fewer co-partisans to their side on foreign than on domestic votes during both eras, in part because they receive relatively high rates of support anyway. Although the differential is not large during the Cold War era, it is measurable in the post–Cold War era, especially when presidents take liberal positions. In contrast, presidents are able to shift a considerably greater number of opposition members to their side on foreign than on domestic policy during both eras, and there is little indication that the effect has weakened from the Cold War to the post–Cold War eras.

Thus, the weaker overall advantage on foreign policy during the post–Cold War era, compared to the Cold War era, is not a function of a declining ability to influence opposition members but of the much greater ability of liberal presidents to gather co-partisan support for their domestic, as opposed to their foreign policy, positions. This pattern of growing ability of presidents to influence co-partisans for their domestic policy positions raises the question of whether it is the decline of the Cold War consensus or the rise of party polarization that better accounts for the patterns detected here. The next section turns to this question.

THE COLD WAR CONSENSUS, PARTY POLARIZATION, AND THE TWO PRESIDENCIES

What better accounts for the patterns noted here, the breakdown of the bipartisan consensus on foreign policy or the increasing polarization between the parties? On one level, both processes are linked over time. On a merely descriptive level, during the era of the Cold War consensus, party polarization was much lower than during the post–Cold War era, with polarization averaging 0.39 during the 1953 to 1973 years but 0.60 from 1974 to 2012.[15] Little research on congressional party polarization, however, compares trends for different policy areas, as is done here.[16] Jochim and Jones (2013, 352), using the Policy Agendas Project framework, find differences "in which individual issues became integrated into the partisan and ideological fabric of the political system."[17] That is, some issues became polarized earlier and/or more strongly than others. For instance, policy areas most closely tied to economic concerns—such as macroeconomics, labor, and housing—consistently showed party differences in voting. But party conflict was appreciably lower for environment, foreign affairs, agriculture, and transportation, and these policy areas were only slowly enveloped into partisan divisions, which became more pronounced from the 1980s onward (Jochim and Jones 2013, 358).

Understanding the causal relationship between the breakdown of the Cold War consensus and party polarization is more complicated. Arguments can be made that the breakdown of the Cold War consensus contributed to the growing polarization between the parties. This process suggests that differences over the best foreign policy for the United States became linked to the platforms and positions of the parties. For example, first an intellectual debate over policy arose, with the two parties eventually adopting differing sides on that debate.

Another perspective suggests that increasing polarization may have forced or motivated politicians within each party to take a stand on foreign policy debates that were consistent with their party. Such a process would also have led to the demise of the Cold War consensus, but rather than ideas and ideology motivating the process, partisan competition structured stances on foreign policy. Intellectual debate is less important in this partisan competition argument. Instead partisan debate on foreign policy may be viewed uncharitably as a rationalization for the foreign policy positions that politicians within the two parties take.

We may not be able to sort out the different causal mechanisms in the breakdown of the policy consensus, the rise of party polarization, and the effects of those two processes on presidential influence in Congress, because the first two are so heavily correlated. Yet it is possible to assess whether polarization in the House affects presidential influence on foreign versus domestic policy and to compare (in a statistical sense) the relative ability of the Cold War consensus and polarization explanations to account for presidential influence in Congress. Table 6.4, model 1, presents estimates that replace the Cold War dummy variable with the party polarization variable, as measured in chapter 5. To test the polarization–foreign

TABLE 6.4 IMPACT OF PARTY POLARIZATION ON PRESIDENTIAL FOREIGN POLICY INFLUENCE, HOUSE OF REPRESENTATIVES, 1953–2012

VARIABLE	(1) OVERALL LIBERAL (%)	(2) SAME PARTY LIBERAL (%)	(3) OPPOSITION PARTY LIBERAL (%)
Presidential position	0.07**	0.03	0.09**
	(0.03)	(0.03)	(0.04)
Foreign policy	−0.08***	0.06	−0.18***
	(0.02)	(0.04)	(0.04)
Interaction (Position × Foreign policy)	0.03	0.12***	−0.08
	(0.03)	(0.04)	(0.06)
House party polarization	−0.12**	0.28	−0.30
	(0.06)	(0.32)	(0.34)
Interaction (Position × Polarization)	−0.12*	0.43***	−0.62***
	(0.06)	(0.06)	(0.08)
Interaction (Foreign × Polarization)	0.09***	−0.19***	0.33***
	(0.03)	(0.06)	(0.07)
Interaction (Position × Foreign × Polarization)	0.01	−0.28***	0.33**
	(0.06)	(0.09)	(0.13)
Constant	0.60***	0.33**	0.68***
	(0.03)	(0.15)	(0.17)
Observations	16,448	16,448	16,448
R^2	0.03	0.12	0.09
F	17.45	238.6	171.2
rss	293.5	1802	2072

Note: Analyses clustered on year, contested roll calls. Robust standard errors in parentheses.
*$p < 0.1$, **$p < 0.05$, ***$p < 0.01$.

policy influence hypothesis requires a three-way interaction: Presidential Position × Foreign Policy × Party Polarization.

Again, since it is difficult to interpret three-way interactions, figure 6.6 presents the predicted percentage voting liberal by presidential position and by foreign versus domestic votes, for different levels of House polarization. The figure indicates that, when the president takes a conservative position, the amount of presidential influence on foreign compared to domestic votes declines as polarization increases, even though conservative presidents are always more influential on foreign than on domestic votes. When polarization is low, the relative influence on foreign versus domestic policy is strong, at 9% (about thirty-nine members), but recedes to 4% (seventeen

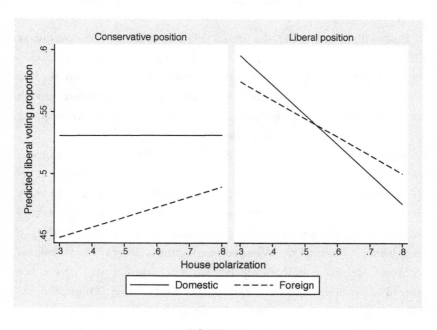

FIGURE 6.6

Impact on overall member voting of presidential position on domestic and foreign policy roll calls, by House party polarization, 1953–2012

Note: Overall liberal voting percentage, presidential position: –1 = Conservative; 0 = No position; 1 = Liberal. House party polarization is the percentage of party roll calls during the year. Based on results from table 6.4, model 1.

votes) when polarization is at its highest. We saw a similar pattern, though not as strong, for the Cold War consensus hypothesis. Conservative presidents have an 8% foreign policy advantage during the Cold War era, which dips slightly to 6% during the post–Cold War era.

Polarization exhibits different conditional effects on influence when the president takes a liberal position. When polarization is low, liberal presidents are more influential on domestic than on foreign policy by about 2% (eight or nine votes), but when polarization is high, liberal presidents become more influential on foreign than on domestic votes, a reversal in their influence patterns. At high polarization levels, the advantage on foreign over domestic votes is again not very strong, at 2%, or about eight to nine votes. Clearly, presidents have more influence on foreign than on domestic votes when they take a conservative position, a relationship that holds at all levels of polarization.

But, as discussed earlier, the figures that look at all members may mask different patterns within the parties. Table 6.4 presents results of models for co-partisan and opposition members (models 2 and 3), but again, because of the complex three-way interaction, we turn to figures to help sort through the complexities. Figures 6.7 and 6.8 present the relevant information for same party and opposition party members.

Figure 6.7 indicates almost no difference in presidential influence on co-partisans on foreign compared to domestic votes when the president takes a conservative position. Although the foreign policy advantage is about 4% (seventeen votes) when polarization is low, the effect of position taking declines as polarization rises: when polarization reaches peak levels, the gap in influence is less than 1%. When comparing the Cold War and post–Cold War eras, we saw a 2% foreign policy advantage during the first era, but instead of being extinguished, as it is when polarization is high, the foreign policy advantage remained at 2% during the post–Cold War era.

Polarization seems to have greater conditional effects when presidents take a liberal position. Repeating the finding for all members, liberal presidents display slightly more influence on foreign than on domestic votes when polarization is low, about 4% (nine votes, assuming a 218 majority). But when polarization rises to its highest levels, liberal positions now show an influence advantage on domestic over foreign policy votes of 20%

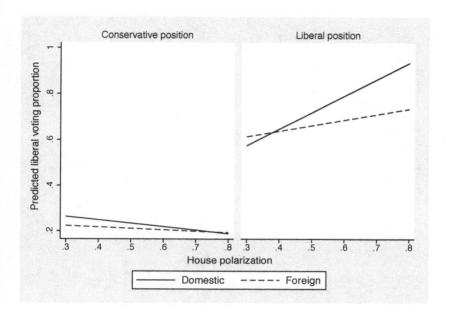

FIGURE 6.7

Impact on co-partisans of presidential position on domestic and foreign policy roll calls, by House party polarization, 1953–2012

Note: Same party liberal voting percentage, presidential position: –1 = Conservative; 0 = No position; 1 = Liberal. House party polarization is the percentage of party roll calls during the year. Based on results from table 6.4, model 2.

(forty-three to forty-four votes with a narrow 218 majority). The reason for this reversal in influence patterns on foreign policy votes is the nearly perfect voting unanimity of same party members on domestic issues when polarization is high. In contrast, during the Cold War consensus era, liberal presidents display a meager 1% advantage on domestic over foreign policy votes, the opposite of the effect found for the low-polarization condition. But, corresponding to the high-polarization condition, during the post–Cold War era, liberal presidents are 11% less influential on co-partisans on foreign than on domestic policy votes.

Finally, turning to opposition members, figure 6.8 indicates that when presidents take a conservative position, they always have more influence on

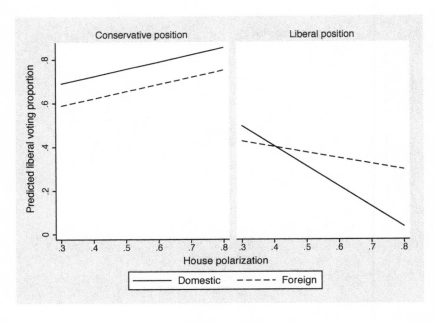

FIGURE 6.8

Impact of presidential position on domestic and foreign policy roll calls on
opposition member voting, by House party polarization, 1953–2012

Note: Opposition liberal voting percentage, presidential position: -1 = Conservative;
0 = No position; 1 = Liberal. House party polarization is the percentage of party
roll calls during the year. Based on results from table 6.4, model 3.

foreign than on domestic votes. Moreover, this influence impact is steady
at differing levels of polarization. For instance, when polarization is low,
there is about a 10% differential. When polarization is at its highest, it is
still 10% (or about twenty-two votes when the opposition holds 217 seats).
Increasing polarization does not seem to affect the additional influence of
conservative-positioning presidents on opposition members on foreign compared to domestic votes. The earlier comparison between the Cold War
and post–Cold War eras showed similar effects, with a 12% foreign policy
influence advantage on opposition members during the Cold War era and
a 10% advantage during the latter era.

In contrast, polarization seems to affect the relative influence of liberal-positioning presidents on opposition members both on foreign and on domestic votes. When polarization is low, presidents have more influence on domestic than on foreign policy votes, 7% (about fifteen votes when the parties hold similar numbers of seats). Matters reverse as polarization increases, with liberal-positioning presidents becoming more influential on foreign than on domestic policy votes by about 26% (a massive fifty-six votes with a narrow 217 minority). Such an effect seems too large to be true; there are probably other, unmeasured factors that are also affecting the roll call behavior of members.[18] But a similar though less extreme pattern is present when comparing the Cold War and post–Cold War eras, as was shown earlier, with Cold War liberal-positioning presidents having 8% more influence on domestic than on foreign policy, an influence gap that expands to 12% during the post–Cold War era.

Overall then, despite minor variations in the magnitude of effects, both the Cold War and polarization hypotheses report similar conditional effects on presidential foreign policy influence. These hypotheses suggest different causal mechanisms, one involving a debate over ideas regarding foreign policy (the Cold War/post–Cold War eras hypothesis) and the other, polarization, emphasizing the politics associated with party competition and how those competitive pressures engulf more and more policy areas until, by the 2000s, competition between the parties largely structures virtually all policy areas. Despite the temporal coincidence of the post–Cold War era with high levels of polarization, which makes separating their statistical effects difficult, each perspective brings a different understanding of presidential influence on foreign compared to domestic policy. The high statistical correlation between the two precludes a definitive test to select one over the other, but we can ask whether both potentially contribute to explaining temporal patterns in presidential influence on foreign compared to domestic policy votes in the House.

Two generally accepted methods for accounting for the comparative model fit of different specifications (on the same data) are the Akaike information criterion (AIC) and the Schwarz's Bayesian information criterion (BIC). Both produce summary statistics for model fit, with one major difference: the AIC penalizes less for additional variables than does the BIC. For each, when comparing two models, the one with the smaller value is preferred. Additionally, one can compare models with different variables, as well as nested models.[19] Finally, the larger the absolute difference between the two models, the stronger the evidence in support of one over the other. Generally, a rule of thumb is that the absolute difference should be greater than 2 (Raftery 1995).

Table 6.5 presents the AIC and BIC statistics for three models, ones that includes the Cold War dummy, a second that includes polarization, and a third that includes both. For all members, both the AIC and BIC point to the combined model as best, suggesting that both the Cold War and the polarization ideas contribute to understanding the influence of presidents on foreign compared to domestic votes. Furthermore, the evidence in support of this is quite strong, with the absolute difference in the statistics for the combined model compared to the other models being greater than 10.[20] The AIC and BIC statistics, however, point in different directions for co-partisans and for opposition party members. Although in both cases the AIC suggests that the combined model is preferred, the BIC supports the polarization-only model. However, the absolute difference for the BIC statistics is much larger than is the case for the AIC. In either event, both the AIC and the BIC criteria indicate that polarization is necessary in accounting for presidential influence on foreign over domestic policy, though it is not clear that the Cold War–era hypothesis is pertinent for explaining the behavior of within-party groups.

A nested regression approach offers another way of assessing the relative importance of the two explanations. Nested regression compares the difference between a restricted model and a full model, where the nested model excludes one or more variables that are included in the full model. For our present purposes, the nested regression would compare the Cold War era–only model with a model that includes the variables to estimate both the Cold War and the polarization models. A second nested comparison would be between a polarization-only model and the full model that includes both the relevant Cold War and polarization variables.[21]

Table 6.6 presents the results of the nested regression analyses on all members. No matter the entry order of the Cold War and polarization block

TABLE 6.5 COMPARISON OF AKAIKE INFORMATION CRITERION AND BAYESIAN INFORMATION CRITERION STATISTICS FOR COLD WAR–ERA, PARTY POLARIZATION, AND COMBINED MODELS

MODEL	ALL MEMBERS		SAME PARTY MEMBERS		OPPOSITION PARTY MEMBERS	
	AIC	BIC	AIC	BIC	AIC	BIC
Cold War	−19,365.87	−19,304.20	10,579.03	10,640.69	12,891.58	12,953.24
Polarization	−19,526.12	−19,464.45	10,318.21	10,380.21*	12,621.85	12,683.52*
Combined	−19,591.43*	−19,498.94*	10,310.60*	10,403.10	12,615.43*	12,707.93

Note: Based on results from tables 6.3 and 6.4. AIC = Akaike information criterion; BIC = Bayesian information criterion. *Indicates best model.

TABLE 6.6 NESTED REGRESSION ANALYSIS OF THE EFFECTS OF THE COLD WAR AND POST–COLD WAR ERAS AND POLARIZATION ON PRESIDENTIAL FOREIGN POLICY INFLUENCE

	ALL MEMBERS					
BLOCK	F	df	df	Pr > F	R^2	Δ IN R^2
Position	4.45	1	59	0.0391	0.0025	—
Foreign	26.65	1	59	0.0000	0.0082	0.0057
Position × Foreign	18.42	1	59	0.0001	0.0106	0.0025
Cold War variables	6.14	4	59	0.0004	0.019	0.0084
Polarization variables	3.31	4	59	0.0167	0.0329	0.0138

	SAME PARTY MEMBERS					
BLOCK	F	df	df	Pr > F	R^2	Δ IN R^2
Position	698.32	1	59	0.0000	0.0994	—
Foreign	14.74	1	59	0.0003	0.1034	0.0041
Position × Foreign	4.24	1	59	0.0439	0.1037	0.0003
Cold War variables	3.83	4	59	0.0080	0.107	0.0033
Polarization variables	12.04	4	59	0.0000	0.1219	0.0149

	OPPOSITION PARTY MEMBERS					
BLOCK	F	df	df	Pr > F	R^2	Δ IN R^2
Position	257.44	1	59	0.0000	0.0656	—
Foreign	0.19	1	59	0.6682	0.0657	0.0001
Position × Foreign	24.68	1	59	0.0000	0.0684	0.0027
Cold War variables	2.44	4	59	0.0577	0.0746	0.0062
Polarization variables	13.92	4	59	0.0000	0.0904	0.0158

of variables, the nested regression analysis points to the same conclusion: both sets of variables independently add to explanation of comparative presidential influence on foreign compared to domestic votes. The F tests for the inclusion of each of these blocks are statistically significance at the 0.02 level or better in all cases. Still, we must temper this conclusion because of the small R^2s and the very large number of cases. With so many cases, small improvements in model fit may appear statistically significant. Yet these results also conform to the AIC and BIC tests.

Table 6.6 also presents results of nested regressions on same party and opposition party members. The F test for the Cold War block of variables is statistically significant for neither of these analyses, reinforcing the results of the AIC and BIC tests. Thus, the Cold War explanation does not add to what the polarization perspective offers, at least for understanding presidential foreign policy influence within each party. Within the parties, it appears that competitive partisan forces account for the influence that presidents possess on foreign compared to domestic policy.

CONCLUSION

The two presidencies thesis is about influence as much as it is about success. Research that only uses roll calls on which the president has already taken a stand can assess who supports or opposes the president and can compare victory rates across different types of roll calls, such as domestic versus foreign. But analyses on such restricted roll calls cannot easily identify whether presidents are influential, or whether presidents move members to their side, and thus cannot address whether influence accounts for the different levels of presidential policy success on foreign compared to domestic policy. The methodology developed for this study uses all roll calls, regardless of whether the president took a position, and thus can compare member voting on presidential roll calls with voting on nonpresidential roll calls, with all the caveats and cautions detailed in previous chapters.

Results here indicate that presidents are indeed *more influential* on foreign than on domestic policy and that the influence margin is large enough to lead to a number of roll call victories that the president would otherwise have lost had he not taken a position. The analysis also found that presidents have a greater ability to influence opposition party members than copartisans on foreign rather than domestic policy. From the perspective used here, this pattern makes sense. Opposition members, on average, start out with policy positions on foreign policy that are more likely to differ with the president's than is the case for co-partisans. Another way of saying this is that there can be no influence if presidents and their co-partisans "naturally" agree on policy because of shared policy preferences, intraparty recruitment of politicians, or other reasons. Thus, presidents have greater *opportunity* to influence opposition members than co-partisans.

Given the difficulty of finding support from the opposition party in general, it is surprising that presidents appear to influence as many opposition members as they do. Part of the reason that presidents can influence opposition members on foreign policy is that other considerations that affect roll call decisions, such as constituency and party, are relatively weak on foreign policy. When the president takes a position on a foreign policy vote, there are few other factors that compete with the president to influence the member's vote. This dynamic accounts for the influence of presidents on opposition party members on foreign as opposed to domestic policy votes.

Finally, this chapter also inspected changing patterns of presidential influence on foreign compared to domestic policy, comparing two explanations—the breakdown of the bipartisan Cold War consensus on foreign policy and the rise of party polarization in Congress. Both ideas predict that the presidential foreign policy advantage on domestic policy has waned over time. When looking at influence patterns on all members, both ideas statistically contribute to the explanation. But when looking at co-partisan and opposition members voting separately, only the polarization dynamic appears to significantly affect presidential influence on foreign compared to domestic policy. The institutional influence perspective developed here, plus comparing additional years of data to past research on the two presidencies, comparing same party with opposition party members, and comparing the Cold War consensus and polarization ideas, has deepened our understanding of presidential influence on foreign compared to domestic policy.

7

PUBLIC OPINION AS A SOURCE OF PRESIDENTIAL INFLUENCE

I S PUBLIC OPINION a source of presidential influence in Congress? This is a venerable question about presidential influence, which can be traced to Richard Neustadt's *Presidential Power* (1960). Neustadt argues that the president's standing with the public, his prestige, could be a potent resource for dealing with Congress. As Neustadt (1960, 64) claims, a president's "public standing is a source of influence for him, another factor bearing on their [members of Congress] willingness to give him what he wants."

Since Neustadt suggested a relationship between presidential prestige and influence in Congress, few questions regarding presidential–congressional relations have been studied so extensively (see Edwards 2009a for a thorough review). Despite the volume of work, there is considerable controversy about whether one aspect of prestige, *presidential approval*, actually provides the president with much, if any, influence with Congress. Some studies find a positive relationship between approval and support, whereas others report weak or modest effects.[1]

This question of whether public opinion is a source of presidential influence in Congress also reflects on issues of representation. Public opinion about the president, such as approval ratings, provides Congress with information about public attitudes. A popular president may indicate public acceptance, support, and approval for the president's leadership, including his policies. Given the visibility and importance of the president to voters, members of Congress may feel that, for their own electoral self-interest, it would behoove them to support a popular president or to oppose an unpopular one (Edwards 2009a). By responding to the president's approval level in voting on roll calls, Congress may be representing the public, at least on this opinion dimension.[2]

This chapter deals with several limitations of the existing literature on the impact of approval (and other aspect of public opinion) on presidential relations with Congress. First, to repeat the main theme of this book, most research looks at presidential success or support exclusively on presidential roll calls. The amount of influence the president has with Congress may be underestimated by not taking into account the influence that presidents accrue from position taking, which transforms a nonpresidential roll call into a presidential one.

Second, presidential influence with Congress may be contingent on the salience of the issue rather than on approval (Canes-Wrone and de Marchi 2002; Eshbaugh-Soha 2010).[3] James Druckman (see also Jones and Baumgartner 2004; Jones, Larsen-Price, and Wilkerson 2009) argues that salience is necessary for evaluating the quality of representation:

> Imagine that citizens care overwhelmingly about tax cuts—all other issues are far less salient. Then, if politicians craft policies that differ from citizens' preferences on tax cuts (even if citizens' preferences are in fact in their long-term interests) but match citizens' opinions on dozens of other low salient issues, would we conclude that there is general congruence? Put another way, studies of representation need to incorporate an explicit consideration of salience. (Druckman 2006, 408)

Members of Congress are more likely to pay attention to the public when it cares a lot about an issue than when the issue hardly registers among voters, because, among other reasons, salience affects whether an issue will affect voters' election decisions. As Shapiro (2011, 986) writes in his review of the literature on public opinion and representation, "The repeated finding of greater or more frequent effects of opinion on more salient policies fits directly with the expectation that political leaders and candidates would be most concerned with matters that are of greatest visibility to (potential) voters." This chapter looks at the conditioning effect of issue salience on presidential influence in Congress, in addition to the effects of approval.

PUBLIC OPINION AND THE PRESIDENTIAL CONSIDERATION

The institutional theory of presidential influence hypothesizes that when presidents take a position, they convert a floor vote from a nonpresidential into a presidential roll call. This alters the voting calculus of members, as greater weight is attached to the presidential consideration. The presidential consideration is weaker or absent for nonpresidential roll calls. Moreover, the greater the weight given to the presidential consideration, the more influence the president will have on member roll call voting. Finally, position taking has an indirect effect by more closely associating the president with other considerations that affect member voting—in this case, with public opinion. Depending on the configuration of public opinion, this indirect, associational process may work to either the president's advantage or disadvantage.

This chapter compares two aspects of public opinion—presidential approval and issue salience—as possible sources of presidential influence in Congress. Each can be viewed as constituent considerations in members' roll call decisions. When the president takes a position, the presidential consideration is linked more strongly to this constituent consideration. How does this process work for these two aspects of public opinion?

Let's take presidential approval first. In deciding how to vote when the president takes a position, members may look to the president's approval level, anticipating the impact of presidential approval on constituent voting in congressional elections (Canes-Wrone, Brady, and Cogan 2002; Gronke, Koch, and Wilson 2003; Lebo and O'Geen 2011). To minimize the risk of losing voter support on election day, members will be more likely to vote on the president's side when the executive is popular but on the opposite side when the president is not popular (Edwards 2009a).

Although the reelection motivation is common in studies of the sources of congressional roll call voting, there is considerable disagreement on whether presidential approval empirically affects congressional roll call behavior.[4] Existing research may have underestimated the amount of influence presidents acquire from their approval, because of the restricted set of roll calls analyzed, that is, they used only presidential roll calls. If, as I argue here, presidents may influence member voting through position taking, the possibility exists that approval has larger effects on congressional roll call voting than extant research suggests. Still, approval is only one constituent (or voter) consideration that may affect a member's roll call vote.

Other constituent considerations, such as issue salience, may condition presidential influence in Congress. Voters, often being uncertain about which solutions will best address their problems, seek leadership from elected officials, especially the president (Jones and Baumgartner 2004). When a president takes a position on an issue of great concern to voters, presidents are, in effect, representing that public concern (Cohen 1997). Members of Congress thus may view the president as representing the public's concern when the president takes a position on an issue of concern to voters. Viewing the president in this way may provide the executive with some advantages in legislative debates about the best policy solution. If the public either is uncertain or does not care about the particular policy solution, and if voters view the president as representing their concerns when the president takes positions on salient issues, members may be inclined to support the president's solution.

Issue salience has implications for voters' decisions. For instance, voters are better able to discriminate among candidates' positions on more salient than on less salient issues, and they are more likely to judge incumbent performance on more salient issues (Belanger and Meguid 2008; Fournier et al. 2003; Rabinowitz, Prothro, and Jacoby 1982). The consequences of issue salience for voters creates incentives for politicians to be responsive to voters on more salient issues but to be less responsive on less salient issues. Thus, presidents are likely to get more of what they want from Congress on issues salient to the public than on less salient ones.

There are two challenges to this perspective linking presidential position taking, issue salience, and influence. First, presidents can increase the salience of an issue by taking a public position on an issue. Second, presidents are strategic in going public (in taking a position), depending on the public's preferences on an issue. What are the implications for presidential influence if presidents can increase public salience when they take a position? (See Cohen 1997; Canes-Wrone 2006.) Do they derive more influence if they increase the salience of an issue or if they take positions only on issues that are already salient? Without data on the causal ordering of public salience and presidential position taking, we cannot test this conjecture definitively.

The second challenge views presidents as strategic in position taking. They will take positions on roll calls conditional on the public's preferences, on their own preferences, and on the status quo location on the issue. As Canes-Wrone (2006) argues, presidents will refrain from going public (or taking a position) when they prefer the status quo to the public's preferences. Her argument is that although the president cannot easily change public preferences on an issue, the president can increase the salience of an issue by going public on the issue. Further, she assumes that, in setting its agenda, Congress is more likely to act on issues highly salient to the public than on less salient issues. And, for electoral and other reason, the public's preferences on salient issues will have a large impact on how members vote. Given these conditions, presidents will not go public (or take a position) on an issue when they prefer the status quo over the public's preferences. By staying silent, presidents aim to dampen public concern on the issue and thus to keep it from coming to the floor for a vote. To test Canes-Wrone's more complex model requires data on public preferences on the roll call—which, again, we lack.

Despite the fact that we cannot investigate all the ways in which public opinion may interact with presidential position taking, we can test these two hypotheses:

1. Popular presidents will have more influence in Congress than will unpopular ones.
2. Presidents will be more influential in Congress on issues of high salience to voters than on issues of low salience.

MEASURING PUBLIC OPINION:
PRESIDENTIAL APPROVAL

To measure approval, I begin with the Gallup question "Do you approve or disapprove of the way [president's name] is handling his job as president?"[5] Using each administration of the question, I create a monthly approval rating. To do this requires dealing with months when Gallup did not ask respondents the question, months when Gallup asked the question multiple times, and variability in "Don't know" responses. Months without the approval question are not common but tend to occur more frequently in the early years of the 1953 to 2012 period, during the final several months of a lame duck president's term, or during the final months of the term of a president who was not reelected. Months with multiple readings have become more common in recent years. Finally, the percentage responding "Don't know" tends to be higher early in a new president's term of office.

To deal with multiple monthly readings, I took the average of all polls during the month. I corrected for "Don't knows" with the formula: Corrected Approval = Approval / (Approval + Disapproval).[6] And I use linear interpolation to create approval values for months without polls.[7] Additionally, in estimations, the prior month's approval reading is used, rather than the contemporaneous approval level, because presidential performance on roll calls and approval are endogenous, that is, presidential approval appears to increase success rates, but winning also seems to improve approval ratings (Cohen 2013; Lebo and O'Geen 2011). Using lagged approval means we lose the transition months when a new president comes into office.[8]

Finally, there is the issue of using monthly approval readings. Edwards (2009a) criticizes the use of monthly approval in studies of president support and success. As he states in his critique of using the most recent approval reading prior to the vote, "There is no theoretical reason to expect such close associations between approval and congressional support" (348). This is because, he argues, approval is a background consideration that members take into account, and thus we should not expect a one-to-one relationship between approval and success. Hence, Edwards argues that studies should use annual measures of approval which "smooth out 'the vagaries of shift-ing sentiment' and provide a better test of strategic influence" (p. 349).

Edwards's theoretical point is well taken. I argue, similarly, that approval is but one consideration that may affect member roll call behavior. But using annual approval is problematic when conducting analyses at the individual roll call level, as is done here. Assume, for instance, that a president's polls in December of a year are considerably lower than in January of the same year. Why would we expect a member to be able to predict accurately how much a president's polls will change over the course of a year? Using annu-alized approval in effect assumes that members are prescient about the future, an untenable assumption.

The real question concerns the time unit that members use when assess-ing the strategic environment associated with approval. Using the most recent poll is just as arbitrary and problematic as using annual approval or any other aggregation, whether monthly, quarterly, or semiannually. It is likely that different members employ different time units and that the ref-erence time unit might change, depending upon how stable or variable the president's approval and other factors have been. Edwards is correct, in thinking theoretically about the relationship between approval and success or influence, that approval should be thought of in strategic terms. But, in another sense, the proper time unit for measuring approval is an empirical question and the selection may differ depending upon the data at hand and the specific research question.

Given all these theoretical qualifications and uncertainties, monthly data are appropriate for purposes of this research. First, many other data—especially data concerning the economy, such as unemployment and inflation—are measured monthly. Due to the monthly reporting of so much data about various aspects of politics and society, we have become accus-tomed to thinking of political and economic time in monthly terms. Sec-ond, although we could easily use the moving average of the previous two or three months—a compromise between Edwards's annual prescription and those who advocate using the most recent prior poll—aggregating to time periods longer than a month would entail losing many more cases dur-ing transition periods from a departing president to a new one.[9] It is important to retain as much data from this transition period as possible, owing to the special characteristics of the "honeymoon" period and the president's first one hundred days, an important marker of the presidency since Franklin Roosevelt (Beckmann and Godfrey 2007; Dominguez 2005; Frendreis, Tatalovich, and Schaff 2001) and a period when, some theories argue, presidents obtain much legislation (Krehbiel 1998). Third, if Edwards is correct in arguing that months are too short a period to observe any relationship between presidential approval and support (or influence), then using monthly approval ratings puts the hypothesis under a stringent test. Finally, presidential approval generally shifts very slowly over time. Rarely are there large monthly swings in approval, or even swings across several months.[10]

MEASURING ISSUE SALIENCE

To measure issue salience, I use the Gallup Most Important Problem (MIP) series, reconfigured to match the Policy Agendas Project (PAP) and Comparative Agendas Project (CAP) major issue codes. I merge these data at the major issue level with each roll call because the PAP/CAP has coded each roll call using this framework.[11] Still, there are two potential problems with the MIP data. First, as Wlezien (2005) and Jennings and Wlezien (2011) maintain, there is a conceptual difference between the most important *issue* and the most important *problem*. As Jennings and Wlezien explain:

> In theory, an important issue refers to a something that people care about, taxes or the economy, for instance. If a lot of people care about an issue, then it is considered an important political issue. An important problem is conceptually different. It captures the importance of an issue *and* the degree to which it is a problem. Something can be a problem but of little importance. Something can be important but not a problem. Both are necessary for something to be an important problem. (547)

Nonetheless, in their analysis using British data, Jennings and Wlezien find a strong correlation between time series of the most important problem and the most important issue.

Second, even though respondents may not rate an issue as among the *most* important, they may view it as important, as something government should address. When asked to rate the importance of an issue, voters rate many more issues as important than is found with the MIP question (Fournier et al. 2003), which asks about the relative importance of problems and restricts the number of issues that can be named. Finally, using the Most Important Problem codes from the PAP/CAP allows us to measure a characteristic of the roll call and not merely an aspect of the larger political environment, as is the case with measuring approval.[12]

APPROVAL AND INFLUENCE AT THE ROLL CALL LEVEL

The roll call data enable tests of each opinion–influence hypothesis. As before, lopsided votes are excluded. To test the opinion hypotheses requires creating an interaction term between the presidential position and the opinion variables—Presidential Position × Approval, and Presidential Position × Most Important Problem, as above.

Table 7.1 presents results of the interactive effects of approval and position taking on all members, co-partisans, and opposition party members. Results indicate statistically significant effects for all members and opposition members but not for co-partisans. In interpreting the coefficients, all variables are scaled zero to 1, and thus are proportions, but these are easily converted into percentages.[13] When the president takes a position, the proportion of members voting with the president rises, compared to when the president does not take a position.

Due to the difficulty of interpreting interaction effects from regression coefficients, marginal effects are presented graphically on Figure 7.1. The left panel plots the predicted proportion of liberal votes for all members, by presidential position taking at different approval levels. The figure

TABLE 7.1 INTERACTION EFFECTS OF PUBLIC OPINION AND PRESIDENTIAL POSITION TAKING ON MEMBER ROLL CALL VOTING, 1953–2012

VARIABLE	(1) ALL MEMBERS	(2) SAME PARTY	(3) OPPOSITION PARTY
Presidential position	-0.05*	0.21***	-0.30***
	(0.03)	(0.04)	(0.05)
Most Important Problem (MIP)	-0.08***	-0.12*	-0.07
	(0.02)	(0.06)	(0.07)
Interaction: Position × MIP	0.10***	0.19***	0.02
	(0.03)	(0.04)	(0.06)
Monthly approval (lagged)	0.05	0.16	-0.14
	(0.05)	(0.29)	(0.34)
Interaction: Position × Approval	0.10**	0.05	0.14*
	(0.04)	(0.06)	(0.08)
Constant	0.50***	0.41**	0.59***
	(0.03)	(0.18)	(0.21)
R^2	0.01	0.11	0.07
N	16,167	16,167	16,167
Degree of freedom	5	5	5
F	9.300	160.5	61.75
Probability of F	0.000	0.000	0.000
Regression sum of squares	293.4	1,796	2,086
Log likelihood	9,470	-5,178	-6,386

Note: Transition month to a new president is dropped from the analysis in order to use the lagged approval variable. Analysis also clusters on year and only includes conflictual roll calls. Robust standard errors in parentheses. $*p < 0.1$, $**p < 0.05$, $***p < 0.01$.

demonstrates that, as approval rises, the percentage of members who vote liberal when the president takes a liberal position also rises. Similarly, as approval rises, the percentage of members who take a liberal position declines when the president takes a conservative position. Moreover, the gap between liberal voting when the president takes a position, compared to when the president does not take a position, widens as approval rises, but the effect does not appear very potent.

For instance, when approval is 45%, there is essentially no difference in liberal voting between the president not taking a position and the president

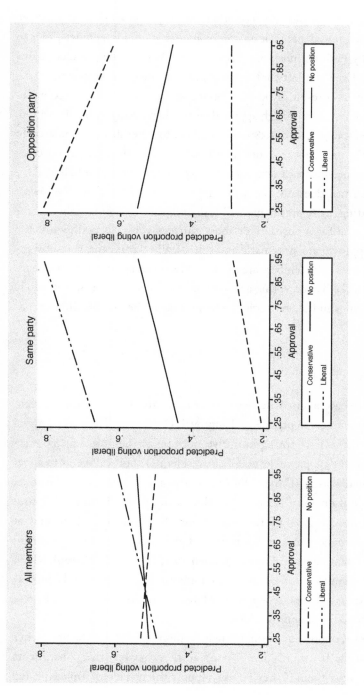

FIGURE 7.1

Interactive effects of presidential position taking and approval on the proportion of members voting liberal on House roll calls, 1953–2012

taking a liberal (or conservative) position. At 55%, approximately the average approval level, presidents pick up approximately 1% more members, four to five votes, by taking a position, a small gain. At 65%, the president gains another 1%. Even at a lofty 85% approval rating, the increase in support for the president as a result of position taking is only about 4%, or sixteen to twenty members. At that high approval level, when taking a liberal position, presidents can expect about 58% of members to vote liberal, compared to 54% when the president does not take a position. When taking a conservative position, presidents can expect about 50% of members to vote liberal.

Low approval does not seem to hurt too much, either. At the lowest approval rating, 25%, presidents will lose only about 3% of members compared to not taking a position, or about thirteen votes. Overall, while the effects of approval are systematic and statistically significant, the substantive effects across all members are modest. Moreover, approval may not have much practical effect on voting across all members because presidents rarely see their ratings in the 80+ region, when it may make notable difference.

APPROVAL AND INFLUENCE AT THE ROLL CALL LEVEL: PARTISAN DIFFERENCES

There is a debate about whether co-partisans are more responsive than opposition members to presidential approval. Dwyer and Treul (2012) argue that co-partisans have strong incentives to support the president, no matter the president's approval level. Since presidential approval seems to affect congressional voting (Canes-Wrone, Brady, and Cogan 2002; Gronke, Koch, and Wilson 2003; Lebo and O'Geen 2011), co-partisans can improve their reelection chances by rallying behind the president, which may at times lead to higher presidential success. Higher success, in turn, appears to lift the president's approval rating (Cohen 2012; Lebo and O'Geen), which leads to stronger electoral performance for both the president and congressional co-partisans. Thus, co-partisans have incentives to support the president, irrespective of approval level.

In contrast, opposition members may be more sensitive to the president's approval rating. If the president is popular, they may fear that constituents will vote against them if they do not support the president. This expected voter reaction may temper how strongly opposition members will work against a popular president's legislative program. But, as approval drops, opposition members can easily oppose the president without fearing much retribution from their constituents. Thus the hypothesis that co-partisans will not be responsive to shifts in the president's approval but that opposition party members will.

Table 7.1 presents results for co-partisans (the middle column) and opposition members (the rightmost column), providing support for the asymmetric effects of approval on co-partisans and the opposition. Where the interaction between approval and position taking does not reach statistical significance for co-partisans, it is positive and significant for opposition members, as hypothesized.

The center panel in figure 7.1 plots the interactive effects of position taking and approval on co-partisans. Although co-partisan voting with the president increases as approval rises, the gap between support when the president takes or not does not take a position hardly varies across approval level. With average approval (55%), about 47% of co-partisans will vote liberal when the president does not take a position. Position taking has about a 24% effect at this approval level, with 71% voting liberal when the president takes a liberal position and 23% when the president takes a conservative position. At 75% approval, the position-taking effect is nearly the same, about 25%. Thus, when the president does not take a position, 52% of co-partisans vote liberal, but 77% of members vote liberal when the president takes a liberal position and 26% vote liberal when the president takes a conservative position. Even when approval falls to its lowest, 25%, the effect of position taking on co-partisans is still around 23% to 25%. At that level, when the president does not take a position, 44% will vote liberal, compared to 67% when the president takes a liberal position and 21% when the president takes a conservative position.

Opposition members are more responsive to rising and falling approval, but the effect is far from overwhelming. The rightmost panel shows that, as approval rises, the gap between opposition voting when the president takes versus does not take a position narrows. This indicates that fewer opposition members vote against the president as approval rises. At average approval levels (55%), about 52% of opposition members vote liberal when the president does not take a position, compared to 73% when the president takes a conservative position and 29% when the president takes liberal position, or about a 21% to 23% position-taking effect. When approval hits 75%, the gap narrows to about 19% to 20%. At that level, about 49% of opposition members will vote liberal when the president does not take a position, compared to 68% when the president takes a conservative position and 29% when the president takes a liberal position. When the president's approval is very low, 25%, 55% of opposition members vote liberal when the president does not take a position, but 81% will vote liberal when the president takes a conservative position and 29% will vote liberal when the president takes liberal position, a position-taking effect of about 26%.

To translate this percentage effect into votes, assume that the opposition holds 217 to 218 seats. In this case, presidents will lose an additional seven to eight opposition votes when their approval is at this bottom level (25%) compared to when it is at the 55% average. The comparative position-taking effect of presidents at 25% to 75% approval is about 6% to 7%, or about fourteen votes when the opposition holds 217 seats—presidents at 75% approval gain fourteen opposition votes compared to when their approval is 25%. As the number of opposition seats grows, presidents will benefit or lose proportionately as their approval rises or falls. But this effect rarely accumulates into enough opposition votes to make a difference on a roll call outcome, except on the closest votes.

THE MOST IMPORTANT PROBLEM AND INFLUENCE AT THE ROLL CALL LEVEL

Approval has statistically significant but substantively small effects on member voting when the president takes a roll call position. This finding is consistent with extant research on the effect of approval on member support for the president (e.g., Edwards 2009a). Although there is considerable research on the approval–support linkage, not much research assesses the effects of issue salience on presidential influence.

Results in table 7.1 suggest a positive and statistically significant inter-active effect of position taking and issue salience on influence. As issue salience rises, so does the percentage of members who vote with the presi-dent when he takes a position. One complication in using issue salience is that most issues, most of the time, do not register with the public. In this sample of roll calls, issue salience is nonexistent (e.g., not one respondent cited the issue area as a most important problem) for about 24% of our roll calls. Thirteen percent of roll calls had salience rates from zero to 1%, and another 8.5% were cited by between 1% and 2% of respondents. Similarly, only about 16% of our roll calls receive salience ratings of 10% or higher. Few issues are important to voters.

Figure 7.2 presents a kernel density plot of issue salience for the roll calls included in the analysis, with normal density overlaid for comparison. The salience distribution is strongly, positively skewed (2.99), which raises concerns about outlier effects from the relatively rare, highly salient issue

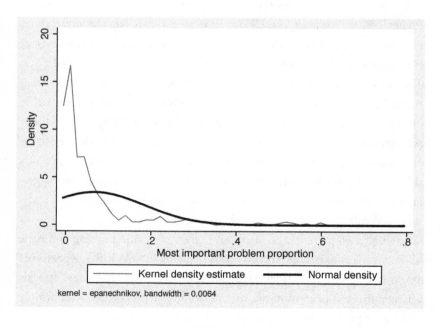

kernel = epanechnikov, bandwidth = 0.0064

FIGURE 7.2

Kernel density plot for issue salience on roll calls used in the analysis

roll calls. Fortunately, this does not appear to be the case. The appendix to this chapter includes two supplementary analyses showing that alternative estimations still report the significant interactive effect of position taking and issue salience.[14]

As for approval, the interaction between position taking and the most important problem is significant across all members. As issue salience grows, so does the presidential position taking effect. The leftmost panel of figure 7.3 presents the marginal effects plot for all members. The figure clearly shows that, as salience grows, the difference in the percentage voting liberal between presidents taking and not taking a position also increases.

There is hardly any position-taking effect when issue salience is zero; whether the president takes a position or not, the percentage of liberal votes hovers around 53%, the mean liberal vote percentage across all votes. Issue salience less than 10% does not lead to much presidential position taking effect either. When issue salience reaches 5%, the position taking effect is only about 1%.[15] At 10% salience, the position-taking effect is only about 1% to 2%.

The position-taking effect becomes more noticeable when issue salience reaches 25%; at that level, presidents can expect to generate about 3% (about thirteen) additional votes. Although it is unclear at what salience level an issue begins to take on important electoral implications, an issue with 25% of voters saying it is the most important problem has probably reached that threshold. When issue salience hits 50%, the issue is probably dominating the political agenda and will likely drive most election campaigns. At that level, presidents can expect 6% to 7% more votes when they take a position than when they do not, or about twenty-five to thirty votes. That many additional supporters for the president's position is substantively consequential and will affect the outcome on many votes, leading to numerous additional roll call victories for the president.

Table 7.1 also presents the interactive effect of position taking and issue salience for co-partisans and opposition members. While co-partisans appear to respond to presidential position taking as salience rises, opposition members appear immune to following the president's lead simply because the public cares about an issue. Among co-partisans, when the issue does not register with voters, there is a 23% difference in member voting, comparing presidential position taking with not taking a position. At this

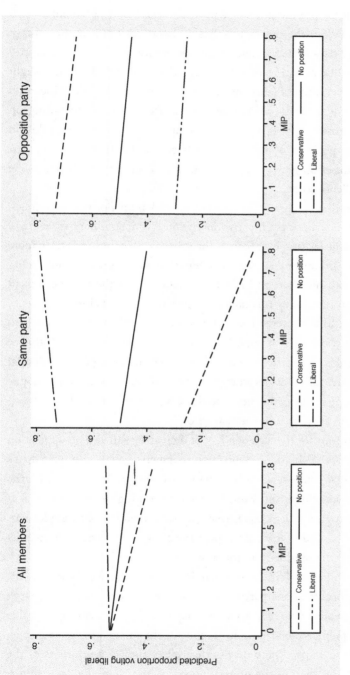

FIGURE 7.3

Interactive effects of presidential position taking and issue salience on member voting, 1953–2012

Note: Based on results from table 7.2; MIP = Most Important Problem.

level, without the president taking a position, about 49.6% of members will vote liberal. When the president takes a liberal position, the percentage voting liberal rises to 72.8%, and when the president takes a conservative position, the liberal voting percentage recedes to 26.4%. There is a slight interactive effect when salience hits 10%; the position-taking effect increases by 2%. At 25%, a highly salient issue, the effect of position taking on co-partisans grows another 3%, to 28%, comparing when presidents do and do not take a position. When the issue becomes dominant, say 50%, the position-taking effect grows to 33%, fully ten points more than when the issue has a zero salience score.

Assuming that the president's party holds a bare majority of 218, presidents can expect about twenty-two more votes for a dominant issue (50%) than for an issue lacking in salience. The salience effect becomes even more substantively important as the president's majority grows. Mobilizing twenty or more members to his side, or about 5% of the membership of Congress, can turn many roll calls from presumed defeats into victories.

In contrast to the interactive effects of position taking and salience on co-partisans, the voting of opposition members hardly budges as salience grows.[16] There is an approximately 22% difference in voting for presidential and nonpresidential roll calls when an issue's salience is at zero. For dominant issues, 50% salience, the difference hovers between 20% and 21%, essentially the same as when salience is at zero.

What accounts for the lack of effect of increasing salience on opposition party legislators? Why don't opposition members move to the president's side on highly salient issues? Why don't we see a polarizing effect, with the opposition distancing itself from the president on highly salient issues? It is over these highly salient issues that the parties tend to compete for voters in elections. Thus, we might expect the opposition party to harden its stance against the president on the most salient issues.

One possibility is that the two parties have different policy agendas. What is important to one party may not be important to the other, especially among voters who identify with the party. As presidents appear able to influence public salience to some degree (Cohen 1997), the Most Important Problem data used here may better reflect the issue priorities of the president's party than of the opposition party. But there does not appear to be much support for this interparty agenda differences hypothesis. Utilizing the new Most Important Problem data set, which is disaggregated to the individual respondent level, Heffington, Park, and Williams (2017) do not find among voters any partisan differences about foreign or economic policy, historically the two issue areas of greatest importance to voters. Thus, it is unclear why salience does not affect opposition members as it does co-partisans. The lack of opposition member movement as issue salience rises, either to the president's side or against the president, is an important question for future research.

CONCLUSION

This chapter has built upon but also extends the research on public opinion as a source of presidential influence in Congress by looking at the effects of issue salience, in addition to presidential approval, which is more commonly studied. Generally, the results suggest that issue salience more strongly affects the roll call behavior of legislators than does approval. Perhaps this is due to the fact that the salience variable measures public attitudes about the roll call itself (or at least the issue area of the roll call), whereas approval is a characteristic of the president across all roll calls at specific point in time. Issue salience, in this sense, is more contextually precise than approval. This suggests that it might be useful to look at policy-specific presidential approval as a presidential influence resource, rather than overall job approval.

Generally, the results reinforce the common understanding of approval's effects, which points to a substantively marginal but still statistically significant impact. Approval's effect on congressional voting, however, is stronger among opposition members than among the president's co-partisans. Co-partisans appear to have incentives to support the president regardless of his approval level. Opposition members, in contrast, have to balance two contrary pulls. One may come from their congressional party, urging them to oppose the president, but when the president is popular, reelection considerations may pull them to support or, less frequently, to oppose the president. Issue salience appears to more strongly affect member voting than does approval. As salience rises, so does the impact of presidential position taking on roll call votes. But this effect seems restricted to co-partisans; opposition members do not change their support for or opposition to the president as salience rises. Moreover, on highly salient votes, presidents can expect to add a substantively significant number of members to their side. This degree of influence on members is enough to convert defeats into victories on a measurable number of roll calls. When presidents take positions on salient issues, they can impact public policy.

The results detailed in this chapter lend support to the theory of institutional presidential influence. By taking a position on a roll call, the president becomes associated with aspects of public opinion, such as approval and salience. This association will work to the president's advantage or disadvantage, depending on the approval level and degree of salience.

APPENDIX

The issue salience variable is highly skewed, with very low values for large numbers of roll calls, but few roll calls are highly salient to voters. Figure 7.2 plots the distribution for the salience variable. A skewed independent variable in itself poses little threat to regression, but it raises the concern that outliers may be driving the statistical results (Choi 2009). As applied here, the statistical relationship between issue salience and presidential influence may be due to the small number of roll calls on highly salient issues.

This appendix employs several methods of dealing with the outlier problem, including deletion of suspect cases and transforming the salience variable. First, I deleted from analysis all cases with salience scores of 0.15 or greater—that is, 15% salient or higher—or about 12.5% of cases. Second, I log transformed the salience score.[17] The log transformation reduces the values of the high salience scores, lessening their outlier impact in the regression. Thus, the log-transformed variable ranges from zero to 4.3, with a mean of 1.3, where the original variable ranges from zero to 0.78, with a mean of 0.06 (or, in percentages, zero to 78%, mean 6%). Although still skewed, the log-transformed variable is much less skewed than the original MIP salience variable, with a skew value of 0.52, compared to 3.15 for the untransformed salience variable. A perfectly symmetrical or normally distributed variable would have a skew value equal to zero.

The results reported here generally remain intact when these outlier correction methods are applied. Whether we delete cases or use the transformed issue salience variable, the interaction with presidential position taking still has a positive and statistically significant effect on all members and co-partisans. However, the interactive effects for opposition members turn negative when the high salience cases are deleted. In the text, the sign for the coefficient was positive but statistically insignificant. But the transformed variable repeats the insignificant results for opposition legislators, as in the text (see table 7.2 for details).

TABLE 7.2 IMPACT OF ALTERNATIVE MEASURES OF ISSUE SALIENCE ON PRESIDENTIAL INFLUENCE IN CONGRESS, 1953–2012

VARIABLE	(1) ALL MEMBERS[a]	(2) ALL MEMBERS	(3) SAME PARTY[a]	(4) SAME PARTY	(5) OPPOSITION PARTY[a]	(6) OPPOSITION PARTY
Presidential position	-0.05*	-0.07**	0.16***	0.17***	-0.24***	-0.29***
	(0.03)	(0.03)	(0.04)	(0.04)	(0.06)	(0.06)
Most Important Problem (MIP)	-0.32***	—	0.06	—	-0.56	—
	(0.08)	—	(0.37)	—	(0.42)	—
Interaction: Position × MIP	0.20*	—	0.84***	—	-0.47*	—
	(0.11)	—	(0.20)	—	(0.24)	—
MIP (logged)	—	-0.01***	—	-0.01	—	-0.01
	—	(0.00)	—	(0.01)	—	(0.01)
Interaction: Position × MIP (logged)	—	0.01***	—	0.03***	—	-0.00
	—	(0.00)	—	(0.00)	—	(0.01)
Monthly approval (lagged)	0.04	0.04	0.17	0.16	-0.17	-0.14
	(0.05)	(0.05)	(0.29)	(0.29)	(0.34)	(0.34)
Interaction: Position × Approval	0.10**	0.11**	0.09	0.06	0.07	0.14
	(0.05)	(0.04)	(0.07)	(0.06)	(0.09)	(0.09)
Constant	0.52***	0.52***	0.40**	0.41**	0.62***	0.61***
	(0.03)	(0.03)	(0.18)	(0.18)	(0.21)	(0.21)
Observations	14,153	16,167	14,153	16,167	14,153	16,167
R^2	0.01	0.02	0.10	0.11	0.07	0.07
N	14,153	16,167	14,153	16,167	14,153	16,167
df_m	5	5	5	5	5	5
F	5.267	15.23	149.1	210.7	70.67	61.76
rss	260.5	291.0	1,560	1,795	1,807	2,084
ll	8,188	9,535	-4,477	-5,171	-5,516	-6,378

Note: [a]Cases restricted to Most Important Problem values less than 0.15, or 15%. Robust standard errors in parentheses. $*p < 0.1$, $**p < 0.05$, $***p < 0.01$.

8

PRESIDENTIAL LOBBYING EFFORT AND INFLUENCE

P REVIOUS CHAPTERS HAVE noted that presidents have more influence than is recognized in past research. Unlike past research, the present study conceptualizes presidential position taking as sometimes a presidential attempt to influence roll call voting. When presidents declare a position on a roll call, it is transformed from a nonpresidential to a presidential vote. This transformation, in turn, affects members' roll call decisions. The president does not factor very much in members' votes on nonpresidential roll calls but can be an important consideration for members on presidential roll calls.

This conceptualization leads to a study design that differs from past research on presidential–congressional relations. Where past research generally looks only at member voting on presidential roll calls, the conceptualization here requires a comparison of member voting on presidential roll calls with voting on nonpresidential roll calls. It is the difference between these two sets of roll calls that enables us to get a handle on how much influence presidents have on members. One difficulty in comparing presidential with nonpresidential roll calls is that we cannot observe the president's position on nonpresidential roll calls; the president is silent about his policy preferences on those roll calls. Instead, we can compare the liberal or conservative voting of members on presidential and nonpresidential roll calls. Any difference in such voting tendencies might be due to the president taking a position and, through that position taking, influencing member voting. The analysis in chapter 4 found that we can attribute to the president some of the difference in member voting on the two types of roll calls and that presidents appear to have more influence on roll calls than existing studies suggest.

This conceptualization of position taking as an influence attempt, that is, as a generic form of presidential lobbying, has another implication. Rather than viewing presidential influence as a personal characteristic of presidents, a function of their skill, personality, background, and the like, as is common in the existing literature (e.g., Wayne 2009), position taking activates aspects of the larger political environment, such as the partisan, policy, and approval contexts, to the *advantage or disadvantage* of the president. The structure of the political environment and context has much to do with the amount of influence presidents have.

But presidential influence is not merely a matter of dumb luck, as research on the president portrays it. Obviously, the president is lucky if the larger political environment is structured to his advantage, such as when his party controls Congress. But presidents also decide whether to engage the policy making process, whether to take a position on a roll call. Presidents are likely to be highly strategic in deciding whether to take a position.

Beyond the decision to take a position, presidents also must decide on the specific strategy and tactics for influencing members. There are at least two strategic decisions presidents may make: the *mode* of lobbying Congress and the *level of effort* to be expended. The lobbying mode refers to the particular behaviors that presidents use, such as, for example, going public (Cameron and Park 2011; Canes-Wrone 2006; Kernell 1986, 2006); threatening vetoes (Cameron 2000; Hassell and Kernell 2016); working with leaders to set the legislative agenda (Beckmann 2008, 2010); bargaining; and the like.

This chapter focuses on lobbying effort. Does the amount of effort presidents exert affect their influence in Congress? There is little direct research on the implications of lobbying effort for presidential influence, but we can extract from the larger literature on presidential–congressional relations several different models of the presumed effect of effort on influence. The next sections review three models that make contradictory predictions about the effectiveness of increasing effort. One model argues that increased effort will not lead to greater influence because presidents cannot easily influence Congress (Edwards 1990, 2006). A second model suggests that increased effort will lead to higher levels of influence, although probably not in a one-to-one ratio (Beckmann 2010; Canes-Wrone 2006). Finally, a third model suggests that increased effort will be associated with lower levels of influence because greater effort is a function of the amount of opposition and resistance to the president's side. Presidents, according to this third model, work harder because they must (Cameron and Park 2011). Obviously, all three of these perspectives cannot be right.

After reviewing these models, I offer a fourth model, which integrates the insights of the positive effects and the negative effects models. This fourth model maintains that increased effort leads to greater influence up to a point, after which additional effort has negative returns. This is based on the assumption that presidents will only work as hard as is needed to win. Each added unit of effort requires expending an additional unit of presidential resources, such as time, favors, and the like. But presidential resources, to some degree, are finite and incur opportunity costs. Presidents will only expend the effort necessary to obtain their goals—which, here, is winning on the roll call. Expending additional effort when they have already met (or think they have met) that goal is wasteful, especially when they can divert that resource unit to another activity or even to another roll call.

This idea leads to the hypothesis that when presidential effort is at low to medium levels, those opposed to the president are in a relatively weak position. Presidents, under this circumstance, possess a high likelihood of influencing member voting and thus of winning on the roll call. However, as presidents work harder, they do so because they confront a potent opposition. Presidents have to work harder to counter a strong opposition but they will not always be successful. Thus, higher levels of effort indicate presidential weakness. This fourth model suggests a curvilinear relationship between presidential effort and influence.

COMPETING MODELS OF THE EFFECTIVENESS OF LOBBYING EFFORT

The literature on presidential relations with Congress offers three perspectives on the effectiveness of lobbying effort. The first model maintains that presidential lobbying is ineffective, that presidents gain nothing from increasing their lobbying effort. Simply put, this perspective contends that presidents cannot influence Congress, the *no effects model*. The second model argues, in contrast, that there is a positive relationship between effort and influence—the more presidents expend on lobbying, the greater their payoff or influence. This is the *lobbying investment model*. A third model suggests that increased lobbying effort will be associated with less influence, because lobbying effort is a function of the degree and strength of the opposition that presidents face (Cameron and Park 2011), or the *counterlobbying model*.

THE NO EFFECTS MODEL

The no effects model argues not only that increased presidential lobbying effort will not lead to greater presidential influence in Congress but also that presidents do not have much influence in any event. To a degree, the results presented in the previous chapters undercut the idea that presidents have no influence in Congress. Still, the present study and the no effects perspective offer different conceptions of presidential influence. Where influence is conceptualized in much of the presidency research as a personal attribute of the president, such as, for instance, whether the president is skillful (Edwards 1980, 116–204; Fleisher, Bond, and Wood 2008; Wayne 2009), presidential influence is here considered to be a combination of structural, environmental, and contextual factors, such as party control, along with the strategic decisions that presidents make in using those factors.

In a series of important studies, George Edwards (1990, 2006) argues that presidents are not very influential, that at best they can affect Congress around the margins. To Edwards and most scholars of presidential–congressional relations, political–structural factors such as party control of Congress are givens—constants within a Congress—that the president

PRESIDENTIAL LOBBYING EFFORT

cannot affect. They have to work within the political environment given to them, which presidents can barely dent. As Edwards (1980, 204) states, "There is little the president can do about his degree of influence in Congress. He cannot affect the party affiliation of members of Congress to a large extent."

In his early book-length study *Presidential Influence in Congress*, Edwards (1980) comprehensively reviews the multitude of activities that presidents can undertake to try to influence members, from midterm campaigning to working with leaders, making personal appeals to members, bargaining, arm-twisting, providing services, going public, and working with interest groups, among other activities (see also Manley 1978). The upshot of his early analysis is that although these activities may garner a vote here or there, he fails to detect any systematic evidence that these activities can move large numbers of members to vote with the president if they otherwise would have voted against the president. These presidential actions cannot overcome the hand already dealt to the president, primarily the partisan composition of Congress. Summarizing the research up to that time, Edwards (1980, 202) asserts that presidential skills "do not appear to be a predominant factor in determining presidential support in Congress on most roll calls and therefore, despite commonly held assumptions, they are not a prominent source of influence. Thus, what seems to be the most manipulatable source of presidential influence is probably the least effective."

Thus, rather than viewing presidents as directors of change who influence members through their persuasive efforts, Edwards views them as facilitators who "understand the opportunities for change in their environments and fashion strategies and tactics to exploit them." (Edwards 2009, 12). Presidents, however, cannot do much about the "contours of the political landscape."

The top left panel in figure 8.1, labeled No Effect, schematically diagrams the relationship between lobbying effort and amount of influence, as the no effects model predicts. The horizontal axis on the figure indicates the amount of effort, and the vertical axis indicates the amount of influence. As effort increases, influence does not. Secondarily, this model predicts low to nonexistent levels of influence, as shown by the point at which the slope intersects the influence axis.

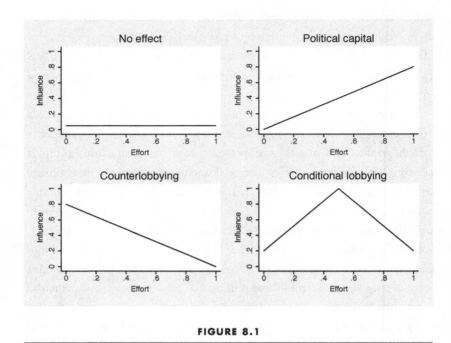

FIGURE 8.1

Hypothetical relationships between presidential lobbying effort and influence in Congress

THE LOBBYING INVESTMENT/POLITICAL CAPITAL MODEL

The lobbying investment, or political capital, model suggests that presidential influence increases as presidents invest more resources and effort into lobbying. The top right panel in figure 8.1, labeled Political Capital, diagrams the prediction of the lobbying investment hypothesis. As presidential lobbying effort increases, influence rises.[1]

Several sets of studies present findings consistent with this view. The first looks at direct lobbying of members of Congress by the president, such as presidential contacting of targeted members and offering favors. A second set looks at indirect lobbying, specifically going public, with the president trying to rally and/or activate public opinion on an issue. A third set focuses on veto threats and bargaining, which one can view from a lobbying perspective. These studies suggest that presidents can gain policy concessions from Congress by threatening vetoes (Hassell and Kernell 2016) or by engaging in a veto bargaining game (Cameron 2000).

Beckmann (2010) develops a theory of direct presidential lobbying as an investment and finds support for it. He assumes that members have multiple goals when deciding how to vote and that their preferences are not fixed but are somewhat malleable. This malleability opens the possibility that presidents, and others, can move members to vote with them. Beckmann identifies two presidential lobbying strategies, vote-centered (endgame) and agenda-centered (earlygame) strategies. Endgame lobbying aims to shift member preferences on roll call votes, while earlygame lobbying aims to limit the alternatives on which members can vote. Although the primary goal of Beckmann's study is to compare the relative efficacy of these two lobbying strategies, Beckmann assumes, for both lobbying approaches, that presidents benefit from greater lobbying effort.

In detailing the effects of endgame (vote-centered) lobbying, Beckmann states, "The president's influence . . . depends on (1) the political capital he spends, and (2) members' responsiveness to that expenditure." Further, he states, "Presidents' vote-centered lobbying activities always improve their legislative prospects. . . . Obviously, the more political capital the president spends, the more influence he exerts." Yet there may be marginally diminishing returns to presidents spending more capital, because "the president must induce more and more pivotal members to move" (49–50). In other words, voter-centered lobbying is more efficient when the president needs to move only a few as opposed to a lot of members. The fewer members the president needs to target, the more concentrated are the president's lobbying efforts and the greater is the amount of presidential resources spent on each targeted member. As the number of members needed to win increases, the president has to spread his lobbying efforts across them, in effect diluting the amount of effort expended (or capital spent) on each member. Returning to figure 8.1, if there are marginal diminishing returns on effort, then, at some point (to be determined empirically), the trend line will flatten.

Agenda setting, or earlygame lobbying, is working with the congressional leadership to restrict the alternatives on which members can vote. With an agenda-centered approach, presidents want to bring proposals to the floor that have a strong chance of acceptance, while keeping alternatives that would beat the president's proposal from reaching the floor. In Beckmann's theory, earlygame lobbying is more efficient than vote-centered lobbying. Presidential effort also has positive implications for agenda-centered lobbying. As presidents work harder with the leadership to shape the roll call agenda, presidents are more likely to see favorable alternatives reaching the floor and unfavorable ones blocked, which leads to greater presidential success on floor votes.

In the empirical tests, Beckmann (chapters 4 and 5) finds strong support for the effectiveness of agenda-centered lobbying, although there does not seem to be much support for endgame efforts. Most important for our purposes here, greater presidential involvement (an indication of presidential effort), primarily in the agenda-setting stages of the legislative process, leads to greater success rates.[2]

Two other studies look at specific types of direct presidential lobbying or targeting of members. Covington (1988) uses data from the Kennedy and Johnson administrations with regard to invitations to members to attend social functions, often at the White House, with the president in attendance. These presidents targeted with invitations specific members, mostly co-partisans who were inconsistent supporters of the president. During the Kennedy–Johnson years, these were mostly southern Democrats. If we view the number of invitations to a member as an indicator of presidential lobbying effort, Covington intriguingly finds that more invitations produce higher levels of support among the targeted group of southern Democrats (258–259).

Finally, Eric Uslaner looks at the effects of President Bill Clinton's lobbying of members in support of the North American Free Trade Agreement (NAFTA) in 1993. To measure presidential lobbying, Uslaner uses data on whether the administration contacted a member.[3] The administration did not equally target all legislators, mostly contacting those who "played coy," who were not firmly committed either for or against the trade pact. In lobbying members, "Clinton reputedly promised support on all manner of other bills in return for the legislator's promise on the trade pact" (Uslaner 1998, 353, 356–357). And the president's lobbying efforts conditionally paid off. Uslaner's results indicate that lobbying increased the probability of a vote for the trade pact among co-partisans but had counterproductive effects on the opposition—Republicans whom the administration lobbied were more inclined to vote against the bill (359–360).[4] But this perverse negative sign seems to be due to the president contacting Republicans already committed to supporting the bill, perhaps a presidential attempt to counterlobby the bill's opponents.

Another set of studies looks at indirect presidential lobbying efforts—primarily, going public. By "indirect lobbying" I mean that presidents do not target members as individuals but rather mobilize external support, such as voters, to pressure members to support the president. Going public is one example of indirect lobbying.

The going public idea, first introduced by Kernell (1986), suggests that presidents have some ability to influence public opinion. Presidents may try to influence opinion about themselves (their approval ratings), influence preferences on the issue, and/or influence the salience of an issue. Members will respond to changes in the opinion climate on an issue and/or on the president for electoral (and perhaps other) reasons. There is extensive literature on presidential attempts to influence the public's issue preferences, issue salience, and/or attitudes toward the president. It appears that presidents are better able to increase issue salience than either their approval ratings or the public's issue preferences.

Taking off from this point, and arguing that the public's policy preferences are fixed and thus unresponsive to presidential attempts to alter them, Canes-Wrone (2006) develops a model in which presidents can raise the salience of an issue by going public, and she argues that presidents only go public on issues when the president's and the public's preferences are close and when the public's preferences are closer than the status quo to the president's preference. In tests, she finds that presidents are more likely to win on budgetary issues that presidents mention in major television addresses than on unmentioned issues. Although Canes-Wrone does not measure how much the president stresses the budgetary item, I have found that public perception of the salience of an issue rises as presidents emphasize the issue (Cohen 1997). If mentioning an issue more frequently is a sign of presidential effort, then coupling these two studies suggests that, the more the president goes public on an issue, the more presidential success on the issue in Congress should rise. These studies offer some support for the idea that lobbying effort has a positive effect on presidential influence in Congress.[5]

Veto bargaining and threats also can be viewed as a form of presidential lobbying. Presidents target the entire Congress when issuing a veto threat or entering into a veto bargaining game; the unit of interest in studies that examine this is the bill or, in the case of Hassell and Kernell's (2016) veto threat study, riders to appropriations bills. These studies tend to measure the bargaining or threat game discretely—the president either threatens a veto or does not—and thus the veto threat or bargaining activity is not measured in terms of effort. But we can suggest that veto bargaining and threats, by their very nature, are high-effort activities. Presidents seem to derive policy benefits from engaging in veto bargaining games (Cameron 2000) and from threatening vetoes, at least on appropriations riders (Hassell and Kernell 2016).

THE COUNTERLOBBYING MODEL

A third model, the counterlobbying model, predicts a negative association between lobbying effort and influence. This hypothesis grows out of and generalizes Cameron and Park's (2011) opinion contest model. In opinion contest theory, the president responds to the climate of opinion on an issue and/or anticipates what that climate will be if he goes public. Cameron and Park outline two presidential scenarios linking going public with the opinion climate. In the first, the opposition goes public first and the president must decide whether to go public in response. Remaining silent may lead to almost certain defeat, whereas responding "may be trying merely to maintain the opinion status quo or salvage his position" (446). Alternatively, presidents may decide to move first. Doing so may stimulate an opposition response. An implication of opinion contest theory is that "greater presidential effort is likely to correlate with worse, not better, performance in Congress" (447). Still, Cameron and Park argue that opinion contest theory also predicts that presidents "*would have done even worse* had they not gone public in a strategic fashion" (emphasis mine). Going public at least allows the president the possibility to mute or counter the effects of a strong opposition.

Cameron and Park provide empirical support for opinion contest theory, using the example of presidential nominations to the Supreme Court. They find that presidents are more likely to go public in support of their nominees in a less favorable political environment, using the number of interest groups that have mobilized publicly against the nominee as an indicator of opposition (461). Plus, they report that, as the number of presidential statements in support of a nominee increases (a measure of lobbying effort), the number of votes the nominee receives in the Senate falls (466).[6] Similarly, Holmes (2007) finds that going public is negatively associated with support for appeals court nominees, presumably because the nominees are in trouble.

We can generalize the opinion climate in Cameron and Park, and thus contested opinion theory, to the entire political environment surrounding any presidential position, which I will term the "opposition environment." The opposition environment encompasses all important political elements that may affect the outcome of bills, including the opinion climate (as in Cameron and Park), the alignment of supporters and opponents within Congress, the mobilization of interest groups on both sides, and the stances and reporting in the news media, among other factors. In its entirety, the opposition environment confronting a president may range from the most advantaged situation for the president, that is, where there are no opponents, to weak opponents, opponents that match the president, or strong opponents, which most seriously disadvantages the president.

As detailed in Cameron and Park, presidential lobbying effort is primarily a response to the opposition environment—presidents will lobby Congress harder when facing strong opponents. This leads to the hypothesis that, everything being equal, the stronger the opposition environment, the more poorly the president's side will do on roll calls. Presidents lobby hard, not to win but to avoid a lopsided defeat, which could (irreparably) harm the president's reputation, affecting other presidential policy goals. The bottom left panel on figure 8.1, "Counterlobbying," diagrams the prediction of this model, that as presidential lobbying effort increases, presidential influence decreases.

AN INTEGRATIVE, CONDITIONAL THEORY OF PRESIDENTIAL LOBBYING EFFORT

This section offers a model that integrates elements of the lobbying investment and opinion climate notions. The lobbying investment theory does not take into account counterlobbying or the relative strength of the president's opponents. That perspective may best be applied to situations where presidential opponents are nonexistent or weak. In contrast, the counterlobbying idea is most appropriate when presidents face a strong opposition.

Additionally, neither perspective accounts for the *joint effects* on congressional voting of the full range of the opposition environment *and* presidential lobbying. Doing so leads to a new hypothesis, that the effect of presidential lobbying effort is curvilinear—increased effort has a positive effect on congressional voting, up to a certain point. After that point is reached, however, increased presidential effort is associated with negative effects on congressional voting. The conditional effects model of lobbying effort combines elements from both investment theory and counterlobbying.

The conditional effects theory of presidential lobbying effort begins with several assumptions. First, presidents confront an opportunity cost problem in deciding how much lobbying effort to exert on a roll call. Expending additional lobbying effort necessitates spending less time, resources, and effort on other activities that the president may find beneficial and/or valuable. For example, lobbying Congress may require the president to stay in the nation's capital and meet with legislators instead of traveling around the nation to burnish his reputation and/or to aid his (and others') reelection campaigns, or visiting other nations in pursuit of some foreign policy ends. Simply put, presidents cannot do two things at the same time, although the institutional resources of the modern White House, such as staffing support, enable presidents to accomplish more than was possible for earlier presidents.

In deciding how much effort to allocate to legislative lobbying, the president must compare the net benefits to be received from lobbying compared to the benefits from another activity, with the net benefits defined as the benefit received minus the costs associated with an activity. When the net benefits of lobbying outweigh those of another activity, the president will lobby. The same logic applies to increases in lobbying effort—each increment of additional effort is weighed against other activities that the president may perform. Finally, presidents will expend only the minimum amount of lobbying effort necessary to win on the roll call.

But at times presidents expend great lobbying efforts. Why? Presidents increase their lobbying effort when winning on the roll call is important *and* they have doubts about the outcome. Since the legislative process is complex, presidents often may be uncertain about the eventual outcome of a roll call (Arnold 1992; Beckmann 2010). Thus, presidents may increase their lobbying effort to increase the odds that they will win.

Attributes of the legislative environment provide the president with clues about the eventual outcome, which they use in deciding how much effort to exert. The strength of the opposition to the president provides information on the likelihood that the president's side will prevail. The weaker the opposition, the higher the likelihood that the president's side will win.

Owing to uncertainty about legislative voting, even in the face of a weak opposition, presidents may overinvest in lobbying, especially on non-lopsided roll calls. Small increases in lobbying effort, which do not chew up too many of the president's lobbying resources, may have large impacts on the final vote when confronting a weak opposition, thus ensuring a victory. As the opposition becomes stronger, presidents need to increase their lobbying efforts. When the opposition is strong but presidents do not care much about the issue, they are unlikely to lobby very hard.

To defeat a strong opposition, presidents have to increase their lobbying effort beyond what the opposition can do. A strong opposition may be able to match increases in presidential lobbying efforts, leading to a lobbying-effort escalation spiral akin to an arms race. At some point, the administration may begin to exhaust the resources that it can deploy against a strong and determined opposition. Finally, if the ratio of presidential to opposition lobbying effort matters for congressional voting, presidential overinvestment against a weak opposition often means that the ratio is more strongly tilted in the president's direction than is the case against a strong opposition.[7] Thus, we are likely to see larger improvements in vote support for the president at lower levels of opposition than at higher levels—a curvilinear pattern, as displayed in the bottom right panel of figure 8.1 labeled Conditional Lobbying.

ISSUES IN MEASURING PRESIDENTIAL LOBBYING EFFORT

Ideally, testing of the conditional lobbying idea would employ data on presidential and opposition lobbying efforts across roll calls. Yet collecting such data is notoriously difficult, if not impossible. Consequently, there are few studies of the effectiveness of presidential lobbying efforts, much less of the relative effects of presidential versus opposition lobbying. One impediment to collecting data on lobbying, presidential or otherwise, is that much lobbying goes undocumented. Even when records of contact between presidents and members of Congress exist, the content of those meetings remains opaque.

For instance, Beckmann (2016) imaginatively uses the presidential Daily Diaries from 1961 to 2000 to measure the frequency of presidential contact with members of Congress. The Daily Diaries provide a minute-by-minute cataloging of the president's activities and whom he met with, yet they do not record what the president or the other party said. As Beckmann observes with regard to collecting data on presidential decision making, data collection hurdles arise because so many of the relevant processes occur behind the scenes, without public comment. And while presidential libraries include a treasure trove of insider materials, minutes, memos, and the like, few collections offer a systematic sample, much less a comprehensive population. Thus, when the president has met in person or talked on the telephone with a member, we do not know exactly what the president and the member said to each other, although, using the Daily Diaries, one can distinguish policy-related from purely social contacts.[8]

Further complicating the measurement of lobbying effort is that presidents have a multitude of ways or modes of lobbying Congress, from going public to offering favors, aiding member reelection campaigns, threatening vetoes, or inviting members to social events at the White House. On any bill, presidents can draw from the large menu of lobbying modes, build a strategy that may employ one or more of these modes, and use them with varying effort. The combination of lobbying modes across issues and bills is likely to vary. Further complicating matters is the difficulty of comparing lobbying effort across modes—how, for instance, do we equate time spent speaking in public about an issue with invitations to the White House?

Research on presidential lobbying generally looks at only one mode at a time. What if a president employs two modes and we only measure one and find significant effects? For instance, assume that the president used both social invitations and going public to lobby Congress, but we only measure going public and find a significant effect from going public. We would conclude that going public affects congressional voting. But it may be that the social invitation was the activity that led members to vote with the president. In effect, we have an omitted variable problem, which leads to faulty causal inference, ascribing causal effects to the measured variable (going public) when the unmeasured variable (social invitation) was the true causal factor. Estimating the effect of presidential lobbying becomes even more complex to deal with if there are joint or interactive effects when the president employs more than one mode. Using the above example, perhaps lobbying is most effective when the president goes public *and* invites members to the White House but neither has much impact when used alone.

MEASURING PRESIDENTIAL LOBBYING EFFORT FROM PRESIDENTIAL PRIORITIES

To estimate the effect of presidential lobbying and lobbying effort, we need a more comprehensive approach than is found in the existing research. We are unlikely to be able to do that by measuring each lobbying mode separately, since so much lobbying activity is not documented. The tack taken here is that we can identify the president's legislative and policy priorities and use those priorities as a signal of the president's lobbying intentions. First, assume that presidents will lobby harder for the passage of high priorities than for low priorities. Second, assume that presidents are truth-ful when they publicly identify their legislative priorities.

I use the Policy Agendas Project/Comparative Agendas Project coding of the State of the Union Address (SUA) to identify the president's policy priorities. Each quasi statement in the SUA was coded according to the same policy scheme that was used previously to code roll calls. For each SUA, the priority accorded to each issue area is defined as the percentage of quasi sentences mentioning the major issue area among all quasi sentences that mention an issue area.[9]

The SUA is traditionally viewed as a statement of the president's policy priorities for the upcoming year and a report on accomplishments from the past year. There is an elaborate process for building the SUA, which includes surveying each department and agency for recommendations about which of their priorities are to be mentioned in the SUA. The amount of attention given to a particular issue reflects the importance of that issue to the presi-dent and to the administration (Cohen 1997; Light 1999; Rudalevige 2002). Although there is some debate about whether the SUA sincerely reflects the president's policy preferences (Cohen 2012, 58–61; Steger 2005), the SUA does sincerely reflect the priorities the president will work on during the coming year (Cummins 2010; Fett 1992; Rutledge 2009).

The priority given to an issue area in the SUA also signals how hard the president will work to realize his policy goals, including the effort the administration will exert in lobbying Congress. If this assumption is valid, we should expect that presidents will be more likely to take roll call positions on issues of high rather than low priority.[10] We can test whether presidential policy emphasis affects presidential position taking. If the SUA sincerely signals presidential priorities and, by implication, how hard a president will work to realize his policy priorities, there should be a posi-tive relationship between policy emphasis and presidential position taking, even though the president does not have complete control over which issues reach the floor.

To test this hypothesis, the presidential position taking variable is recoded such that 1 equals "president takes a position" and zero equals "pres-ident does not take a position." Then, using a logit estimation, this variable is regressed on policy emphasis in the SUA on all conflictual votes from

1953 to 2012. The estimation also includes several control variables that might predict whether presidents take a position, including being a Democrat, whether the public is in a liberal mood, the president's approval level, whether the president's party controls the House, and the level of party polarization in the House.

As shown in table 8.2 in the appendix to this chapter, all of the control variables except for party control of the House are statistically significant predictors of presidential position taking. Most important, so is presidential policy emphasis. Figure 8.2 plots the predicted probability that the president will take a position, by policy emphasis. As policy emphasis increases, so does the probability that the president will take a roll call position.

For example, when the president does not mention a policy area, the probability of position taking is 0.19, that is, presidents take positions on about 19% of roll calls. When the policy area receives 10% of the space in

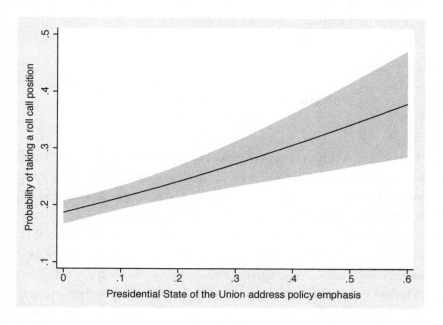

FIGURE 8.2

Impact of presidential policy emphasis in the State of the Union Address on presidential roll call position taking, conflictual roll calls, 1953–2012

the SUA, slightly higher than the average attention given to a policy area (7%), the probability of the president taking a position rises to 21%. At 20% attention, the probability of position taking rises to 24%, about 5% more than when the president does not take a position. Presidents rarely give an issue area 30% or more of the space in the SUA, only 3% of the time. Issue areas that attain that much attention are probably the highest presidential priorities, although there is no definitive dividing line to distinguish the highest priorities from other issue areas. At 30% attention, the probability that a president will take a roll call position is 0.27. For the very few issue areas receiving 40% attention, the probability of position taking tops 30%. Given the inability of the president to determine which issues will receive roll calls, as well as events after the SUA that may alter the priorities of both Congress and the president, these figures are substantively impressive.

Issue attention predicts whether a president will take a position, but does issue attention also indicate the effort presidents exert in lobbying Congress? And does such lobbying effort affect presidential influence on House roll calls? The next section addresses these questions.

PRESIDENTIAL LOBBYING EFFORT AND INFLUENCE

My argument is that the emphasis presidents give to an issue in the SUA signals to Congress how hard presidents are likely to work, to lobby, to get their preferred policy. We cannot test this assumption directly, lacking data on presidential lobbying effort. But, as has been shown, presidents are more likely to take positions on issue areas emphasized in their SUAs. Policy attention in the president's SUA is more than merely symbolic politics; it has implications for presidential engagement with the legislative policy-making process.

But how do other participants in legislative policy making react to such presidential policy attention? If policy emphasis signals the effort presidents will expend on an issue, opponents may decide to countermobilize. Presidential policy emphasis also may deter opponents from mobilizing against the president.

We lack the data to test whether policy emphasis leads to countermobilization or deterrence among opponents of the president's policy aims.[11] Still, we can test whether policy emphasis, an indirect measure of lobbying effort, affects influence on roll calls. That presidential policy emphasis only indirectly measures lobbying effort may work to our advantage in testing this chapter's theory, by making it difficult to find a relationship between emphasis and influence. If the policy emphasis measure affects influence as hypothesized, therefore, it should bolster confidence in the theory developed here.

Table 8.1 presents the results of interacting presidential position taking with policy emphasis. Models 1 and 2 compare the linear and curvilinear hypotheses. For the linear hypothesis, position taking is simply interacted with policy emphasis. The no effects model predicts that the interaction will not be statistically significant, the political capital model predicts a positive and significant coefficient, and the counterlobbying model predicts a negative sign. Results from model 1 suggest support for the political capital model. The coefficient for the interaction term is positive and statistically significant—the more the president emphasizes an issue area, the greater is his influence over member voting. Assuming that policy emphasis measures presidential policy effort to some extent, this result provides support for the political capital model of lobbying effort.

Model 2 tests the curvilinear idea by adding the square of policy emphasis, and its interaction with presidential position taking, into the estimation. Support for the conditional model will be found if the squared interaction term is negative and statistically significant and the linear interaction of position taking and policy emphasis remains positive and significant.

This is what the results of model 2 show. The coefficient for the position taking–policy emphasis interaction is $b = 0.22$, $p < 0.01$, while for the squared interaction it is $b = -0.37$, $p < 0.05$. Figure 8.3 presents the marginal effects of presidential position taking at different policy emphasis levels.[12] When presidents do not mention a policy area, there is no difference in liberal voting, whether the president takes a position or not. Presidents realize some influence, about 3% to 3.4%, or thirteen to fifteen additional votes, at emphasis levels of 20% to 40%, which we might consider to be a medium amount of presidential lobbying effort. This influence effect is large enough for the

TABLE 8.1 PRESIDENTIAL LOBBYING EFFORT AND INFLUENCE ON CONFLICTUAL ROLL CALLS, HOUSE, 1953–2012

VARIABLE	(1) ALL MEMBERS	(2) ALL MEMBERS	(3) SAME PARTY	(4) SAME PARTY	(5) OPPOSITION PARTY	(6) OPPOSITION PARTY
Presidential position	0.01	0.00	0.24***	0.24***	-0.22***	-0.23***
	(0.01)	(0.01)	(0.01)	(0.01)	(0.02)	(0.02)
Policy emphasis	-0.05	-0.22**	-0.12	0.20	-0.03	-0.56
	(0.03)	(0.09)	(0.11)	(0.37)	(0.13)	(0.42)
Interaction: Position × Emphasis	0.10***	0.22**	0.14***	0.18	0.02	0.34*
	(0.04)	(0.09)	(0.05)	(0.15)	(0.06)	(0.18)
Emphasis-squared	—	0.48**	—	-0.90	—	1.51
		(0.19)		(0.91)		(1.03)
Interaction: Position × Emphasis-squared	—	-0.37**	—	-0.02	—	-0.96**
		(0.18)		(0.32)		(0.41)
Constant	0.53***	0.53***	0.50***	0.49***	0.52***	0.53***
	(0.01)	(0.01)	(0.05)	(0.05)	(0.06)	(0.06)
Observations	15,787	15,787	15,787	15,787	15,787	15,787
R^2	0.00397	0.00745	0.101	0.103	0.0680	0.0723
Regression mean squared error	0.135	0.135	0.337	0.337	0.362	0.362
Regression sum of squares	287.3	286.3	1,797	1,793	2,072	2,063
Log likelihood	9,223	9,251	-5,246	-5,231	-6,372	-6,335

Note: Robust standard errors in parentheses. $^*p < 0.1$, $^{**}p < 0.05$, $^{***}p < 0.01$.

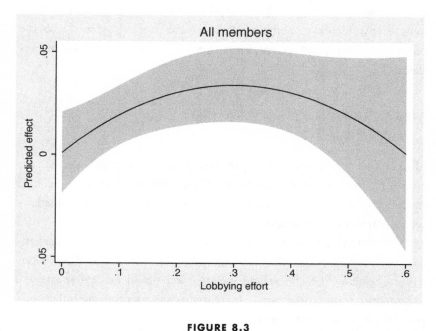

FIGURE 8.3

Impact of presidential lobbying effort on member voting, conflictual
roll calls, 1953–2012

Note: Based on results from table 8.1, model 2.

president to win on almost all close votes. Modest policy emphasis, that is, lobbying effort, can have substantively consequential policy implications.

But once presidents begin to lobby Congress heavily, at 40% or more, their influence flags. At 50% policy emphasis, presidential influence declines by 2% compared to the 40% policy emphasis. Influence recedes further as emphasis climbs higher. When emphasis reaches its peak of 60%, presidents have essentially no influence on member voting, much like the effect when presidents take a position but do not mention the issue in their SUA. This curvilinear pattern is exactly what the conditional effects theory predicts.

In interpreting these results, it is important to keep in mind that policy emphasis is an indirect and crude measure of presidential lobbying effort. Better data on presidential lobbying effort, such as actual indicators, might reveal even stronger effects. Still, presidential lobbying is unlikely to result in massive influence on member voting. But the crude measure of lobbying effort used here provides empirical support for the conditional effects theory.[13]

PARTISAN RESPONSES TO PRESIDENTIAL LOBBYING EFFORT

How do the members of the two parties respond to the president's lobbying effort? Do they respond similarly or display different patterns? Table 1, models 3 through 6, present results of the linear and curvilinear estimations for co-partisan and opposition party members.

When lobbying effort across all members displays a curvilinear pattern, co-partisans respond positively to increasing presidential issue attention, in a linear fashion. At each level of issue attention, presidents realize increasing support from co-partisans. Increased issue attention mobilizes co-partisans behind the president.

Co-partisans always support the president at high levels (as shown in the left panel on figure 8.4). When presidents do not mention an issue area, there is about a 24% vote shift to the president's side when the president takes a position compared to the president not taking one. Assuming the bare minimum majority control, 218 seats, this amounts to about fifty-two votes. At the middle range of issue attention, 30%, presidents can expect a 28% difference in co-partisan support between position taking and not taking a position. With a 218-seat majority, this will produce about nine additional votes over that produced when the president did not mention the policy area. When issue attention reaches its maximum, 60%, the co-partisan rally to the president reaches 32% to 33%, which is 8% to 9% more than when the president did not mention the issue. Again, assuming the bare minimum majority control, 218 seats, the president can expect about twenty more votes from co-partisans than if he did not mention the policy area. Twenty additional votes may be enough to carry the day for the president's side on a large number of roll calls, assuming a bare co-partisan majority. These are substantively strong effects of presidential issue attention, and presumably lobbying effort, on co-partisans.

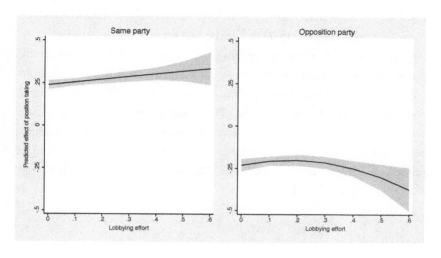

FIGURE 8.4

Impact of presidential lobbying effort by member party, conflictual roll calls, 1953–2012

Note: Based on results from table 8.1, models 4 and 6.

Opposition party members initially respond positively to presidential lobbying efforts (see the right panel on figure 8.4). When the president does not mention a policy area, the president can expect a 23% difference in opposition member voting, to the president's *disadvantage*, when taking versus not taking a position, or a deficit of approximately fifty votes when the opposition holds 217 seats. This deficit recedes slightly as presidents modestly emphasize an issue. At 20% policy emphasis, the gap due to position taking drops to 20%, or forty-three votes among 217 seats. The small uptick in support from the opposition at modest emphasis levels may reflect the weakness of those opposed to the president. For instance, opposition party members and/or their constituents may be split on the issue, or there may be little interest group mobilization in opposition to the president's position. When faced with a weak opposition, presidents may be able to move some opposition members to their side on a roll call, with modest effort.

But once the policy area rises on the president's agenda, the opposition starts to recoil from the president in large numbers. At 40% emphasis, the gap from position taking grows to 25%, or a deficit of fifty-four votes when the opposition occupies 217 seats. For the highest presidential priority, 60%, the gap from position taking reaches 37%, or eighty members. This strong counterreaction to the president offsets the gains the president receives from congressional co-partisans, an estimated seventy-two votes when his party controls 218 seats. The net effect is a loss of eight votes at the highest issue attention, or lobby effort, level when each party holds a comparable number of seats. Under these circumstances—evenly matched parties and high presidential attention to an issue—presidents can expect to lose on a large fraction of close roll calls.[14]

ROBUSTNESS TESTS

The estimation results presented in table 8.1 are bare-bones and sparse, including only whether the president took a position and his issue attention (that is, his lobbying effort). But more factors than just these affect presidential influence in Congress. Do these lobbying effort results hold up with controls for those factors? Including several interaction variables that all use presidential position taking as a component raises multicollinearity concerns. With severe multicollinearity, small changes in model estimation may lead to erratic changes in the coefficients and significance tests of affected variables.

Bearing this in mind, I added several variables and interactions to the models estimated in table 8.1, specifically the three-way interaction between House party control, House party polarization, and position taking (as in chapter 5), and the interaction between position taking and monthly lagged approval.[15] Results of this fuller estimation (see table 8.3 in the appendix) repeat the findings reported previously—there is a small curvilinear effect of lobbying effort on all members, a linear effect on co-partisans, and a curvilinear effect on opposition members. Although this is far from a definitive test, due to the limitations of the lobbying effort variable (issue attention) and to the inability to control for all of the other variables explored in previous chapters, analysis continues to find support for the conditional lobbying effects theory.

CONCLUSION

This chapter has asked whether presidential lobbying can affect member roll call behavior. The question is quite important and strikes at the heart of any discussion of presidential influence in Congress. Previous chapters looked only at the impact of presidential position taking on member voting. Generally, when presidents take a position they do influence member voting, but from those analyses one cannot distinguish between the two major processes that might lead to presidential influence, that is, the indirect effects that strengthen the association between the president from the factors that tend to affect roll call behavior (such as party or issue type) through direct presidential lobbying. If presidents have any agency, and if their behaviors have any impact on Congress, the president's lobbying strategy—which lobbying modes to employ, who to target, and how much effort to exert—should affect members' voting on roll calls. The question of presidential influence becomes less interesting if strategic presidential behavior does not affect members' roll call voting.

There is disagreement in the literature over whether presidential lobbying can affect member voting. Some argue that presidents cannot affect members through lobbying. Others suggest that increases in lobbying effort result in greater influence. A third perspective suggests a negative relationship between lobbying effort and influence, as presidents lobby harder when they face strong opposition. The theory proposed here argues that the effects of presidential lobbying effort are conditional. When presidents lobby at low to medium levels, it indicates a weak opposition, and thus there should be positive effects from lobbying. But when the president exerts strong lobbying effort, there should be negative effects, because presidents lobby hard only when they face a strong opposition.

Testing for the effects of presidential lobbying is difficult because presidents may use numerous lobbying modes. Systematically collecting data on all modes employed across all, or even a large number, of roll calls is impossible, primarily because many ways in which presidents lobby are not well documented. This may lead to omitted variable bias—ascribing effects to a measured lobbying mode (such as going public) when an unmeasured lobbying mode (such as bargaining or doing favors) actually affected member voting. Because of these issues, the research strategy here employed an indirect measure of presidential lobbying effort, arguing that presidents signal how hard they are willing to work on an issue by the emphasis they give to an issue in their State of the Union Address.

Analysis using this indirect measure found support for the conditional theory of lobbying effort. Presidential lobbying leads to gains in members supporting the president, but only at low to medium effort levels. Once presidential lobbying reaches a higher effort level, the impact of each additional increment of effort is associated with a reduction in the number of members voting with the president. The effect of presidential lobbying across all members, although statistically significant, is not very large, with the largest effect being about 3% to 3.4%, or thirteen to fifteen members.

The analysis also showed that members of the two parties respond differently to presidential lobbying effort. Co-partisans always respond positively to increased lobbying effort. As presidential lobbying efforts increase, more co-partisans rally behind the chief executive. In contrast, opposition party members display a curvilinear pattern. At low to medium lobbying levels, they gradually increase their support for the president. But when lobbying grows more intense, so does their opposition to the president. When presidents lobby very hard, members of the two parties increasingly polarize.

This pattern builds on research showing polarization in member voting when the president takes a roll call position. In her groundbreaking study, Frances Lee (2008, 2009) documents the party polarization effects in Congress of presidential position taking. She did not, however, distinguish presidential lobbying efforts, as is done here. This research extends her work, showing that polarization effects heighten when presidents work very hard on an issue. At lower levels of presidential effort, there may be a slight convergence between the parties.

Why does party polarization in Congress grow only when the president lobbies hard, but not at lower levels of presidential lobbying effort?[16] The decision to lobby is a decision about allocating a scarce resource, presidential lobbying resources. As that resource is finite and lobbying is costly, presidents will only consume as much lobbying resources as is necessary to realize their goals. When the opposition on an issue is relatively weak, presidents do not have to lobby hard to win. But as the opposition becomes stronger, presidents must intensify their lobbying to counter that opposition. Against the strongest opposition, perhaps the best the president can hope for is to minimize the size of his defeat. Being trounced on a roll call important to the president may have spillover effects onto other roll calls, fostering an image of a weak president who can be challenged successfully and thus emboldening the president's opponents across various issues.

An attendant process also sets in as presidents lobby hard. The issue becomes more closely tied to the president, helping to define the president and what he stands for, as well as defining the president's party and the opposition. For instance, the huge effort Barack Obama put into passage of health care reform became the signature policy of his administration, a foundation of his legacy, and the rallying cry of the Republican Party, which campaigned and ran against Obama *and* the Democrats from the passage of the Affordable Care Act, in 2010, through the 2016 presidential elections. Obamacare, in effect, defined not only the president but also his party and the opposition party.

Still, there is much we do not know about the linkage between presidential lobbying, presidential policy emphasis, and party polarization. The parties could have staked out different positions on an issue and then the president decided to work hard on it. This is likely the case with issues that traditionally divide the parties, such as economic policy. In such situations, the president, as the most important figure for the party, may feel compelled to adopt and represent the party (Wood 2009). To some degree, the president's nomination and election are due to his positioning on and prioritizing of issues. But presidents can have an independent effect on their parties, and on voters' image of the parties as well, as presidents decide which issues to prioritize, which solutions to propose, and which issues to lobby hard on. In Daniel Galvin's (2014) phrase, presidents are sometimes "agents of change."

This research only scratches the surface on these complex processes. Most important for present purposes, this chapter demonstrates that presidents can influence Congress, and the decisions they make in allocating lobbying resources is important to understanding presidential influence in Congress. In other words, presidents have agency, or institutional agency (Jacobs and King 2010), and the exercise of their institutional agency has implications for their influence in Congress and for the production of public policy.

APPENDIX

TABLE 8.2 PREDICTING PRESIDENTIAL POSITION TAKING ON CONFLICTUAL ROLL CALLS, 1953–2012

VARIABLE	POSITION TAKING (= 1)
Presidential policy emphasis	1.73***
	(0.40)
Public mood (centered)	0.07***
	(0.02)
Monthly approval (lagged)	1.39***
	(0.36)
Democratic president (= 1)	0.46***
	(0.14)
Democratic House (= 1)	0.42***
	(0.15)
House party polarization	-2.19***
	(0.63)
House party control (= 1)	0.01
	(0.12)
Constant	-1.59***
	(0.55)
Observations	14,314
Pseudo R^2	0.0543
Wald X^2	143.0
Probability of Wald X^2	0.001
Degrees of freedom	7
Log pseudolikelihood	-6,912

Note: Robust standard errors in parentheses.

*$p < 0.1$, **$p < 0.05$, ***$p < 0.01$.

TABLE 8.3 PRESIDENTIAL LOBBYING EFFORT AND INFLUENCE ON CONFLICTUAL ROLL CALLS, WITH ADDITIONAL CONTROLS, HOUSE, 1953–2012

VARIABLE	(1) ALL MEMBERS	(2) SAME PARTY	(3) OPPOSITION PARTY
Presidential position	0.09***	−0.18**	0.31***
	(0.03)	(0.07)	(0.08)
Presidential lobbying effort	−0.23***	0.23	−0.63*
	(0.08)	(0.30)	(0.36)
Interaction: Position × Lobbying	0.30***	0.25	0.32*
	(0.09)	(0.15)	(0.17)
Lobbying effort–squared	0.46***	−0.79	1.48*
	(0.17)	(0.76)	(0.88)
Interaction: Position × Lobbying effort–squared	−0.65***	−0.18	−0.98**
	(0.19)	(0.39)	(0.43)
House party control (1 = majority)	−0.10**	0.78***	−0.94***
	(0.04)	(0.29)	(0.29)
Interaction: Position × House party control	−0.12***	−0.10	−0.06
	(0.03)	(0.12)	(0.11)
House polarization	−0.16**	0.72**	−0.78**
	(0.06)	(0.35)	(0.39)
Interaction: Position × House polarization	−0.25***	0.55***	−0.91***
	(0.04)	(0.08)	(0.10)
Interaction: Party control × Polarization	0.16*	−1.22**	1.42**
	(0.09)	(0.59)	(0.61)
Interaction: Position × Party control × Polarization	0.37***	0.22	0.19
	(0.05)	(0.17)	(0.15)
Monthly approval (lagged)	−0.02	0.32	−0.31
	(0.05)	(0.29)	(0.32)
Interaction: Position × Approval	0.04	0.12*	−0.02
	(0.02)	(0.07)	(0.08)
Constant	0.64***	−0.13	1.20***
	(0.04)	(0.20)	(0.20)

(*continued*)

TABLE 8.3 PRESIDENTIAL LOBBYING EFFORT AND INFLUENCE ON CONFLICTUAL ROLL CALLS, WITH ADDITIONAL CONTROLS, HOUSE, 1953–2012 *(CONTINUED)*

VARIABLE	(1) ALL MEMBERS	(2) SAME PARTY	(3) OPPOSITION PARTY
Observations	15,637	15,637	15,637
R^2	0.05	0.18	0.17
F	34.62	226.4	77.02
Probability of F	0.0000	0.0000	0.0000
Regression sum of squares	271.9	1,616	1,825
Log likelihood	9,492	−4,443	−5,395

Note: Robust standard errors in parentheses.

$^*p < 0.1$, $^{**}p < 0.05$, $^{***}p < 0.01$.

9

MODERNITY AND PRESIDENTIAL
INFLUENCE IN CONGRESS

T HE MODERN PRESIDENCY thesis is one of the most influential accounts
of the evolution of the office. According to this perspective, modernization led to the office becoming central to policy making and
governing. Bailey (2002, 35) summarizes the main thrust of the modern
presidency idea: "The modern president is said to routinely wield more
power than ever imagined by premodern presidents." The modern presidency thesis does not argue that modern executives can dominate Congress and get everything they want but that modern presidents are more
influential than premodern executives, including in the legislative arena.[1]

In fact, the suggestion that modern presidents have more power than
premodern ones contrasts with research on legislative relations of modern
presidents, which represents the bulk of research on the question and which
stresses presidential struggles and barriers to winning congressional acceptance of their policies. It appears, from this research, that dumb luck or a
favorable context determines presidential success in Congress (Rockman
1981), while president-centered factors have, at best, a marginal or modest
impact on success (Bond and Fleisher 1990; Edwards 1990).

To a degree, this research paints the president as either a captive or a
beneficiary of the political environment. In accounting for presidential
success, it matters little what presidents do; they have no agency in the
legislative policy-making process. Presidents take positions on legislative

matters not because of the potential to affect outcomes but because of public expectations and pressures for presidential policy activism. Overall, presidents appear relatively weak or incapable of helping themselves. The combination of weakness and public expectations leads to a gap between what people expect of presidents and what they can deliver, the expectations gap. This expectations gap, furthermore, may lead to public disillusionment with politics (Jenkins-Smith, Silva, and Waterman 2005; Waterman, Jenkins-Smith, and Silva 1999; Waterman, Silva, and Jenkins-Smith 2014).[2]

Can we reconcile these two pictures of modern presidents in the legislative policy-making process? First, just because presidential influence has increased from the premodern to modern periods does not mean that modern presidents possess much capacity to influence legislative outcomes. But the limited ability of presidents to influence Congress calls into question the usefulness of the modern presidency notion, as some have done.[3] Second, research may have underestimated the amount of influence modern presidents have, as the institutional influence perspective presented here maintains. Yet the institutional influence theory does not argue that presidents are so influential as to get all they want, only that the context and dumb luck accounts may underestimate the amount of presidential influence with Congress.

To answer the question of whether modern presidents possess more influence in Congress than premodern executives requires *comparable data* spanning both eras. The methodology developed here to measure presidential influence can be applied to presidents serving in the premodern era. Chapter 10 uses that methodology to estimate presidential influence in Congress from 1877 to the present.[4]

Before turning to that exercise, this chapter reviews the modern presidency thesis in detail to show why it argues that presidential influence increased as a result of modernization. As the modern presidency idea is built in part on the view that presidents of the Reconstruction–Gilded Age period (the late 1800s) were very weak, I review what research has to say about the influence of these presidents. Although there is debate about the weakness and legislative ineffectiveness of the Reconstruction–Gilded Age presidents, no study directly compares their influence with that of the modern presidents. Next I review the scant literature that has compared presidents across the premodern–modern divide. This literature, too, is found to be lacking. Although it assesses presidential success, it does not raise the question of influence, which is at the heart of the premodern—modern distinction. Presidents can be successful without having much influence, as the context–dumb luck perspective claims.

THE MODERN PRESIDENCY AND PRESIDENTIAL INFLUENCE

With Franklin Roosevelt's presidency, all the attributes necessary for the modern office came together for the first time (Greenstein 1978; 1988). Greenstein (1988, 4) identifies four factors that define the modern presidency and distinguish it from the premodern or traditional office: heightened visibility with voters, providing presidents with a unique political resource; the ability to set the policy agenda for Congress and the nation; the accumulation of staff resources especially for policy advice; and the increasing use of unilateral instruments for making policy. These factors provide modern presidents with bargaining and other advantages that premodern presidents lacked in dealing with Congress. As Patterson (1976, 56) observes, "The rapidity with which Franklin Roosevelt and his successors extended their power after 1940 suggests the potency ... of forces assisting ambitious Presidents."[5] Consequently, modern presidents should be more influential than premodern executives, but not so influential as to dominate the legislative policy-making process.

The literature on the modern presidency is not always explicit about how these factors lead to greater presidential influence, but it is useful to be specific for our purposes here. First, heightened public visibility gives the president a political resource to use with Congress, and several aspects of public visibility have implications for presidential influence. Public expectation about presidential policy leadership not only pressures presidents to develop policy alternatives and to work to see their enactment but also compels Congress to at least consider the president's initiatives, even if most members disagree with the policy solution.[6] In addition, the notion that voters view the president as a national representative but see each member as primarily a representative of a locality reinforces the pressures on Congress to put the president's policy proposals on its legislative agenda. As the public visibility of the president has risen, so have the electoral implications of public support for the president, with regard to members' careers. But public support for the president (such as job approval ratings) is a two-edged sword—it gives the president leverage when he is popular but undercuts his position when he is unpopular.[7]

Public visibility is closely tied to the idea that the president sets the national and congressional policy agendas.[8] By setting those agendas, presidential prioritization of an issue induces Congress to expend energy, time, and attention on that issue, diverting attention away from other issues. Presidents set the terms of debate on the nation's priorities and on what Congress should be doing with its legislative time.

Increased staffing adds to these presidential advantages. A larger staff, especially with policy expertise, allows the president to be active and to provide leadership across a large number of issue areas. These staffers, and others in line agencies such as the Bureau of the Budget/Office of Management and Budget, are important in helping the administration draft legislation to submit to Congress (Rudalevige 2002).

Critically, the development of staffing led to the institutionalization of the president's program. The president's program was formalized during the Truman administration and has been a fixture since Eisenhower. Congress began to expect and to rely on a program from the president, appearing unable to address the nation's problems without it (Huntington 1965; Neustadt 1954, 1955). The process of central clearance, a part of building the president's program, is especially important to understanding the influence presidents derive from the legislative program. Central clearance not only determines whether an agency's legislative recommendations are consistent with the administration's but also restricts direct communication between agencies and Congress. Prior to the institutionalization of central clearance, agencies could contact Congress independently of the president and without restriction; Congress also could initiate such communications. Congress thus had access to the information and intelligence of the bureaucracy, unfiltered by the administration.

With central clearance, the administration would control all communication between an agency and Congress. Agency heads at congressional hearings could not air policy disagreements between their agency and the administration. Consequently, when communicating with agencies Congress would learn only of the administration's line on policy, not about whether the agency held alternative preferences. This made Congress increasingly dependent on the presidency for policy information and expertise. And policy information and expertise became increasingly important to policy making as problems grew in technicality and complexity. Congress would have to either develop in-house expertise—in units like the Congressional Budget Office, for instance—or rely on nongovernmental expertise from think tanks and the like. Yet the politicization and advocacy of think tanks undermined their utility in countering the administration's choke hold on bureaucratic expertise. Previously (Cohen 2012), I have found support for the importance of central clearance in accounting for the legislative success of modern presidents. But, as has been noted, success and influence differ. I did not test the implications of central clearance for presidential influence in Congress.

Finally, modern presidents increasingly use unilateral devices for making policy. One reason they do so is because of frustrations with Congress, with both the slowness of the legislative process and the uncertainty about the policy products of that process. But presidents also may threaten to use executive orders and the like as a bargaining tool to extract what they want from Congress, much as they employ veto threats. Implicit in such use of executive order threats is that if Congress wants input on a policy, it will have to legislate. Otherwise, the president alone will promulgate a policy, which might be less desirable to Congress than one produced through legislation.[9]

For such reasons, modern presidents should have more influence in Congress than premodern ones. This does not mean that modern presidents will necessarily be more successful in legislation than premodern presidents or that premodern presidents lack influence in the legislative process. These factors and public expectations for presidential leadership may push presidents to support legislation with uncertain chances of enactment. Premodern presidents, in contrast, may be more circumspect in supporting legislation. If premodern presidents ask for less, compared to modern presidents, and only take sides on less controversial legislation, their success rates may be higher than that of modern presidents.

Presidential influence and success are separate, albeit connected, questions. We know relatively little about the legislative involvement and influence of premodern presidents. Recent research has begun to question the portrait of premodern presidents as impotent in congressional affairs, especially presidents during the Reconstruction and Gilded Ages, roughly 1866 to 1900. The next section reviews that literature. Still, resolving the question of the relative influence of premodern and modern presidents requires data enabling comparison across both epochs, the task of chapter 10.

LEGISLATIVE INFLUENCE OF THE GILDED AGE PRESIDENTS

There are two ways that one can assess the influence of modern presidents. First, one can look directly at the attributes of the office in the modern period, arguing that those attributes endowed the office with a certain degree of influence. Second, one can compare modern presidents with earlier occupants of the office to test whether modern executives are more influential. For the second approach, presidents serving during the Reconstruction and Gilded Ages, roughly from Andrew Johnson through William McKinley, are of critical importance. These late nineteenth-century presidents are commonly portrayed as weak and ineffectual, mere pawns of their respective parties, nothing more than clerks who rubber-stamped congressional decisions. Even contemporary observers viewed these presidents that way, as shown, for instance, in two influential publications, Woodrow Wilson's *Congressional Government* (1885) and Lord Bryce's *The American Commonwealth* (1889).

In a now famous passage, Wilson ([1885] 1981, 170) describes late nineteenth-century presidents: "The business of the President, occasionally great, is usually not much above routine. Most of the time it is mere administration, mere obedience of directions from the masters of policy, the Standing Committees [of Congress]." And Bryce asks why great men are not chosen as president, implying that presidents since Lincoln were unimpressive, accomplishing little of note.

Keller (1977, 544) depicts Gilded Age presidents as "small in scale and limited in power, caught up more in the vicissitudes of party politics and patronage than in the formulation and conduct of public policy." According to Patterson (1976, 39), "The presidency remained relatively weak throughout most of the nineteenth century. For several extended periods—1810 to 1829, 1849 to 1860, 1868 to 1898—it was an insignificant institution." In his seminal study of influence on the enactment of ninety major pieces of legislation from 1873 to 1940, Lawrence H. Chamberlain (1946, 47–49) finds predominant presidential influence on nineteen (21%) and shared influence with Congress on twenty-nine (32%). Most telling is that presidential influence is more common beginning in 1933, with Franklin Roosevelt. Presidents were influential, predominantly or jointly, on twenty-two of twenty-four (92%) enactments from 1933 to 1940, on twenty-four of fifty-one (47%) from 1900 to 1932, but on only two of fifteen (13%) from 1873 to 1899, figures in line with the portrait of late nineteenth-century presidents as weak.[10] Other prominent historians, such as Richard Hofstadter ([1948] 1989) and Wilfred Binkley ([1947] 1962), offer similar assessments of the late nineteenth-century presidents.

Reasons offered to explain the ineffectiveness of Reconstruction–Gilded Age presidents include congressional encroachment on presidents' ability to shape their administration (such as through the Tenure of Office Act) and the lack of presidential involvement in the passage of landmark legislation. In recounting the legislative accomplishments during Benjamin Harrison's term, Sidney Milkis and Michael Nelson (2015, 216) report, "A burst of important legislation during the first two years of Harrison's term, including the protectionist McKinley Tariff Act, the Sherman Anti-Trust Act . . . , the Sherman Silver Purchase Act . . . , the Dependent Pensions Act . . . , and increased spending on internal improvements and on the navy marked the rise of party discipline and congressional efficiency," but nowhere do they cite Harrison as being involved in or important for the passage of any of these major laws.

Moreover, the strong House speakership emerged in the late nineteenth century, especially with Speaker Thomas Reed (1889 to 1891 and 1885 to 1899) (see Jenkins and Stewart 2013). Reed formally concentrated the organizational and procedural power in the speakership through the Reed Rules, by which the Speaker could determine whether a quorum was present, which was necessary for Congress to conduct business, even if a member refused to answer the quorum roll call.[11] Critics of Reed derisively called him Czar Reed. The rise of the strong speakership had policy-making and institutional power implications as well: nothing could be legislated without the involvement and consent of the Speaker. Presidents were relegated to a secondary, peripheral role in policy making, due to the concentration of institutional power in the speakership.[12]

The weakness of the Gilded Age presidents is important to the hypothesis of concern here, that modern presidents are more influential in Congress than are premodern ones. Their supposed weakness and ineffectiveness provide a stark contrast to modern presidents, making it relatively easy to argue that the office has gained influence as it has modernized, especially in comparison to the Gilded Age presidents.[13]

CHALLENGES TO THE PRESIDENTIAL MODERNITY PARADIGM

There is broad agreement with Greenstein's (1988) description of institutional changes in the presidency coalescing in the 1930s. But several research strands suggest that those developments may not have had as much impact on presidential influence in Congress as the Greenstein paradigm implies. These strands include revisionist literature on the Gilded Age presidents, suggesting that they were not as weak as the standard portrait indicates, and the fact that premodern presidents at times engaged in modern-like behavior, often with similar motivations and outcomes.[14]

REVISIONIST ASSESSMENTS OF LATE
NINETEENTH-CENTURY PRESIDENTS

Over the past several decades a revisionist scholarship has emerged that challenges the portrait of Gilded Age presidents as lacking influence, unwilling to protect the office from congressional encroachment, and mere rubber stamps for their congressional parties (Calhoun 2002). Although it does not claim that these presidents were enormously influential or assertive in legislative and policy debates, this research suggests that the standard interpretation of Gilded Age presidents as weak, ineffective, and feckless overstates the case. The revisionist school brings several types of evidence to make its case, including the success of these presidents in wresting and/or maintaining control over the dispensing of patronage, the eventual repeal of the Tenure of Office Act, and (limited) presidential activism on several critical policy fronts.

Since the invention of the spoils system, with Andrew Jackson, the dispensing of federal patronage was crucial to the electoral fortunes of parties and to building loyalty to often highly fractious parties (DiSalvo 2012; Folke, Hirano, and Snyder 2011; Sorauf 1959). Presidents from Andrew Jackson until Reconstruction had a major say in naming patronage appointees, although they often deferred to Congress in specific instances. From 1876 onward, presidents battled with Congress several times over control of patronage appointments. The outcome of these disputes, often to the president's advantage, would have major implications for the relative power of the two branches of government. Through control over patronage, presidents possessed some leverage for passage of legislation they favored.

Early in his administration, for instance, Rutherford B. Hayes, who owed his presidency to the infamous "corrupt bargain of 1876,"[15] tangled with perhaps the most powerful member of Congress from his own party, Roscoe Conkling, senator from New York, over patronage. The Hayes–Conkling dispute arose over an investigation into practices associated with the New York Custom House, which were found to be corrupt. Control over appointment to that customhouse was crucial because it was the most important source of federal revenue collection. The Conkling faction had long controlled appointment to that post, which was an important foundation of the group's political power. After a protracted struggle, Hayes succeeding in removing Chester A. Arthur, a member of Conkling's faction, from the leading position in the New York Custom House, placing in office his own nominee. Hayes also extended some early civil service standards for appointment to lesser offices at the customhouse, which further weakened the Conkling faction's hold on the customs office (Hoogenboom 1988, 1995; Paul 1998; Vazzano 2006). Despite the overall interpretation of Hayes as a weak president, he was assertive and successful in these struggles with perhaps the most powerful faction within his party.

A second contest over patronage, again involving the New York Custom House and Roscoe Conkling, was perhaps more telling and consequential. This time, James A. Garfield, like Hayes a supporter of civil service reform, removed a Conkling-allied customs collector and appointed to the post a New York–based rival to Conkling. In an attempt to demonstrate their political prowess, both Conkling and Thomas Platt, also a Republican New York senator, resigned their seats and then sought reelection from the New York legislature. But the legislature refused to reseat them, paving the way for Senate confirmation of Garfield's nominee.[16] Garfield effectively rid the Senate of two key opponents from within his party.

Conkling thought that his prospects for patronage control were improved with the assassination and death of Garfield and the ascendency of Conkling protégé Vice President Chester A. Arthur to the presidency. But like Hayes and Garfield before him, Arthur asserted his independence and refused Conkling's entreaties over patronage (Doenecke 1981; Reeves 1975). By the time of the Arthur administration, the presidency had reclaimed its traditional role and had protected its independence from Congress, at least on patronage matters. Despite these victories against congressional dictating of patronage, Patterson (1976, 47) maintains that the presidency did not emerge as a strong or forceful institution but "remained on the defensive" until at least the end of the century.

One cannot point to the forceful personality or tenacity of any president during this time period for (re)securing patronage power. None of these presidents, Hayes, Garfield, or Arthur, had a reputation for being strong or assertive; still, they fought with Congress over control of major patronage posts, and won.[17]

Although they are instructive as cases, did the Gilded Age presidents actually have any systematic influence on patronage, and did they have more influence on patronage than Congress did? Rogowski's (2016) recent study presents the first systematic evidence on these questions. Post offices and postmaster positions were the most important source of federal patronage in the late nineteenth century. Rogowski (2016, 327) notes that 18% of federal expenditures were devoted to post offices in 1895, making the postal service among the largest and most important elements of the federal establishment in the late nineteenth century. Not only was postal patronage important to the political parties and to the growing administrative state (Carpenter 2000; Skowronek 1982) but also postal patronage was fundamental to presidential influence with Congress (Rogowski 2015, 2016).

Rogowski's research is all the more important because the dominant theme of the distribution of particularistic goods such as rivers and harbors, of public improvements, and even of the development of the bureaucracy in the late nineteenth century emphasizes the role of Congress and hardly mentions the presidency (Carpenter 2000; Kernell and McDonald 1999; Wilson 1986). Using the geographic location of post offices from 1876 to 1896, the period of greatest postal expansion and historically reputed to be an era of weak presidents, Rogowski finds that congressional membership in the president's party, whether the majority or the minority, affects the distribution of post offices. In contrast, neither membership in the congressional majority, being on relevant committees, nor holding a congressional leadership position affects whether a member's district receives a post office. And contrary to the congressional dominance school, the president, but not Congress, influences the location of post offices. As Rogowski (2016, 336–337) summarizes his findings: "Across a wide range of model specifications . . . I find strong, consistent, and robust evidence that counties represented by legislators who shared the president's party received substantially more post offices. At the same time, the results provide limited or no evidence that counties represented by members of the House majority party, key committees, or who served as committee chairs or ranking members received increased numbers of post offices."

At least with regard to the distribution of particularistic benefits to localities, Rogowski's findings resemble findings for presidents of the modern era (Berry, Burden, and Howell 2010; Dynes and Huber 2015; Hudak 2014; Kriner and Reeves 2015a, 2015b).

It is hard to square Rogowski's findings, which directly compare presidential and congressional influences on the location of post offices, with the view that Gilded Age presidents lacked influence in Congress. Still, there are two limitations of Rogowski's study with regard to the hypothesis that modern presidents are more influential than premodern, and especially Gilded Age, presidents. First, Rogowski's evidence only speaks to dispensing of patronage. He does not offer evidence of premodern presidential influence on substantive policy making. Other studies find, for example, that premodern presidents took comparatively few positions on legislation compared to modern ones (Cohen 2012). Second, Rogowski's evidence does not compare the influence of modern presidents with that of premodern presidents. Only data spanning the two eras, with comparable indicators, can test that hypothesis, as is done in chapter 10 of the present study. Still, Rogowski's study is important as the first systematic test of the influence of presidents on one of the most important decisions at the time. His evidence, coupled with the struggles and victories of Hayes, Garfield, and Arthur, suggests that we need to revise the portrait of Gilded Age presidents.

MODERN BEHAVIOR IN THE PREMODERN PRESIDENCY

A second critique of the modern presidency thesis is that premodern presidents at times behaved similarly to modern presidents, from controlling the bureaucracy to dealing with Congress and speaking to the public. Numerous studies of the "great" or "historically notable" premodern presidents, such as Thomas Jefferson (Bailey 2007), Andrew Jackson (Yoo 2007), and especially Abraham Lincoln (McPherson 1992), have shown that they employed modern-like behaviors. This critique is only important to the hypothesis considered here if less great or less historically notable presidents also engaged in modern-like behavior, and if they did so often enough to suggest a behavioral pattern. None of the Gilded Age presidents, no matter how generously defined, can be considered a great or historically notable president. If modern-like behavior of premodern presidents is observed only occasionally, and merely as a response to extraordinary circumstances, then it is hard to argue that the difference between premodern and modern presidents is not as great as is generally assumed.

In detailing the differences between premodern and modern presidents, Greenstein (1988) implies that there is a difference in the pattern of behavior of modern and premodern presidents, that *all* modern presidents typically behave as moderns, and that there is little variability in the behavior of modern presidents. As Neustadt (1991, 6), also a proponent of the modernity model, contends, "A striking feature of our recent past has been the transformation into routine practice of actions we once treated as exceptional. A President may retain liberty, in Woodrow Wilson's phrase, 'to be as big a man as he can.' But now he cannot be as small as he might like."

With regard to the bureaucracy, Moe (1985) argues that the defining traits of modern presidents are the *politicization* of appointments to the bureaucracy and *centralization* of policy making in the White House, both of which reduce the influence of bureaucrats and Congress, to the president's benefit. Presidents politicize and centralize because of the gap between public expectations for their policy leadership and the structure of government, which limits presidential influence over policy. Where Moe focuses on the expectations gap, a feature of the modern era, in motivating presidents to politicize and centralize, Galvin and Shogan (2007, 481) argue that the incentive for politicization and centralization derives "from the ambiguity of executive power and the elusiveness of authority that is inherent in the office itself" and thus has roots in the nature of the office, not in modernization.

To make their case, Galvin and Shogan use the examples of three premodern presidents, John Tyler, James K. Polk, and Rutherford B. Hayes.[18] Tyler is very important to their argument because, as a Whig, he and his party argued against the way Andrew Jackson aggrandized the executive. Tyler inherited a cabinet composed of loyalists to his predecessor, William Henry Harrison, many of whom possessed independent power bases. Traditionally, presidents dating to Thomas Jefferson ceded much authority to their cabinet secretaries. However, in a series of actions, such as the replacement of sitting secretaries, Tyler reshaped the cabinet in his image, wresting authority and influence from his secretaries to himself. Galvin and Shogan (2007, 501) summarize the behavior of these three presidents thusly: "The thread that binds them together is their common impulse to push the envelope of executive power and their manipulation of structural arrangements to pursue their policy program. As these cases demonstrate, the tendency for presidents to seek control, authority, and autonomy is not only a modern phenomenon."

A second behavioral pattern relates to presidential particularism. Recent research has begun to challenge the congressional dominance explanations of distributive, pork barrel policy making. Presidents use their position and authority to direct federal grants where it will be most electorally beneficial to them, an action termed "presidential particularism." Most of this research focuses on the modern age (Berry, Burden, and Howell 2010; Hudak 2014; Kriner and Reeves 2015a, 2015b). Earlier, we reviewed Rogowski's (2016) related work on postal patronage in the late nineteenth century, which also found strong presidential effects. None of these studies, however, explicitly compares premodern and modern presidents with regard to distributive benefits.

Lowande, Jenkins, and Clarke (2018) look at presidential particularism in trade policy from 1917 to 2006. Presidents can use unilateral directives, such as executive orders, memoranda, and, most commonly, proclamations. Thus, Lowande, Jenkins, and Clarke can compare premodern with modern presidents on the same policy area, using the same types of policy instruments, although their data do not extend into the Gilded Age, when presidents were supposedly weaker and less assertive.[19] Surprisingly, they demonstrate that premodern presidents from 1917 to 1933 were more inclined than succeeding presidents to issue protectionist directives for their particularistic electoral needs. We would expect modern presidents to be more assertive in their use of unilateral directives and to be more particularistic in their behavior. Thus, while Lowande, Jenkins, and Clarke (2018) reveal differences between modern and premodern presidents, those differences are contrary to expectations based on the modern presidency thesis.

LEGISLATIVE INTERACTIONS OF PREMODERN PRESIDENTS: VETOES

Since this study is concerned with legislative influence, it is important to ask whether premodern presidents interacted with Congress in ways that resemble the interactions of modern presidents. In what ways did they interact with Congress, how frequently and typically did they employ modern presidential methods, and to what extent did such interactions result in influence with Congress?

Like modern presidents, premodern presidents may threaten vetoes, bargain with Congress, and/or go public in attempts to influence Congress. Although there is an extensive literature on vetoes and several studies of vetoes from the early days of the Republic to the present (Copeland 1983; Lee 1975; McCarty 2009; Spitzer 1988; Watson 1993), there is no systematic study of veto threats or veto bargaining by premodern presidents. It is probably safe to assume that premodern presidents did not use veto threats or engage in sequential veto bargaining games with Congress (Cameron 2000) as much as modern presidents do.

Still, there are several historical accounts of Gilded Age presidents using veto threats. After the 1878 midterm elections, the Democratic majority began a legislative effort to repeal aspects of the Reconstruction laws, especially provisions on placements of federal troops and marshals at polling places in the formerly secessionist states and the requirement of a loyalty oath for jurors in those states. The Democrats' legislative strategy was to apply riders to appropriations bills. President Hayes signaled his opposition, prior to these provisions being tied to appropriations bills, and his intention to veto bills with such riders if they reached his desk. Challenging the president, the Democrats passed a bill, which Hayes swiftly vetoed. Congress upheld Hayes's veto. In all, Democrats sent seven appropriations riders to Hayes, who vetoed them all, and Congress sustained all the vetoes. Eventually, Congress sent the president appropriations bills lacking the riders (Vazzano 1993). Otherwise, Hayes rarely vetoed legislation (only thirteen times, including the riders' legislation) or threatened vetoes.[20]

Chester A. Arthur may have entered into what appeared to be a sequential veto bargaining game with Congress over the exclusion of Chinese laborers. He vetoed the first bill sent to him on the topic because it imposed a twenty-year exclusionary period, which he argued violated several treaties, although in his veto message he expressed support for exclusion. Congress then sent him a second bill, which shortened the exclusionary period to ten years, which Arthur signed (Calhoun 2002, 247).[21]

Grover Cleveland wielded the veto pen frequently and consistently. In his eight years of office, he issued 584 vetoes (on average, seventy-three times per Congress). Only Franklin Roosevelt vetoed more frequently, 635 times (though this was only fifty-three times per Congress). Mostly, Cleveland vetoed bills concerning pensions to Civil War veterans and what he considered to be pork barrel spending. Cleveland was consistent in signaling to Congress his position on these issues, yet, despite the Democrats being in the majority for six of Cleveland's eight years, Congress still sent bills to him that he vetoed.

Thus, while we have examples of presidents using veto threats or engaging in sequential veto bargaining games, we lack systematic evidence on anything other than the incidence of premodern veto behavior. Outside of veto threats and veto bargaining, it is not clear what influence premodern presidents derive from vetoes, other than to block legislation they oppose.

LEGISLATIVE INTERACTIONS OF PREMODERN PRESIDENTS: SELECTIVE INDUCEMENTS

President also may use positive inducements aimed at individual members to secure their support. There are numerous ways in which presidents can try to induce members to support them, such as by doing favors, dispensing patronage, and so on (Edwards 1980; Wayne 2009). Most relevant discussions focus on modern presidents, perhaps assuming that premodern presidents did not actively participate in shaping legislation, except on rare occasions, and thus had little reason to try to induce member support with favors and other incentives.

There also is little systematic information on presidential use of favors and inducements to influence member roll call voting. Paul (1998, 75) contends that one reason presidents of the Gilded Age, like Hayes, fought with Congress over control of patronage appointments was to use them "in return for congressional support," as bargaining chips. But there are few recorded instances of premodern presidents offering members inducements for their support on legislation.

Even among modern presidents, it is unclear whether inducements are an important source of influence, other than on an occasional member on a particular vote (Edwards 1980). Presidents and members of Congress also may want to stay private when they strike such bargains. Not only may they fear public outcry against such practices but also presidents, with a limited supply of inducements to offer, may not want to develop a reputation as an easy mark, which may lead many members to demand such "payoffs" frequently.

LEGISLATIVE INTERACTIONS OF PREMODERN PRESIDENTS: GOING PUBLIC

Going public (Kernell 1986; 2006) is a presidential strategy to mobilize voters to pressure Congress on behalf of the president's legislative goals. To Kernell, going public only became an important presidential tool as institutional pluralism in Congress gave way to individual pluralism, sometime in the mid-1970s (see also Cohen 2010). During the era of institutional pluralism, the 1950s to 1970s, presidents would rarely go public. Instead, they worked with key members of Congress, such as party leaders and committee chairs, who could deliver large numbers of votes.

Some studies detect presidential going public before the onset of individual pluralism, but this still is restricted to modern presidents. Greenstein (1988) implies that the tightened relationship between the president and the public, a characteristic of the modern presidency, could provide presidents with a source of influence in Congress. In *Presidential Power*, Neustadt (1960) suggests that the president's standing with the public could affect his influence in Congress, but neither Neustadt nor Greenstein discuss presidential actions to bolster their support among voters.

Still, some research suggests premodern presidential outreach to voters. Tulis (1987) argues that Theodore Roosevelt, and especially Woodrow

Wilson, would go public to rally public opinion on issues and legislative battles (see also Ceaser et al. 1981). Tulis's seminal conceptualization and study raises a number of questions about presidential public rhetoric in general and as it applies to legislative interactions: How much do presidents speak publicly, who does the president target, what does the president speak about, and what is the role of presidential surrogates? (See Bimes 2009; Bimes and Skowronek 1996.)

There are notable examples of premodern presidents publicizing their positions on issues before Congress and taking their case to the voters, sometimes by touring the nation (Bimes 2009, 214). Bimes mentions James Monroe, Andrew Jackson, Martin Van Buren, Zachary Taylor, and Andrew Johnson doing so. Calhoun (2002, 241) notes Hayes's domestic travel, and Ellis (2008) details the extent of presidential travel throughout the premodern era. Again, however, the data are not systematic and are presented more as illustrations than as hypothesis tests, and we know little about the impact of such public activities on roll call voting.

COMPARING THE LEGISLATIVE INTERACTIONS OF MODERN AND PREMODERN PRESIDENTS

At times, premodern presidents behaved similarly to modern presidents, including in their interactions with Congress. There also are examples of Gilded Age presidents winning battles with Congress over patronage, and evidence that premodern presidents influenced the dispensing of patronage during the Gilded Age (Rogowski 2016), all of which belies the stereotype of Gilded Age presidents as weak, inept, and ineffective. But to assess the relative influence of premodern and of modern presidents with Congress requires comparable data spanning the two eras. Few studies employ such data.

In an early paper (Cohen 1982), I looked at presidential success from 1861 to 1972. I measured success as the percentage of presidential proposals mentioned in the State of the Union Address that Congress enacted. Consistent with the view of Gilded Age presidents as weak, I found presidents serving from 1861 to 1894 to be the least successful (39.4%), compared to early twentieth-century presidents (1895 to 1932, 51.8%) and to modern presidents (1933 to 1972), who were the most successful set, at 57.9% (519). Moreover, I found differences in the bases of success across the three periods—strong legislative parties always help presidents, wars are more consequential to success for premodern presidents, and presidential activism is only associated with success for modern executives.

In a second study (Cohen 2012), I used a larger data set, comprising all presidential proposals for legislation from 1789 to 2002, again assessing presidential success. As in my earlier study, there are some continuities and similarities across the premodern–modern divide, as strong legislative parties are always associated with presidential success. Reiterating my earlier finding, presidential activism, or the number of legislative proposals, is positively associated with success for modern presidents but is negatively associated with success for premodern presidents. This comparison is suggestive of changing norms for legislative leadership from the president.

The major limitation of these studies for understanding presidential influence is that they assess success, not influence. As I argue here, however, influence and success, although related, differ. Chapter 10 will use the methodology developed here to compare the influence of modern and premodern presidents.

CONCLUSION

The modern presidency thesis implies that modern executives are more influential in Congress than are premodern executives. Modernizing the office endowed it with the capacity to influence legislators in ways that premodern presidents could not. Modern executives could draw on larger and more expert staff, mobilize public support, and set the congressional agenda, none of which premodern presidents could do systematically.

This chapter detailed the linkages between the modernization of the office and influence in Congress. The chapter also examined the relationship between presidents from Reconstruction through the end of the nineteenth century, the Gilded Age presidents, who are so important to the argument that modern presidents have more influence in Congress than premodern ones. Revisionist research on Gilded Age presidents suggests that the stereotype of them may be overdrawn, whereas other research even suggests that they may have had more influence over congressional policy making than is typically recognized.

Still, it is possible that, even if the Gilded Age presidents were not so beleaguered in their dealings with Congress as the traditional view of them holds, they still were less influential in Congress than are modern presidents. To resolve these differing viewpoints requires comparable data on presidential–congressional interactions and influence spanning the two eras.

10

COMPARING THE INFLUENCE OF PREMODERN AND MODERN PRESIDENTS

T HE MODERN PRESIDENCY thesis suggests that modern presidents should be more influential with Congress than are their premodern predecessors because the modernization of the office endowed it with resources that could influence Congress, institutional resources unavailable to premodern executives. Chapter 9 offered two critiques of the modern presidency thesis: first, that premodern presidents, especially those of the Gilded Age, were not as weak or as impotent with Congress as is often portrayed, and second, that premodern presidents at times exhibited modern-like behavior, although probably not as frequently or as routinely as modern presidents.

To test the modern presidency influence hypothesis requires comparable data spanning the two eras. In two previous studies (Cohen 1982, 2012), I employed such data but focused on presidential success, not influence. The next section applies the methodology for measuring presidential influence in Congress, as it is developed here, back to 1877. These data are then used to test the premodern–modern hypothesis.

IDENTIFYING PRESIDENTIAL POSITIONS
ON ROLL CALLS IN THE PRE-*CONGRESSIONAL*
QUARTERLY AGE

To compare the legislative influence of premodern and modern eras requires identifying presidential positions on roll calls. For much of the modern era, we have such information. Since 1953, the *Congressional Quarterly* (*CQ*) service has catalogued all public presidential positions on congressional roll calls. Although the *CQ* data are not without their limitations (Bond and Fleisher 1990; Edwards 1985), almost all studies of presidential success and influence in Congress, including the present study, utilize the *CQ* data.

This study begins with the *CQ* data as a baseline and guide for collecting data on presidential roll call positions prior to 1953. Those positions then are identified on roll calls from 1877 to 1952, the 45th through 82nd Congresses (Rutherford B. Hayes through Harry S. Truman). The aim is to replicate as closely as possible the *CQ* procedure for identifying presidential positions on roll calls.

The 1961 *CQ Almanac* defines a presidential position on a roll call when "it is possible to say that the President, were he a Member of Congress, would have voted 'yea' and 'nay' on the basis of his personal messages and statements issued before the vote was taken." To identify a president's positions, *CQ* reviews all public statements and messages, only including roll calls in cases where the language of the roll call and the president's position are similar. *CQ* excludes roll calls that are extensively amended and/or that differ greatly from the president's public position, conditions that render it impossible to determine the president's position on the roll call. Votes to recommit, reconsider, or table are included, but appropriations are not, except when they deal with specific funds that the president requested be added or deleted.

There are some major hurdles in constructing *CQ* presidential positions. First, presidential public rhetoric in the modern period is voluminous. Second, there is a degree of judgment in deciding whether a president's public position matches a roll call. In addition, premodern presidents are less likely to speak publicly on legislative matters and thus there is less of a public record to use in identifying a president's position.

With these issues in mind, to identify presidential positions I begin with the *Database of [United States] Congressional Historical Statistics, 1789–1989* (Swift et al. 2001). Within the massive data collection are two data files pertinent to identifying presidential positions. First is the presidential request file, the Request Table, which consists of all public presidential requests for legislative action from 1789 to 1992. This data file uses messages sent to Congress, compiled from sources like Richardson's *Compilation of Messages and Papers of the Presidents*, for presidents Washington through Wilson's first term; the *Congressional Record* for 1917 to 1929; Samuel I. Rosenman's (1969) compilation of Franklin Roosevelt's papers; and, for president Hoover and for Truman through Bush, the *Public Papers of the Presidents* series.

Using these official and public sources, data collector Michael Malbin and his team define a presidential proposal for legislation as a message from the president to Congress, published in one of the above noted sources. Excluded are requests or recommendations delivered privately, verbally, or through an intermediary, including official, approved administration requests from a cabinet secretary. Moreover, requests for Congress *not* to act are excluded; this includes vetoes and proposals subject to a legislative veto, such as executive branch reorganization plans. Treaties are included only if they meet the publication tests above and all nominations are excluded. Appropriation requests are generally excluded, unless they represent new policy initiatives.[1] Discrete requests are listed separately, even if they form part of an integrated policy package. Beginning with Truman (the first president to leave office at the end of a term after the 20th Amendment), presidential requests made after the last day of the final congressional session in that president's term are not included, except for treaties (see Swift et al. 2001, Request Table).

These requests are then linked (matched) to specific congressional roll calls in the *Database*'s Rollreq Table (Swift et al.). This database aimed to replicate *CQ* as closely as possible, with the exceptions of excluded vetoes and nominations, which *CQ* includes. The difference is that *CQ* is interested in presidential positions whereas the *Database* is interested in the president's legislative requests.

Fortunately for our purposes here, the *Database* presidential positions are recorded in Voteview's roll call files.[2] Yet presidents may and do take positions on roll calls besides requests for legislation.[3] To follow *CQ* for premodern presidents, I add presidential positions on vetoes and nominations and use other ways of identifying whether the president took a public position, as follows.

I use the Senate's comprehensive list of vetoes to locate the number of the bill the president vetoed for the 45th through 82nd Congresses. I then used the RCtext file from the Swift et al. (2001) database, the historical database that includes the Rollreq file, to locate the bill number and accompanying roll call number for each of these presidential vetoes. The RCtext file contains text descriptions of each roll call.

Why include vetoes to measure influence, when presidents issue them after the vote? First, as we have seen, vetoes are a common form of presidential–congressional interaction during the premodern era. Ulysses S. Grant, Grover Cleveland, Franklin Roosevelt, and Harry Truman—presidents for whom we do not have *CQ* data—vetoed frequently. More important is whether presidents signaled their veto intentions to Congress prior to the roll call. If they routinely threaten to veto legislation, then presidents are taking a position on the bill before the roll call is cast.

We do not know how frequently premodern presidents used veto threats, although the anecdotal evidenced reviewed earlier indicates that at times they did. Nonetheless, even if premodern presidents did not threaten vetoes overtly, they tended to veto certain types of bills routinely, especially on pensions for Civil War veterans. Cleveland, further, routinely vetoed bills that would subsidize special interests. The presidents' routine and frequent use of vetoes against the same types of bills suggests that members can anticipate the president's position and the potential for a veto before the roll call is held, even if the president does not publicly threaten a veto. For these reasons, I included vetoed bills in identifying presidential positions.

Second, I used the RCtext file from the *Database* to locate all presidential nominations, to make these data comparable to the later *CQ* procedure. To locate nominations, I conducted keyword searches on the text description of all roll calls, using terms such as "nominate" and "nomination," "appoint" and "appointment," and the like. Further, I scanned the text file for terms associated with vetoes and overrides of presidential vetoes, as a double check on the official Senate list. Finally, I did a keyword search for terms that would name the president and/or his administration, such as "president," "administration," "executive," and so on. Then the text of each roll call was read to determine whether the president had publicly announced a position on the roll call and, if so, the specifics of the president's position.

TRENDS IN PRESIDENTIAL ROLL CALL POSITIONS

Premodern presidents take fewer positions on roll calls than do modern presidents, even considering the increase in congressional roll calls over time. From 1953 to 2012, the years of the *CQ* data, presidents averaged 146.5 House positions per Congress, whereas pre-*CQ* presidents, 1877 to 1952, took an average of 19.3 positions.[4] Although this appears to be a stunning increase in the number of presidential positions, the number of roll calls also increased, from 235.8 to 897.4. The difference in the percentage of positions is not so great, once we consider the greater frequency of congressional roll calls: presidents from 1877 to 1952 took positions on 9.1% of roll calls, compared to 23.8% for presidents from 1953 to 2012.

Figure 10.1 plots the percentage of presidential positions for all Congresses from 1877 through 2012. There is a notable spike in positions during the 84th to 90th Congresses (1955 to 1968), with presidents taking positions on 49% to 56% of roll calls—more than twice as frequently as the next-highest years, when they took positions on about 20% of roll calls. Still, there is an upward trend in position taking from the 45th through the 73rd Congresses, the years prior to Franklin Roosevelt.[5]

The congressional reforms of the 1970s, in part, account for the decline in presidential positions after the 91st Congress. With the Legislative Reorganization Act of 1970, the House changed procedures for recorded votes and paved the way for electronic voting, which would speed up the counting of roll call votes. Prior to electronic voting, roll call counting could be time consuming and cumbersome. For a teller vote, members pass between two tellers, first the yeas and then the nays, to record their vote. For a roll call vote, the presiding officer, usually the Speaker, reads the name of each member, who responds yea or nay. Since these procedures were time consuming, voice or division votes were often used, in which members answered either yea or nay as a group, or stood up (or raised hands), and the Speaker

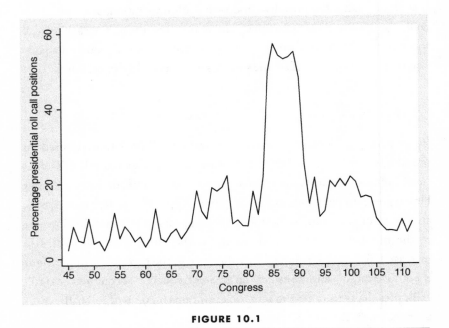

FIGURE 10.1

Presidential positions on House roll calls as a percentage of total House roll calls, by Congress, 45th to 112th Congresses, 1877–2012

decided which side had won. This gave the Speaker great power to decide who won and members did not have to go on record. Part of the movement toward electronic voting, and thus toward more recorded votes, was to increase transparency and to enable constituents to better learn how their representative voted (Kravitz 1990; Lynch and Madonna 2013).

Controlling for this reform and for the greater frequency of position taking by presidents from the 84th to 90th Congresses (1955 to 1968), results still find modern presidents (Franklin Roosevelt and after) taking more positions, as a percentage, than premodern ones. Table 10.1 presents results using the following variables: a modern presidency dummy (45th to 72nd Congresses = 0; 73rd to 112th Congresses = 1); a dummy for 84th to 90th Congresses, a period when presidents took an unusually large number of positions; a dummy for the post-reorganization Congresses (91st to 112th); and a counter (45th to 112th Congresses).

TABLE 10.1 TRENDS IN PRESIDENTIAL POSITION TAKING ON
CONGRESSIONAL ROLL CALLS, 45TH TO 112TH CONGRESSES

	(1) POSITIONS OUT OF TOTAL ROLL CALLS (%)	(2) POSITIONS OUT OF TOTAL ROLL CALLS (%)
Modern dummy	9.58***	7.56***
	(2.41)	(1.20)
Active era	38.56***	38.07***
	(2.42)	(1.95)
House reform era	1.61	—
	(2.71)	—
Congress counter	−0.09	—
	(0.09)	—
Constant	12.35*	7.20***
	(5.25)	(0.89)
N	68	68
R^2	0.89	0.89
Adjusted R^2	0.89	0.89
F	131.5	266.4

Note: Standard errors in parentheses. See text for procedure to determine presidential positions on congressional roll calls. Modern dummy: 45th–72nd Congresses = 0; 73rd–112th Congresses = 1. Active era: 84th–90th Congresses = 1; otherwise = 0. House reform era: 1st–90th Congresses = 0; 91st–112 Congresses = 1. $*p < 0.05$, $**p < 0.01$, $***p < 0.001$

Results indicate that the presidents of the highly active period of position taking (84th to 90th Congresses) take positions, on average, 39% more often than do other presidents and that modern presidents take about 9.6% more positions than do premodern ones. Neither the congressional counter nor the post-reorganization dummy is statistically significant. Dropping these variables changes the story only slightly—now modern presidents take positions about 7.6% more frequently than do premodern ones. The increase in position taking by modern presidents represents approximately a doubling in the number of positions, compared to premodern executives, who take positions on an average of 7.2% of roll calls. Modern presidents are more legislatively active, at least in the sense of taking positions on roll calls.

THE PREMODERN VERSUS THE MODERN PRESIDENCY AND INFLUENCE

Are modern presidents more influential in Congress than premodern executives? The same techniques used thus far to estimate presidential influence now are used to address this question. Recall that, first, the roll call data for each Congress are arrayed in long form, with the dependent variable defined as the individual member's vote. Each member's vote then is rescored, with a liberal vote set to 1 and a conservative vote to -1, using the Fowler and Hall (2013) method.

The previous analysis for 1953 to 2012 suggests that presidential influence enables the president's side to win on a significant number of roll calls that the opposing side would have won had the president not taken a position. Furthermore, presidential influence is greater among co-partisans than among opposition members, greater on foreign than on domestic policy, and greater when presidential legislative effort is at moderate levels. For the pre-1953 period, however, there is scant data on bill characteristics and presidential effort, limiting what can be said about these factors and presidential influence. Even so, it is possible to compare presidential influence on co-partisans with influence on opposition members.

First we must ask whether premodern presidential position taking has a causal impact on member voting. If position taking does not have a causal effect, it makes little sense to analyze the sources of presidential influence, because premodern presidents lack influence. As in chapter 4, to assess the causal effect of position taking, the analysis first uses regression and then turns to treatment effects analysis.

THE CAUSAL EFFECT OF PREMODERN POSITION TAKING ON MEMBER VOTING

It can be difficult to establish causal effects with observational data like that which is used here. Presidents may take a position on an expected lopsided vote to claim credit and/or to be identified with the winning side.

Presidents may not have any influence on such "hurrah" votes; rather, the congressional alignment leads the president to take a position, that is, *Congress influences the president*. Including hurrah votes may inflate the estimated amount of presidential influence. Since presidential position taking and congressional roll call results may be endogenous (Canes-Wrone, Howell, and Lewis 2008; Howell, Jackman, and Rogowski 2012; Howell and Rogowski 2013), estimating presidential influence requires taking into account this potential endogeneity, as much as is possible.

Further, presidents do not take positions on a random subset of roll calls. They may be more inclined to take positions on votes they think they can affect, because of public and political pressures, and/or because of strongly held beliefs about the desirability of certain policy directions, among other reasons. Consequently, we cannot simply compare the expected liberal voting tendencies on presidential and nonpresidential roll calls to ascertain the amount of presidential influence. The two sets of roll calls may systematically differ in ways other than just the president taking a position or not. Chapter 4 used two techniques to adjust for these problems: eliminating hurrah votes and using quasi-experimental analytic techniques. These techniques also are applied to the premodern presidential data.

To begin the causal assessment of premodern influence, as in chapter 4, analysis first regresses the percentage of liberal votes on the president's position (1 = liberal, -1 = conservative, and zero = no position). Table 10.2 reports results of three regressions. The first is for all members from the 45th through the 82nd Congresses (Hayes through Truman), while the second and third split the Congresses list into two subsets, the premodern (45th through 72nd, Hayes through Hoover) and the early modern (73rd through 82nd, Franklin Roosevelt through Truman). The estimation clusters on Congress to control for Congress-specific factors that might affect results, such as the number of roll calls and presidential positions. This initial analysis does not distinguish lopsided votes from contested ones.

For each estimation, the sign on the presidential position-taking variable is positive, indicating that, as premodern and early modern presidents take positions, members have a tendency to shift from their established voting patterns to the president's side. For the entire period, the regression coefficient is 0.06 ($p < 0.004$) and is statistically significant. Since the

TABLE 10.2 IMPACT OF PRESIDENTIAL POSITION TAKING ON MEMBER ROLL CALL VOTING, 45TH TO 82ND CONGRESSES

VARIABLE	(1) 45TH–82ND CONGRESSES	(2) 45TH–72ND CONGRESSES	(3) 73RD–82ND CONGRESSES
Presidential position	0.06***	0.03	0.06*
	(0.02)	(0.03)	(0.03)
Constant	0.50***	0.49***	0.55***
	(0.02)	(0.02)	(0.02)
Observations	8,962	7,064	1,898
R^2	0.00	0.001	0.01
Adjusted R^2	0.004	0.001	0.01
df	1	1	1
F	8.15	1.45	4.01
rss	576.8	451.9	118.2
Log likelihood	−424.2	−312.9	−58.41

Note: Robust standard errors in parentheses. Clustered on Congress. Dependent variable is the percentage of liberal votes on a roll call. Presidential position: 1= Liberal; 0 = No position; –1= Conservative.

$^*p < 0.1$, $^{**}p < 0.05$, $^{***}p < 0.01$.

dependent variable is a percentage, there are 6% more liberal votes when the president takes a liberal position and 6% fewer liberal votes when the president takes a conservative position, compared to not taking a position. This effect is comparable to that detailed in chapter 4 for the 1953 to 2012 period. Still, pre- and early modern presidents take many fewer positions than do presidents from 1953 to 2012, about 8% in this analysis.[6] Thus, while early presidents appear to influence voting patterns when they take positions, they take relatively few positions. Hence, they will have only a limited impact on legislative production, although they may affect the outcome of the select votes when they take a position.

Premodern presidents also are less influential than the early moderns, Franklin Roosevelt and Harry Truman. The coefficient for the premodern presidents is 0.03 ($p = 0.12$, not significant), indicating an approximate 3% shift in votes from position taking, compared to 0.06 ($p = 0.04$, significant) for Roosevelt–Truman. The limited effect of premodern presidents may be due to the rarity of their position taking. Premodern presidents took positions on only about 6% of roll calls, whereas Roosevelt and Truman took positions on 14%.[7]

LOPSIDED, ROLLS, AND CONTESTED ROLL CALLS

Chapter 4 distinguished three types of roll calls that are relevant for understanding presidential influence: lopsided votes, rolls, and contested votes. Lopsided votes were defined as those with 80% or more on the winning side. Rolls are when 80% or more members voted against the president. Contested votes are those with less than 80% on the winning side. Lopsided votes and rolls do not provide good tests of presidential influence— even if the president could shift a large number of members, the president would be unlikely to move enough to carry the day. By definition, rolls suggest that the president lacks influence, since large majorities, including many co-partisans, opposed the president. Influence is most interesting, theoretically, when it provides the winning margin, that is, when the president's side would have lost had the president not taken a position.

During the premodern and early modern eras, lopsided votes are not uncommon, but they are less common than for the 1953 to 2012 era. From the 45th through 82nd Congresses, and for each subperiod, about 26% of roll calls are lopsided.[8] Across the entire period, 15% (113) of presidential positions were taken on hurrah votes. For the premodern presidents, the figure is seventy (15%), while Roosevelt and Truman took hurrah positions on forty-three (15%). These presidents are sometimes rolled—on forty-eight votes (6.6% of presidential positions) across the entire period, with premodern presidents rolled on thirty-one (6.8%) and Roosevelt and Truman rolled on seventeen (6.1%) of their positions.

Table 10.3 reports the results of the effect of position taking on contested votes. Across all Congresses, presidents are marginally influential, with a coefficient of 0.03 ($p = 0.05$, one-tailed), about half the magnitude of considering all roll calls. This 0.03 effect equals about thirteen additional votes, which is not many but is enough to carry the day on very closely contested votes. The premodern (pre-Roosevelt) presidents do not appear to be influential at all, with a coefficient of −0.01 ($p = 0.70$). In contrast, Roosevelt

TABLE 10.3 IMPACT OF PRESIDENTIAL POSITION TAKING ON
MEMBER VOTING, ROLL CALL LEVEL, EXCLUDING LOPSIDED
VOTES, 45TH TO 82ND CONGRESSES

VARIABLE	(1) 45TH–82ND CONGRESSES	(2) 45TH–72ND CONGRESSES	(3) 73RD–82ND CONGRESSES
Presidential position	0.03	–0.01	0.06**
	(0.02)	(0.02)	(0.02)
Constant	0.50***	0.48***	0.53***
	(0.01)	(0.01)	(0.02)
Observations	6,612	5,220	1,392
R^2	0.00	0.00	0.02
Adjusted R^2	0.004	0.00	0.02
df	1	1	1
F	2.83	0.16	7.37
rss	130.8	97.25	30.43
Log likelihood	3,587	2,989	685.8

Robust standard errors in parentheses. Clustered on Congress. Dependent variable is the percentage of liberal votes on a roll call. Presidential position: 1 = Liberal position; 0 = No position; -1 = Conservative position. Lopsided votes defined as those with 80% or more on the winning side. $^*p < 0.1$, $^{**}p < 0.05$, $^{***}p < 0.01$.

and Truman appear to be about as influential on contested as on all votes, with a coefficient of 0.06 ($p = 0.01$, one tailed). A coefficient of this magnitude produces about twenty-six additional votes, enough to win on a large number of contested roll calls. Furthermore, the effects for Roosevelt and Truman are in line with historical accounts of these presidents and with the modern presidency thesis that these presidents, like the moderns to follow, are somewhat influential in Congress.

Overall, the presidents from 1877 to 1952 appear somewhat more influential than those serving from 1953 to 2012; chapter 4 reported a 1.5% to 2% position taking effect for the modern presidents on non-lopsided votes. The greater influence of the premodern presidents is surprising, given the comparatively vast institutional resources of the post-1953 presidents. The increased position taking of post-1953 presidents may account for their weaker influence compared to the pre-1953 presidents. Expectations of presidential involvement across a host of issues not only may dilute the influence resources at the president's disposal but also may lead post-1953 presidents to take many positions on which they would be unable to influence members. Political and representational factors may motivate presidential position taking during the post-1953 period (Cohen 1997), whereas premodern presidents may not feel these forces as strongly, allowing premodern presidents to be more selective in position taking. It is also important to note that most of the influence of pre-1953 presidents is associated with Franklin Roosevelt and Harry Truman, not with their predecessors. Still, we should not push this line of argument too far, as the regression results do not establish unambiguously the causal impact of presidential position taking on congressional voting. The next section turns to a treatment effects analysis, a superior technique for establishing causal effects with observational data.

A QUASI-EXPERIMENTAL TREATMENT ANALYSIS OF PREMODERN POSITION TAKING

If can be difficult to sort out causal effects on observational data such as is used here. Chapter 4 employed a quasi-experimental treatment effects approach, using inverse probability weights–regression adjustment (IPWRA) and augmented inverse probability weights (AIPW). That chapter details the reasons for using these estimations, which also are applicable to the pre-1953 data.

Both IPWRA and AIPW estimators employ two equations, one to predict the treatment and another for the outcome. The treatment equation is useful for correcting bias associated with nonrandom assignment of the treatment, in this case, position taking. The outcome equation can include covariates that also are hypothesized to affect the outcome—here, the percentage voting liberal. These covariates act as control variables, much as they would in multiple regression.

Chapter 4 employed a relatively rich set of variables to predict the outcome. First was a set of dummy variables: whether there was a Democratic majority in the House (= 1), whether the vote was on foreign policy (= 1), whether the president's party was the majority in the House (= 1), and whether the president was a Democrat (= 1). There also were two scaled variables: presidential approval during the month of the vote and party polarization in the House. The treatment equation in chapter 4 likewise employed two variables: the dummy variable for whether the president was a Democrat (= 1) and the scaled variable, the public mood. That analysis found significant effects of presidential position taking on member roll call votes.

Unfortunately, with regard to these historical data, we do not have as rich a set of variables to use for the outcome or treatment equations. Data are lacking for policy type (such as foreign versus domestic), presidential approval, and the public mood. The treatment effects analysis may not correct for bias as effectively in these pre-1953 roll calls as in votes from 1953 to 2012. The outcome equation for the 1877 to 1952 votes employs these covariates: a dummy variable for Democratic majority in the House (= 1), a dummy variable for majority party president (= 1), a dummy variable for Democratic president (= 1), and a scaled variable, party polarization in the House.[9] The treatment equation employs two variables: presidential party (Democrat = 1) and the percentage of presidential positions on roll calls per Congress. Presumably, presidents are more active when they think they possess enough influence to affect member voting (Cohen 2012).

Table 10.4, models 1 and 2, presents the results of the treatment effects analysis on non-lopsided votes. (Complete results are presented in table 10.8 in the appendix to this chapter.) The IPWRA and AIPW estimations produce highly similar results. Across the entire period, when a president takes a liberal position, the liberal roll call percentage increases by about 3% to 3.6% (statistically significant at $p < 0.05$ in both cases). In contrast, when presidents take a conservative position, they appear unable to influence member voting. The coefficients for both treatment estimations are close to zero (0.01) and fall short of statistical significance at the 0.05 level. These treatment effects analyses suggest much less presidential influence than is found using regression. But when presidents take a liberal position, there is a measurable and significant amount of influence over member voting, even if it is less than that observed in chapter 4 for presidents serving from 1953 to 2012.

That only liberal position taking leads to presidential influence hints that this finding may be due to Franklin Roosevelt and Truman, the early

TABLE 10.4 TREATMENT EFFECTS ANALYSIS OF PRESIDENTIAL POSITION TAKING ON ROLL CALL LIBERAL VOTING PERCENTAGE, NON-LOPSIDED VOTES, 45TH TO 82ND CONGRESSES

	MODEL (1)	MODEL (2)	MODEL (3)	MODEL (4)	MODEL (5)	MODEL (6)
Congress	45th–82nd	45th–82nd	45th–72nd	45th–72nd	73rd–82nd	73rd–82nd
Estimation	IPWRA	AIPW	IPWRA	AIPW	IPWRA	AIPW
Average Treatment Effect						
Liberal Position	0.036*	0.0340*	0.02	0.022	0.058***	0.058***
	(0.014)	(0.014)	(0.017)	(0.017)	(0.012)	(0.012)
Conservative Position	0.009	0.012	0.009	0.009	0.088***	0.086***
	(0.011)	(0.011)	(0.010)	(0.010)	(0.021)	(0.020)
Outcome Mean	0.49***	0.49***	0.48***	0.48***	0.53***	0.55***
	(0.002)	(0.002)	(0.002)	(0.002)	(0.004)	(0.004)
N	6,612	6,612	5,220	5,220	1,392	1,392

Note: Standard errors in parentheses. House polarization defined as the absolute difference in the mean Democratic and Republican DW-NOMINATE first dimension score. AIPW = augmented inverse probability weights; IPWRA = inverse probability weights–regression adjustment.

$*p < 0.05$, $**p < 0.01$, $***p < 0.001$.

modern presidents, who took more positions than the premodern executives. Table 10.4, models 3 and 4, presents results of the treatment effects analysis on the premodern presidents serving from the 45th through 72nd Congresses (presidents prior to Roosevelt). Because House polarization was not a significant predictor of presidential position taking during this period, the analysis drops that variable from the treatment equation.[10] The premodern presidents lack influence over member voting. Whether the president is taking a liberal or a conservative position, the resulting coefficients fall far short of statistical significance. This finding confirms, using regression, premodern presidents' lack of influence.

Next, a treatment effects analysis is performed on Roosevelt and Truman. Because both are Democrats, we have to drop the presidential party variable. Similarly, Democratic Party control of the House is collinear with divided government, as the Republicans held the House only once during these terms, during the 79th Congress. Table 10.4, models 5 and 6, presents the results. When Roosevelt or Truman takes a liberal position, the percentage of members voting liberal increases by about 6%, which is both statistically and substantively significant.

One advantage of the treatment effects analysis is that we can decompose presidential influence effects depending on whether the president takes a liberal or a conservative position. When Roosevelt or Truman takes a conservative position, results suggest negative influence: the percentage voting liberal is higher than when they take a liberal position or when they do not take a position. The coefficient is nearly 0.08, statistically significant, about 2% higher than when they take liberal positions. Yet Roosevelt and Truman rarely take conservative positions—only on about 11% of their total positions.

To summarize, the treatment effects analysis confirms the findings of the regression analysis from the previous section. Overall, the pre-1953 presidents appear able to influence members' voting, but only when they take a liberal position. Presidents from 1877 to 1932, however, appear to have little to no influence in Congress on contested votes, the same result as in the regression analysis. In contrast, Roosevelt and Truman appear able to influence members, but only when they take a liberal position. Conservative position taking by these two presidents leads to recoil effect, in which members are more likely to vote against the president.

PARTY DIFFERENCES IN PRESIDENTIAL INFLUENCE

Chapter 5 found that presidential influence was almost completely restricted to co-partisans. Position taking appeared to have no effect on opposition member voting during the post-1953 period. Such a finding has important implications, not only for understanding the nature of presidential influence but also for presidential impact on legislative outcomes. When the president faces an opposition-controlled Congress, even if the president can rally his co-partisans, there may not be enough co-partisans to lead to a victory. Do similar patterns hold for premodern, pre-1953 presidents?

Table 10.5 presents results of position taking of pre-1953 presidents by member party. When we look at all presidents from 1877 to 1953 (models 1 and 2), presidents appear to strongly influence the voting of co-partisans, but opposition members oppose the president with a coefficient of the same magnitude. The coefficient for co-partisans is 0.24, while that for opposition members is -0.24. Whether a president can rally enough members to his side to win is entirely a function of the size of the two parties.

For example, when the president's party controls the House with the slimmest of majorities, 218 seats, there is essentially no net benefit from position taking. Even when his party has a twenty-one-seat advantage (that is, 228 to 207), the net effect will only be five votes, barely enough to win on most close votes. With a comfortable seat margin of forty-one in the House (238 to 197), the net effect of position taking is a modest ten votes.

What about the effects of Roosevelt–Truman compared to the earlier presidents? Table 10.5, models 3 and 4, presents the findings for the premodern presidents (1877 to 1932). While those presidents appear to rally co-partisans to their side with a healthy 0.16 coefficient, opposition party members vote against the president even more strongly, with a coefficient of -0.20. Presidents thus require a large co-partisan majority to win. The break-even point between co-partisans gained and opposition members lost is a majority of forty-six seats (241 to 194); such large majorities rarely exist.

In contrast, Roosevelt and Truman fare much better with co-partisans than with the opposition, with coefficients of 0.06 for co-partisans and zero

TABLE 10.5 IMPACT OF PRESIDENTIAL POSITION TAKING ON ROLL CALL VOTING OF CO-PARTISANS AND OPPOSITION PARTY MEMBERS, 45TH TO 82ND CONGRESSES

VARIABLE	(1) SAME PARTY	(2) OPPOSITION PARTY	(3) SAME PARTY	(4) OPPOSITION PARTY	(5) SAME PARTY	(6) OPPOSITION PARTY
Congress	45th–82nd	45th–82nd	45th–72nd	45th–72nd	73rd–82nd	73rd–82nd
Presidential Position	0.24***	−0.24***	0.16***	−0.20***	0.06**	0.00
	(0.02)	(0.02)	(0.04)	(0.03)	(0.02)	(0.03)
Constant	0.42***	0.54***	0.34***	0.62***	0.74***	0.21***
	(0.05)	(0.05)	(0.06)	(0.06)	(0.01)	(0.02)
Observations	6,612	6,611	5,220	5,219	1,392	1,392
R^2	0.04	0.04	0.01	0.02	0.01	0.00
Adjusted R^2	0.04	0.04	0.01	0.02	0.01	−0.00
df_m	1	1	1	1	1	1
F	117.5	240.1	18.5	34.2	8.9	0.00
rss	809.9	821.3	595.9	597.7	51.85	58.83
Log likelihood	−2,440	−2,487	−1,743	−1,751	314.8	226.9

Note: Robust standard errors in parentheses. Clustered on Congress. Dependent variable is the percentage voting liberal on the roll call.

*$p < 0.1$, **$p < 0.05$, ***$p < 0.01$.

for the opposition. At bare majority control, or 218 seats, they can expect to pick up a net of thirteen seats. But both of the presidents generally held larger majorities. Their party was in the minority during only one Congress (Truman and the 80th Congress, 1948 to 1949). Otherwise, the smallest majority was for the 78th Congress, 1944 to 1945, when the Democrats held 222 seats to 209 seats for the Republicans, with four seats going to other parties. Assuming the four independents would vote with the opposition, Roosevelt and Truman could expect thirteen additional votes from taking a position. This may understate the impact of position taking during this Congress, since it occurred during the Second World War. For the other Congresses, Democratic majorities ranged from 234 to 333, comfortable margins that would result in a victory on most contested votes.

PRESIDENTS AND CONGRESSIONAL INFLUENCE FROM 1877 TO 2012

The previous section detailed the impact of position taking from 1877 to 1952 and thus did not directly test the modern presidency hypothesis, that modern presidents will be more influential than will premodern ones. It provided a hint of the effects of the modern presidency by comparing the early moderns, Roosevelt and Truman, with the premodern presidents from Hayes through Hoover.

This section pools all roll calls from 1877 to 2012, which allows a direct test of the modern presidency hypothesis. There are several issues of concern in performing this analysis. First, some of the variables important for understanding influence in the modern period (1953 to 2012), such as presidential approval and policy type, do not exist for prior years.[11] Second, there are many more roll calls from 1953 to 2012 than from 1877 to 1952. Statistically, the 1953 to 2012 roll calls could overwhelm the sparser number of earlier roll calls.[12] Thus, the analysis clusters by Congress, which helps to adjust for this problem, and it controls for unmeasured factors that vary from Congress to Congress and that may affect member roll call voting. To test the modern presidency hypothesis, as well as a Roosevelt–Truman sub-hypothesis, I interact position taking and two modern periods, the early modern (73rd to 82nd Congresses, 1932 to 1952) and the later modern (83rd to 112th Congresses, 1953 to 2012).

ARE MODERN PRESIDENTS MORE INFLUENTIAL THAN PREMODERN ONES?

Table 10.6 presents the results on four dependent variables: all members, all roll calls; all members, contested roll calls; same party, contested roll calls; and opposition party, contested roll calls. To test the modern presidency hypothesis and to distinguish the early modern from later modern presidents, there are two interaction terms, one between presidential position taking and the early moderns (1932 to 1952) and another between presidential position taking and the later moderns (1953 to 2012).

Turning to all roll calls (model 1), neither of the interactions between presidential positions and the two modern periods reaches statistical significance.[13] Since regression results may obscure interaction effects, table 10.7 presents results of the effect of position taking for each of the three periods. These results indicate modest position taking effects for all three periods, with slightly greater impact during the two modern periods than for premodern presidents. Premodern position taking is associated with a 3% increase in members voting with the president. Presidents of both the first and the second modern periods show a modest improvement in influence over that of premodern executives, another 3%, for a total impact of 6%.

But recall that using all roll calls may inflate presidential effects, due to the inclusion of lopsided votes. Model 2 therefore drops the lopsided votes, revealing dramatically different findings. Now premodern position taking appears to undercut presidential influence, with a *negative* 3% effect. It is puzzling that premodern presidents, who normally refrain from engaging in congressional policy making, have a negative impact when they take a position. This negative influence may indicate that premodern presidents actively participate in the congressional policy-making process on more contentious and hard-fought issues but lack the resources or reputation to influence members. I previously have shown that premodern success declines

TABLE 10.6 IMPACT OF THE MODERN PRESIDENCY ON INFLUENCE IN CONGRESS, 1877–2012

VARIABLE	(1) ALL MEMBERS, ALL ROLL CALLS	(2) ALL MEMBERS, CONTESTED ROLL CALLS	(3) SAME PARTY, CONTESTED ROLL CALLS	(4) OPPOSITION PARTY, CONTESTED ROLL CALLS
Presidential position	0.03	−0.04*	0.13***	−0.22***
	(0.02)	(0.02)	(0.03)	(0.03)
Modern 1 (73rd–82nd Congresses)	0.07***	0.07***	0.35***	−0.30***
	(0.02)	(0.02)	(0.05)	(0.05)
Interaction: Position × Modern 1	0.03	0.04	−0.09**	0.13***
	(0.04)	(0.03)	(0.04)	(0.03)
Modern 2 (83rd–112th Congresses)	0.12***	0.04*	0.12	−0.09
	(0.03)	(0.02)	(0.08)	(0.08)
Interaction: Position × Modern 2	0.02	0.05**	0.12***	0.01
	(0.03)	(0.02)	(0.04)	(0.03)
Constant	0.49***	0.49***	0.37***	0.60***
	(0.02)	(0.02)	(0.05)	(0.05)
Observations	35,878	25,306	25,292	25,271
R^2	0.03	0.01	0.12	0.09
df	5	5	5	5
F	8.270	2.672	115.7	96.96
rss	2,710	855.9	2,945	3,220
ll	−4,570	6,944	−8,695	−9,824

Note: Robust standard errors in parentheses. $*p < 0.1$, $**p < 0.05$, $***p < 0.01$.

as presidents are more active in submitting legislative proposals to Congress (Cohen 2012).

Both early and later modern presidents appear more influential than premodern presidents on contested roll calls, but they still are not very influential. Estimates from table 10.7 suggest that Roosevelt and Truman, while

TABLE 10.7 IMPACT OF PRESIDENTIAL POSITION TAKING FOR
THREE PRESIDENTIAL ERAS

ERA	ALL MEMBERS, ALL ROLL CALLS	ALL MEMBERS, CONTESTED ROLL CALLS	SAME PARTY, CONTESTED ROLL CALLS	OPPOSITION PARTY, CONTESTED ROLL CALLS
Premodern (1877–1932)	0.03	−0.03	0.13	−0.22
Modern 1 (1933–1952)	0.06	0.01	0.04	−0.10
Modern 2 (1953–2012)	0.06	0.02	0.25	−0.21

Note: Based on results from table 10.9.

being 4% more influential than premodern presidents, only move about four to five net members to their side through position taking. Presidents serving after Truman are not much more influential—the 2% effect translates into eight to nine additional votes.

Disaggregating by party shows that presidents positively influence co-partisans, as the large estimates on table 10.7 indicate. Opposition party members, however, recoil from the president; sometimes this effect is larger than the rally in support among co-partisans. Where premodern presidents see a 13% effect on co-partisans, opposition party members move away at a 22% rate. This difference is too large to overcome, except when the president's party possesses massive majorities, which is very rare in the premodern era. The imbalance in co-partisan/opposition response to position taking accounts for the net negative effect of premodern presidents.

Similarly, Roosevelt and Truman more strongly repel opposition members than they attract co-partisans, although the differential is not as large as for the premodern presidents (4%). Frequently during their tenures, Roosevelt and Truman benefited from immense majorities, which produced net advantages for them even though opposition members recoiled from the president more strongly than co-partisans rallied. From the 73rd through 75th Congresses, Roosevelt had House majorities of 313 or more. With 313 seats (73rd Congress), his 6% positive effect on co-partisans from position taking would elicit about nineteen additional votes. In contrast, even though the recoil effect on the opposition was 10%, with only 117 seats Roosevelt would only lose about twelve votes, for a net plus of seven (19 to 12). The break-even point, where presidential position taking generates additional seats among co-partisans equal to the loss among the opposition, is a lofty 270 seats.[14] But even when the Democrats held only 234 seats (the 82nd Congress), the net loss is only six votes. In contrast, the later modern presidents have a larger attraction effect on co-partisans than a recoil effect on the opposition, 25% compared to 21%, or about seventeen votes with an even split in seats between the two parties. Even with the narrowest of party majorities, therefore, the president's side will likely win the roll call.

CONCLUSION: THE MODERN PRESIDENCY AND INFLUENCE IN CONGRESS

According to the modern presidency thesis, by the late 1930s and over the course of the twentieth century, the presidency evolved from a limited and secondary office into one with energy and a policy-making leadership role. An implication of this evolution is that modern presidents will have more influence in policy-making venues, including but not limited to Congress, than did premodern executives. This chapter has tested this hypothesis.

Several types of analyses were used to test the modern presidency hypothesis, including regression and treatment effects. Results generally provided support for the modern presidency hypothesis, but the later modern presidents (1953 to 2012) appeared more influential than the early moderns, Franklin Roosevelt and Harry Truman, especially among co-partisans. Roosevelt especially benefited from massive Democratic majorities during most of the 1930s. But he did not have to influence very many co-partisans to win on roll calls, and his relative lack of influence compared to later presidents may be a function of the large majorities of like-minded representatives, who shared many of his policy orientations.

Although they are considered modern presidents, the institutional resources of the office were not as well developed for Roosevelt and Truman as for later presidents. I have found that the development of central clearance, only possible because of the institutional resources of the office, led to modern presidents seeing greater success than premodern presidents in the enactment of the president's legislative proposals (Cohen 2012). Although central clearance began during the Truman years, it was only institutionalized later. Thus, the increased presidential influence noted here and the legislative success noted in my earlier work have similar timing and are associated with the later modern presidents. The increased influence of later modern presidents may account for their greater success, suggesting another theoretical connection between influence and success.

Moreover, when comparing the influence of premodern and modern presidents, it is important to note that premodern presidents take many fewer roll call positions than do modern presidents, both in terms of total positions and as a percentage of all roll calls. Even if premodern presidents could move large numbers of members to their side, the fact that they took many fewer roll call positions also means that they would have less impact on the production of public policy, on the number of laws enacted.[15]

In several senses, then, there are important differences between premodern and modern presidents. Premodern presidents have less influence, even among co-partisans, when compared to late modern presidents, and they less frequently participate in the legislative policy-making process. Although premodern presidents can at times influence members and/or leave a stamp on policy, as the historical discussion in chapter 9 pointed out, they are less consequential for congressional policy making than are modern presidents, especially late-modern executives.

APPENDIX

Table 10.8 presents the complete results of the treatment effects analysis of presidential position taking for the 45th through 82nd Congresses (1877 to 1952).

TABLE 10.8 TREATMENT EFFECTS ANALYSIS OF PRESIDENTIAL POSITION TAKING ON ROLL CALL LIBERAL VOTING PERCENTAGE, NON-LOPSIDED VOTES, 45TH TO 82ND CONGRESSES

	MODEL (1)	MODEL (2)	MODEL (3)	MODEL (4)	MODEL (5)	MODEL (6)
Congress	45th–82nd	45th–82nd	45th–72nd	45th–72nd	73rd–82nd	73rd–82nd
Estimation	IPWRA	AIPW	IPWRA	AIPW	IPWRA	AIPW
Average Treatment Effect						
Liberal Position	0.0360*	0.0340*	0.0228	0.0217	0.0580***	0.0582***
	(0.0141)	(0.0143)	(0.0173)	(0.0174)	(0.0119)	(0.0119)
Conservative Position	0.00858	0.0117	0.00889	0.00889	0.0877***	0.0862***
	(0.0110)	(0.0112)	(0.0102)	(0.0102)	(0.0208)	(0.0197)
Outcome Mean	0.493***	0.493***	0.484***	0.484***	0.529***	0.529***
	(0.00179)	(0.00179)	(0.00194)	(0.00194)	(0.00428)	(0.00428)
Outcome: No Position						
Divided (=1)	0.0116*	0.0117*	0.0284***	0.0279***	-0.0366*	-0.0342
	(0.00473)	(0.00471)	(0.00531)	(0.00529)	(0.0177)	(0.0177)
House Polarization	-0.00549	0.000681	0.202***	0.209***	1.290***	1.314***
	(0.0147)	(0.0147)	(0.0309)	(0.0309)	(0.168)	(0.167)
Democratic House (=1)	0.0423***	0.0423***	0.0404***	0.0416***	—	—
	(0.00495)	(0.00494)	(0.00573)	(0.00571)	—	—
Democratic President (=1)	0.0170***	0.0162**	0.00750	0.00690	—	—
	(0.00499)	(0.00498)	(0.00536)	(0.00534)	—	—
Constant	0.462***	0.457***	0.297***	0.291***	0.00683	-0.00425
	(0.0120)	(0.0119)	(0.0248)	(0.0248)	(0.0689)	(0.0689)

(continued)

TABLE 10.8 TREATMENT EFFECTS ANALYSIS OF PRESIDENTIAL POSITION TAKING ON ROLL CALL LIBERAL VOTING PERCENTAGE, NON-LOPSIDED VOTES, 45TH TO 82ND CONGRESSES (CONTINUED)

	MODEL (1)	MODEL (2)	MODEL (3)	MODEL (4)	MODEL (5)	MODEL (6)
Outcome: Liberal						
Divided (=1)	−0.0796*	−0.0921**	−0.0706*	−0.0839*	0.0278	0.0206
	(0.0328)	(0.0324)	(0.0324)	(0.0337)	(0.0861)	(0.0857)
House	−0.0701	−0.172*	0.510	0.435	2.405***	2.268***
	(0.0845)	(0.0679)	(0.332)	(0.339)	(0.387)	(0.360)
Polarization	0.0508	0.0232	0.0934*	0.0610	—	—
	(0.0344)	(0.0339)	(0.0374)	(0.0420)		
Democratic House (=1)	−0.0355	−0.0381	−0.0699*	−0.0631	—	—
	(0.0358)	(0.0340)	(0.0323)	(0.0330)		
Democratic President (=1)	0.586***	0.678***	0.113	0.191	−0.393*	−0.336*
	(0.0730)	(0.0611)	(0.271)	(0.279)	(0.162)	(0.151)
Constant						
Outcome: Conservative						
Divided (=1)	0.0989***	0.0989***	0.125***	0.133***	−0.137**	−0.149*
	(0.0258)	(0.0261)	(0.0290)	(0.0267)	(0.0465)	(0.0585)
House	0.0690	−0.0163	−0.00795	−0.0938	3.638***	3.447***
	(0.104)	(0.0937)	(0.128)	(0.119)	(0.751)	(0.882)
Polarization	0.0765**	0.0741**	0.0468	0.0393	—	—
	(0.0275)	(0.0269)	(0.0311)	(0.0275)		
Democratic House (=1)	0.0401	0.0420	0.0477	0.0492	—	—
	(0.0257)	(0.0247)	(0.0291)	(0.0265)		
Democratic President (=1)						

Constant	0.365*** (0.0817)	0.439*** (0.0744)	0.421*** (0.103)	0.498*** (0.0953)	-0.853** (0.301)	-0.771* (0.364)
Treatment: Liberal						
Democratic	1.308*** (0.164)	1.308*** (0.164)	1.038*** (0.188)	1.038*** (0.188)	—	—
President (= 1)					—	—
President (%)	0.107*** (0.0102)	0.107*** (0.0102)	0.0919*** (0.0278)	0.0919*** (0.0278)	0.0619*** (0.0157)	0.0619*** (0.0157)
Positions						
Constant	-4.908*** (0.160)	-4.908*** (0.160)	-4.790*** (0.246)	-4.790*** (0.246)	-2.743*** (0.264)	-2.743*** (0.264)
Treatment: Conservative						
Democratic	-1.088*** (0.195)	-1.088*** (0.195)	-0.518** (0.165)	-0.518** (0.165)	—	—
President (= 1)					—	—
President (%)	0.0766*** (0.0153)	0.0766*** (0.0153)	0.139*** (0.0170)	0.139*** (0.0170)	0.100 (0.0638)	0.100 (0.0638)
Positions						
Constant	-3.436*** (0.120)	-3.436*** (0.120)	-3.892*** (0.150)	-3.892*** (0.150)	-5.686*** (1.117)	-5.686*** (1.117)
N	6,612	6,612	5,220	5,220	1,392	1,392

Note: Standard errors in parentheses. House polarization defined as the absolute difference in the mean Democratic and Republican DW-NOMINATE first dimension score. AIPW = augmented inverse probability weights; IPWRA = inverse probability weights–regression adjustment.

*p < 0.05, **p < 0.01, ***p < 0.001

11
CONCLUSIONS

Presidential Influence in Congress

THERE ARE SEVERAL competing viewpoints on presidential influence in Congress. Some argue that presidents do not have much influence and that we should be more concerned with understanding presidential success than presidential influence (e.g., Bond and Fleisher 1990; Edwards 1990). Others contend that presidents can be highly influential in Congress, a perspective often found in the popular press, among voters, in American politics textbooks, and among scholars subscribing to the heroic conception (Bailey 2002; Roper 2004; Vaughn and Mercieca 2014.).[1] As Charles O. Jones (2000, xiv–xv) says, "Journalists, bureau chiefs, editors, political activists and reformers, Washington insiders, even presidents and their staffs" cling to the notion that policy making and power in Washington is presidency-centered, by which he means that presidents are extraordinarily powerful, that politics and policy making revolves around the president, and that little can get done without presidential involvement. A third perspective views influence as a personal characteristic of a president. Thus, presidents vary in their ability to influence Congress, depending upon their personality, background, and other individual characteristics. Some presidents establish reputations for being highly skilled in legislative affairs, such as Lyndon Johnson and Ronald Reagan (see Wayne 2009).

The present study rehabilitates the idea of presidential influence in Congress. Instead of viewing influence as derived from personal characteristics, this study conceptualizes presidential influence in institutional terms. The major finding here is that presidents have a measurable amount of influence. Although presidents do not possess enough influence to dominate Congress, to force the legislature to accede to their every demand, they do possess enough influence to win on a significant number of roll calls that the president's side would otherwise lose. By winning on more roll calls because of this influence, presidents can affect the public policies produced through the legislative process.

This study conducted several types of analyses to estimate the amount of presidential influence. Since it can be hard to isolate causal effects with observational data, this research paired regression with quasi-experimental treatment effects analyses. The treatment effects analysis for the years 1953 to 2012 suggests that when the president takes a roll call position, the president's side will win an additional 9% of House floor votes, or about five out of the fifty-four roll call positions that presidents take, on average, annually. Although five additional victories may not sound like much, if it leads to five major policy enactments, it may be consequential for the lives of citizens.[2]

Moreover, five additional pieces of legislation add up over the years—in a four-year term, there might be twenty additional enactments. From another perspective, Ansolabehere, Palmer, and Schneer (2016, 2018) estimate that there are eight or nine major legislative enactments per Congress from 1789 to 2010 and about seventeen from 1953 to 2010. The estimated five additional pieces of legislation presidents receive from position taking is nearly 30% of major enactments in the late modern period, assuming all the additional presidential wins are on major legislation. Through position taking, presidents can have consequential impacts on the nation's policies.

As conceptualized here, presidential influence is rooted in the office and in the surrounding political environment, termed "institutional presidential influence." There is some similarity between this conceptualization of influence and studies that emphasize the importance of contextual and political factors for presidential success (Bond and Fleisher 1990; Edwards 1990). But presidents still must decide whether to apply those institutional and contextual levers of influence; they need to be strategic decision makers, too. Hence, presidential influence is not merely a matter of dumb luck

(Rockman 1981). Some presidents may be luckier than others, in that the office and the political environment provide them with greater resources, such as party control, upon which they can draw. But presidents still decide whether, when, how, and with whom they will exert effort, and how much, when trying to influence Congress.

This perspective asserts that presidents have agency, in the sense of being able to influence his or her environment and/or the behaviors of others, such as the voting behavior of members of Congress (Bandura 2000), or what Jacobs and King (2010) call "structured agency." If presidents have no influence with Congress, if what they do or do not do has no implications for how members vote, then presidents are not very interesting to study, at least with regard to the legislative process. If presidents are mere pawns of the situation at hand, then it does not matter whether they take a position on a roll call or not. Their actions will not affect how members vote and will not have consequences for the output of the congressional policy-making process. If this is the case, if presidents are so powerless or lack in influence with Congress, then why study them?[3]

Moreover, exclusively studying presidential success in Congress, as is the case for much research, ignores the possibility that presidents may have some influence. But whether presidents have enough influence to affect roll call voting and the policies that Congress produces is an empirical question. This study empirically assessed whether presidents have enough influence to affect member roll call voting, whether they have enough influence to convert an expected defeat into a victory, and whether they win on enough roll calls to have consequences for the nation's public policies.

Presidential influence appears to meet these standards of changing the votes of enough members to affect the outcome of enough votes to affect the nation's policies. Yet the amount of presidential influence is not constant over time or in various contexts. It rises and falls with aspects of the political context, the historical epoch, the nature of the vote, and the president's lobbying effort. Presidential influence is consequential enough to be reincorporated into studies of presidential–congressional relations, but doing so requires redefining influence and revamping study designs aimed at estimating the amount of influence the president has with Congress, a redefinition and revamping I offer here.

THE DEFINITION AND MECHANISMS OF
PRESIDENTIAL INFLUENCE

I have explicitly defined presidential influence to make it clear how it is being used in the present study. "Influence" and related concepts such as "power" are often used loosely and are not always clearly defined. I begin with Dahl's (1957) seminal definition of "power," which he at times uses interchangeably with "influence." Dahl's definition is implicit in much work on presidential power and influence, such as in Neustadt (1960, 1991). Power or influence exists when X acts on Y to do something Y would otherwise not do. This study of presidential influence falls squarely into the behavioral tradition of power and influence studies.[4] This is admittedly a narrow orientation toward presidential influence, but it has the virtue of being empirically tractable. Empirical tractability is important for estimating how much influence presidents have and thus for engaging debates within the literature over the nature and amount of presidential influence.

From this behavioral perspective, influence is relational and requires an action on the president's part to enable us to observe whether the president influenced anyone. Additionally, presidents are assumed to be rational and purposive when they are trying to influence members of Congress. Past research has underestimated the amount of potential presidential influence because it looks only at roll calls on which the president has already taken a position. Such designs overlook the influence that presidents acquire from position taking itself. To assess accurately the amount of influence presidents have requires estimating the amount of influence at two stages: when the president decides to take a position and, once a position is taken, when the president deploys resources targeted at specific members and in particular ways.

This perspective suggests that the distinction between Congress-centered and presidency-centered factors is not so clear. By taking a position, presidents may activate Congress-centered and other contextual factors. Rather than categorizing factors that affect congressional voting as either Congress- or presidency-centered, it might be better to think of a continuum from purely Congress-centered factors to purely presidency-centered factors. Depending on the context and on presidential behavior, many factors may be a mixture of Congress- and presidency-centered.

The theory proposed here contends that, often, when a president takes a position, the president is trying to influence the voting behavior of members of Congress. But sometimes other goals, such as representing voters and their parties, among other motivations, are more important than influencing Congress. If the president does not take a position on how to vote on a roll call, the president will not factor heavily into the members' voting calculus. Once the president takes a position, however, members begin to weigh the president more heavily into their roll call decision process.

Presidential position taking can influence members either indirectly or directly. The indirect pathway suggests that position taking tightens the linkage between the president and those factors or elements of the political context/environment that may affect member voting. Party is often a strong influence on member voting. When the president takes a position, the president's position also becomes the party's position on the roll call. Partisan forces on member voting may intensify when the president takes a position, which usually leads to greater party polarization on presidential than on nonpresidential roll calls. In this sense, partisanship, conventionally considered a Congress-centered factor, is also presidency-centered, at least to some degree. Once a president takes a position, it is best to think of party as a mixed Congress- and presidency-centered factor. This indirect process also applies to other factors that influence member voting, such as constituent opinion and policy type. The indirect pathway of associating or linking a factor with the president because of position taking forces us to reconceptualize how we think about presidential influence.

Presidents also can influence congressional voting directly, through their active lobbying. Active lobbying, beyond merely announcing a position, requires that the president formulate a lobbying strategy. A presidential lobbying strategy involves deciding which members to target, what tactics or lobbying modes to employ, and how much effort to expend. To some degree, presidents are reactive in developing their lobbying strategies. As a rational actor with finite lobbying resources, presidents want to minimize the lobbying resources they consume on a particular bill. Presidents need not exert very much effort when facing a weak opposition. However, they may need to increase their effort level when confronting a stronger opposition, to avoid an embarrassing legislative defeat, for instance. In this sense of taking into account the opposition, presidential lobbying strategies are reactive.

This theory leads us away from the dumb luck or determinist explanations of presidential–congressional relations, with presidents viewed as mere hostages or captives of the larger environment. Although presidents may not be able to reshape the political environment very much, at least in the short run, they can use or leverage that environment to their advantage and, in that process, influence congressional voting behavior.

The theory developed here also steers us away from personal-based accounts to a more institutionally based understanding of presidential influence. An institutionally based theory of influence focuses on the advantages that accrue to the president from the office itself, its location in the governmental and policy-making processes, the linkages of the office to the larger political environment, and the strategic decisions that presidents make to exploit those resources.

It is one thing to say that presidents can do nothing to further their ends, that all that matters is the contextual hand dealt to them. It is quite another thing to say that presidents make decisions within that context, that context affects their decisions about position taking and lobbying strategies. The theoretical perspective developed here leads to the finding that presidents have a measurable and consequential, if not determinative, amount of influence, and that they have more influence than dumb luck, context-only based theories contend. Presidential influence matters for member roll call voting and for the production of public policies.

SUMMARY OF MAJOR FINDINGS

Presidential influence through position taking varies across members and conditions. Much of the empirical analysis in this book details the varying impact of position taking. Using existing research, three classes of factors that could mediate the effect of presidential position taking were identified:

partisanship, issue type, and public opinion. The empirical analysis also looked at the effect of presidential lobbying effort on influence, integrating several prominent theoretical perspectives. Finally, this research looked at the impact of the evolution of the office, from the traditional to the modern presidency, on influence in Congress, arguing that the modern presidency orientation is at least implicitly about the rise in presidential influence.

When a president takes a position on an issue, not only is that issue converted into a presidential issue but also certain aspects of the political and policy context become more closely associated with the president's position. Through the process of association, the indirect pathway, these contextual factors are mobilized to the advantage or disadvantage of the president, depending upon the alignment of that contextual factor.

For instance, party becomes more closely associated with the president when he takes a position on an issue. There are two dimensions to partisanship: party control of the chamber and a member's partisan affiliation. Presidents are more influential when their party controls the House and among co-partisans. The effects of partisanship as an indirect pathway of presidential influence are often quite stunning. For instance, presidents win an additional 30% of roll calls when their party is in the majority. Such a large increase in floor victories can have substantial consequences for public policy.

The analysis also suggests that position taking has asymmetric effects on members of the two parties. Theoretically, it is plausible that position taking could rally co-partisans by heightening their sense of party loyalty and/or shared fate with the president, while at the same time repelling opposition members for similar reasons. Results here suggest a one-sided process in which co-partisans unite behind the president, but there is little reaction among opposition members to presidential position taking. Thus, as Frances Lee (2008, 2009) first noted, presidential position taking polarizes voting in Congress, increasing the spread between the parties on roll calls, but that polarization effect is primarily a function of co-partisan movement in support of the president.

A large number of studies have asked whether presidents are more influential (and successful) on some types of issues than on others, particularly on foreign versus domestic issues—the two presidencies thesis. Overall, results here suggest that presidents are not more influential on foreign than on domestic policy, which is contrary to much of the two presidencies research. The lack of difference in presidential influence on foreign and domestic roll calls is a function of two countervailing processes. First, presidents appear to have more influence on domestic than on foreign issues among co-partisans. At the same time, presidents appear to have more influence on foreign than on domestic issues among opposition members, the reverse of what was found for co-partisans. The combination of these two processes accounts for the finding of little difference in presidential influence on foreign and on domestic issues and may help resolve some of the debate in the literature over the two presidencies effect. Ironically, support from opposition members on foreign policy votes often provides the margin of victory for the president on that issue area. This analysis also reinforces a theme found in much research on American politics, that domestic issues divide the parties more than foreign policy debates.

Still, bipartisanship on foreign policy has broken down in recent decades. This analysis provides some support for the notion that the parties have become increasingly divided on foreign policy issues over the past few decades, which has implications for presidential influence. As foreign policy has increasingly divided the parties, presidential influence on foreign policy has also waned, compared to the days of bipartisan consensus. The finding that presidents could influence the voting of opposition members on foreign but not on domestic votes provides an account for this decline in foreign policy influence. As partisan patterns of voting on foreign policy resemble those on domestic policy, presidents are less able to influence opposition member voting on foreign policy.

Few questions have animated as much research as the question of whether public opinion is a resource that presidents can use to influence member voting. Where most research on public opinion as a presidential resource in Congress focuses on approval, the present study opened up a new question, about whether issue salience could also be thought of as a presidential resource. Both approval and salience affect presidential influence; presidents are more influential when they are popular and when issue salience is higher. Plus, approval and salience have greater effects on presidential co-partisans than on opposition members. But salience appears to have stronger and more substantively meaningful effects than does approval. These findings with regard to salience should open up a host of new questions about public opinion and presidential influence (and success) in Congress.

One reason why salience has stronger effects on member voting than does approval may have to do with measurement. Approval has the same value across all roll calls during the same period of time, whether it is the month, the year, and so on. Issue salience, in contrast, is a characteristic of the specific roll call. One reason for stronger salience than approval effects may have to do with the ability to measure salience for each roll call. Rarely do studies of presidential support or success look at characteristics of the roll call vote in question. This suggests that, as there are now numerous polls gauging presidential approval on specific policies, it might be useful to test whether policy-specific approval has a stronger impact on member voting than does overall approval.[5]

Lobbying strategies also may affect the amount of presidential influence in Congress. There is considerable debate over the effects of presidential lobbying of Congress. As the review in chapter 8 showed, some contend that presidential lobbying will have no more than marginal effects (Edwards 1980, 1990). Others suggest an investment notion, in which greater presidential lobbying effort will have a positive impact on legislative voting (Canes-Wrone 2006; Beckmann 2010). Still others suggest a negative effect of increased lobbying effort, as presidents work harder when the opposition is stronger (Cameron and Park 2011). These varying perspectives can be integrated into a more general understanding of the effects of lobbying, a curvilinear relationship. At low to medium levels of effort, presidential lobbying will have a positive effect on roll call voting, but as effort rises to high levels, the effect of lobbying will decline, eventually turning negative. This is because presidents only lobby hard when they have to—when the opposition is strong.

The amount of attention presidents give to a policy area in the State of the Union Address is offered as an indirect measure of lobbying effort. Empirical results find support for the curvilinear model of lobbying effort, although lobbying, even when most effective, does not appear to rally many votes, at most thirteen to fifteen. But lobbying appears to operate differently

on members of the two parties. Co-partisans always respond to greater lobbying effort with higher support for the president. Opposition members,
however, respond in curvilinear fashion to lobbying effort. At low to
medium effort levels, they display increased support for the president, but
as lobbying effort rises, they pull away from the president. This curvilinear
pattern probably reflects the nature and mobilization of those who oppose
the president's position on the issue. Opposition members are freer to support the president when those who oppose the president are weak and not
mobilized. But as presidential opponents become stronger, so do the forces
acting to distance opposition members from the president. These results are
important because they demonstrate the influence that presidents derive
from actively engaging the policy-making process—presidential lobbying
activities have some influence over members, but the influence derived from
active engagement is conditional on presidential opponents.

The final set of empirical results tests the modern presidency thesis—
that modern presidents will be more influential in Congress than premodern executives. Although this hypothesis is rarely stated so explicitly, it is
implied in much of the relevant literature. The general thrust of the results
is that traditional-era presidents (1877 to 1932) have only limited influence
on member voting. This, coupled with the relative rarity of their position
taking, implies that traditional presidents have limited impact on policy
production. Franklin Roosevelt and Harry Truman, the early modern presidents, do not appear as influential as the later moderns to follow, perhaps
because the resources associated with the modern presidency had not yet
been institutionalized.

LIMITATIONS OF THIS STUDY AND DIRECTIONS
FOR FUTURE RESEARCH

No single study can say everything there is to say about a question, and no
study design is without compromises or limitations. This study is no different. Progress in (social) science is based in part on explicitly recognizing
those limitations and making realistic recommendations about how to

address them. This section reviews several of the most important limitations of this study, and while I call for refinement and more research on these issues, I am not always able to suggest improvements.

METHODOLOGICAL ISSUES IN MEASURING PRESIDENTIAL INFLUENCE

Perhaps the most fundamental limitation of this study relates to the identification and measurement of presidential influence. First, influence is defined behaviorally, relying heavily on Robert Dahl's (1957) seminal definition. Members have to change their voting behavior in response to a presidential action for us to observe influence. There is a great deal of literature on the meaning and nature of influence and power, which I will not delve into here, other than to suggest the pertinence of other definitions to understanding presidential influence. The definition of power as agenda control may be especially useful in this regard. Presidents may derive much influence over Congress through their ability to shape the congressional agenda, such as by limiting what members get to vote on (e.g., Beckmann 2010) or by directing legislative energies to some topics over others (Lovett, Bevan, and Baumgartner 2015). This study was not designed to address the question of how much of the influence found here is due to the president's ability to affect the congressional agenda.

The specific methodology used here compares member voting on nonpresidential and on presidential roll calls. This method is an empirical compromise. Ideally, one would like to know how a member would vote on a bill prior to the president taking a position on it. Such data are hard, if not impossible, to come by. Members may not have even decided how to vote on a bill until the president takes a position on it. Presidential position taking, in some instances, elevates the priority of an issue, leading members to spend some time considering how they will vote. Some issues may not register on a member's agenda until the president weighs in. It may not be possible to discuss a member's *expected vote* on an issue until the president has entered the policy debate. This is one illustration of the influence the president acquires through his ability to alter the congressional agenda, to focus attention on issues.

Consequently, the method here compares member voting on presidential and on nonpresidential roll calls, suggesting that the difference between voting patterns on these two types of roll calls may be attributed in part to the president's influence, what is termed "potential presidential influence." But there are complications in comparing member voting on presidential and on nonpresidential roll calls for estimating influence. Most importantly, presidential roll calls are not a random subset of all roll calls; there are systematic differences between presidential and nonpresidential roll calls.

These systematic differences include, but are not limited to, the mix of policies, salience, presidential motivations to take positions on some types of issues over others, and the transformative effects of presidential position taking. For example, presidents are more likely to take positions on foreign policy than on other types of roll calls, perhaps because of the special responsibilities of the office. Presidents, too, may be more likely to take positions on salient issues, where they feel political pressures to become involved. When an issue is highly salient to the public, modern presidents may have a difficult time staying on the sidelines.[6] By taking a position, the president transforms the issue in several possible ways. The issue gets redefined, turning it into a presidential issue, whereas before it was a nonpresidential issue. This transformation may raise the salience of the issue to voters, the mass media, the political parties, and members and may affect the implications of the issue for member career and reelection prospects. Moreover, at least in the modern era, presidents appear compelled to weigh in on issues that are already salient to voters (Cohen 1999; Hill 1998). Thus, it may be the case that presidential roll calls are more salient on average than nonpresidential roll calls. For these and other reasons, one cannot simply compare member voting on presidential and on nonpresidential roll calls to estimate presidential influence. Presidential and nonpresidential roll calls differ systematically.

How, then, can we increase the comparability of presidential and nonpresidential roll calls to accurately estimate the amount of voting difference that is due to the president? This study employed several methods. Our confidence that we have estimated presidential influence with some degree of accuracy will be bolstered if differing methods lead to similar conclusions. This study employed two types of methods: regression with controls and quasi-experimental treatment effects. The regression analysis dropped sets of roll calls and controlled for variables that may differentiate presidential from nonpresidential roll calls. Lopsided votes were eliminated from much analysis because they are theoretically uninteresting from a presidential influence perspective. The regression analysis also employed statistical controls such as policy type (for instance, foreign versus domestic policy).

Another approach utilized quasi-experimental treatment effects techniques to compare voting patterns on nonpresidential and on presidential roll calls. This approach aims to simulate randomized experimental designs on observational data, arguing that randomized experiments provide one of the strongest methods for isolating the causal impact of a treatment. Both approaches, regression and quasi-experimental, suggest some degree of presidential influence, with the treatment effects analysis indicating somewhat greater effects than regression using only contested roll calls.

There are other possible approaches for estimating presidential influence on these two types of votes. One approach would look at influence by issue type. To some degree, this was done when testing the two presidencies thesis that presidents have more influence on foreign than on domestic policy. But the point being made now is somewhat different. *Within* issue areas, can presidents influence member voting? On foreign policy issues (or on macroeconomic issues, civil rights, and so on), do we observe shifts in member voting between nonpresidential and presidential roll calls? The point is not that one approach is superior to another for estimating presidential influence; each has its own strengths and weaknesses. Instead, various methods should be employed; a multimethod or mixed method approach may be superior, especially when dealing with complex data and processes (Brewer and Hunter 1989).

ENDOGENEITY BETWEEN POSITION TAKING AND ROLL CALL OUTCOMES

A related concern is the endogeneity between the presidential decision to take a position and the outcome of the roll call. As we have noted, presidents are more likely to take positions on foreign policy than on domestic policy and on more salient rather than less salient issues. But, to some degree, presidents also anticipate the consequences of taking a roll call position. Such anticipations of future consequences may affect whether they take a position or not. For instance, presidents may be concerned with the policy implications of taking a position, as Canes-Wrone (2006) argues, and they may be less inclined to take positions on issues if the odds of being on the losing side is high, as I (Cohen 2012) and Marshall and Prins (2007) argue.

When trying to estimate how much influence presidents have in Congress, and when they have influence, we have to do a better job of taking into account the endogeneity between position taking and the outcome of a roll call. Very little existing research consciously deals with this endogeneity issue (but see Canes-Wrone 2006; Howell, Jackman, and Rogowski 2013; Howell and Rogowski 2013). Chapter 8 tried, to a limited degree, to incorporate factors relevant to this endogeneity concern.[7]

Future research needs integrate the position-taking decision into studies of presidential influence. When we have a better handle on why presidents take positions, we will better understand presidential influence and how presidential motivations to take a position may affect their influence. It may be that presidential influence varies with the motivation to take a roll call position. For instance, presidents may be less influential when they feel compelled by public pressures and expectations to take a position. Strong public pressures may override presidential sensitivity or concern with the congressional environment. Similarly, presidents may be less influential when personal beliefs or ideological orientations drive them to take a position, perhaps because such beliefs limit how much the president is willing to bargain with members. These are just a few examples of, or hypotheses about, the implications of the possibility that motivations for position taking may affect the president's influence in the legislative policy-making process.

WHAT IS PRESIDENTIAL LOBBYING OF CONGRESS?

Another issue that this study raises concerns presidential lobbying of Congress. The study viewed position taking as a generic form of presidential lobbying and did not differentiate the many forms that such lobbying may take, from going public to veto threats, offering inducements, contacting members, trading votes across roll calls, and so forth. There are several issues in trying to study the effectiveness of presidential lobbying efforts. First, presidents have a multitude of direct lobbying forms or modes that they can use. The sheer number of lobbying modes makes data collection a daunting task. Perhaps more important, much presidential lobbying is not recorded and occurs out of public view.

The inability to collect systematic data on presidential lobbying has implications for estimating the effectiveness of those lobbying efforts. For instance, we may attribute effectiveness to a tactic for which we can collect systematic data, such as going public, when an unmeasured tactic was the truly effective lobbying mode. In other words, omitted variable bias may exist when we are unable to collect data on a particular lobbying tactic or mode.

Second, rather than looking at the effectiveness of individual tactics, we should be thinking of effectiveness at the strategic level. Presidents construct lobbying strategies, which involve deciding which members to target with their lobbying efforts, which tactics or modes to use on which (sub)set of members, and how much effort to exert across each mode and member. Presidential lobbying strategies are complex and are likely to vary greatly across roll calls. Thus far, research generally has approached presidential lobbying of Congress in a piecemeal fashion.[8]

For these reasons, this study looked at a generic form of presidential lobbying, position taking, and measured lobbying effort by the priority presidents give an issue in their State of the Union Addresses. The justification for this indirect measure of effort is the assumption that presidents will work harder, will exert more effort, on issues of higher rather than lesser priority. Still, this is a crude indicator of lobbying effort.

It is possible to test the assumption that issue priority in the State of the Union Address signals how much lobbying effort presidents are willing to, and do, expend. For instance, do presidents go public (and go public more frequently) on high-priority issues? Are they more inclined to issue veto threats on high- rather than lower-priority issues? There should be a relationship between the priority of an issue for the president and lobbying effort.

This discussion does not exhaust what we would like to know about the effectiveness of presidential lobbying of Congress. Another important dimension is the president's willingness to compromise or to bargain with members versus being resolute. As with other aspects of presidential lobbying, it is difficult to measure presidential resoluteness on an issue. In a recent paper, Rogowski (2017) suggests one approach based on presidential use of unilateral policy devices such as executive orders. His argument is that when presidents issue executive orders and the like, they are signaling their resoluteness to Congress; the more they use unilateral devices, the less likely it is that they will be willing to compromise with Congress. Such resolve may signal, especially for opposition party members, presidential unwillingness to bargain or compromise, and thus we can expect legislative negotiations over policy to break down when the opposition controls Congress. In an imaginative test using budgetary data from 1947 to 2003, Rogowski finds support for his hypothesis, as budget allocations are closer to the president's request when his party controls Congress than when Congress is under opposition control.

Finally, it may be useful to think of presidents as sometimes policy-motivated actors. They have at their disposal two routes for the realization of their policy goals: legislative, as reflected in the present study, and unilateral, or what Belco and Rottinghaus (2017) term the "dual executive." Some existing research suggests that presidents turn to unilateral approaches for policy making when prospects for legislative success appear dim (Belco and Rottinghaus 2017; Howell 2003).[9] Rogowski's (2017) paper suggests that the connections between unilateral and legislative modes for making policy are more complex than the simple trade-off models found in most of the literature. Despite the progress on the question of presidential lobbying of Congress, there still are many unanswered questions, leaving a rich agenda for future research.

EXTENSIONS TO OTHER SETTINGS

Compared to other research on presidential–congressional relations, this study employed a longer span of data. Where the bulk of previous research uses only data since 1953, when *Congressional Quarterly* started its important data collection, this study extended the time frame to 1877 and the end of Reconstruction. The longer time frame employed here allowed a test of the modern presidency thesis that modern presidents are more influential in Congress than are premodern presidents. Although the modern presidency thesis is one important account of the evolution and development of the office, it has rarely been subject to systematic empirical testing, as is done here. Still, the presidency did not commence in 1877—there is nearly another century of presidential experience prior to 1877.

It would be useful to look at presidential influence across the full expanse of US history. The modern presidency thesis contends that the accumulation of institutional and staff resources added to the president's bargaining and leadership relationship with Congress, providing modern presidents with somewhat more influence with Congress than premodern presidents enjoyed. But the Gilded Age, from approximately 1877 until the turn of the twentieth century, is also considered the nadir of presidential influence and leadership. Comparing modern presidents with Gilded Age executives may, in one sense, stack the deck in favor of the modern presidency thesis, if Gilded Age presidents are the least influential. Formally, the analysis here did not compare only Gilded Age with modern presidents but also included premodern twentieth-century presidents as well. The Gilded Age presidents account for half of the premodern presidents analyzed here, and their heavy representation may have affected the results of the analysis; including more premodern presidents would dilute their impact on the findings.

Moreover, this study looked only at the House of Representatives, but there are two coequal legislative chambers. Are presidents similarly influential in the Senate and in the House? Do the same factors that condition influence in the House affect influence in the Senate? There are numerous differences between the House and the Senate, three of which may be especially important for presidential influence: the Senate's supermajority voting rules (such as the filibuster); its staggered terms; and the fact that senators were not popularly elected until the 17th Amendment was enacted, in 1913, and became effective nationally, in the November 1914 elections.

In comparison to simple majority roll calls, supermajority voting rules, especially the filibuster, create a higher hurdle to overcome in winning on a roll call (Bond, Fleisher, and Cohen 2015). We can only speculate about the implications of supermajority voting rules for influence, but it is likely to have implications for the presidential decision to take a position and for the president's lobbying strategy. Staggered terms may reduce the amount of influence that presidents have in the Senate. When deciding how to vote, the cohort of senators up for reelection should feel greater constituent pressures than cohorts not up for reelection (Kuklinski 1978). Similarly, constituent opinion should be a less important element of senators' roll call calculus prior to their direct election (Meinke 2008). The implication for the president is that constituency opinion should be a less important pathway for influence in Congress among cohorts not running for reelection and prior to the direct election of senators. Staggered terms and direct election of senators suggest two sets of hypotheses, one comparing presidential influence within the Senate and the other comparing influence across the two chambers.

These extensions all refer to the presidency, but underlying presidential influence, as it is used in this study, is the more general concept of executive influence. Shifting a legislator's vote is not specific to presidents but is theoretically applicable to any legislature that deals or interacts with executives. Thus, studies like the one conducted here can be applied to US state governors, presidents of other nations, and even a comparison of presidents and prime ministers. Variance in institutional arrangements across governorships and other presidents opens a host of hypotheses about the impact of those arrangements on executive influence and success.[10] The concept of executive influence provides another basis for building a comparative theory of executives.

MODERNIZATION THEORY, THE PRESIDENCY, AND CONGRESS

A fourth limitation of this study relates to the question of the relative influence of modern versus premodern presidents. For the most part, this study merely compared the influence of presidents of the two periods, but there are several issues with such comparisons. First, although such a simple temporal comparison might tell us whether modern presidents are more influential, it does not tell us why this is so or what aspects of the modern office presidents can use to increase their influence in Congress. What is it about presidential modernity that translates into greater influence with Congress?

For instance, I argue that the central clearance process associated with the president's program increased influence because that process prohibited agency personnel from communicating directly with Congress about policy and legislative matters (Cohen 2012). All communications had to be cleared through the White House to ensure adherence to the president's legislative priorities. No longer would Congress have direct and unfiltered access to the expertise and advice of the bureaucracy. The president would now control information flowing from the bureaucracy to Congress. Insofar as bureaucratic expertise is important to legislative decision making, the president's control of that expertise could be used to influence legislative policy making.

With regard to executive drafting of legislation, an activity also associated with the modern presidency, Rudalevige (2002, 144–145) argues that where a bill is drafted may matter for its success in Congress, and this may be extrapolated to influence as well. Rudalevige finds that the more the White House controls bill drafting, as opposed to allowing agencies a greater role, the less likely it is that Congress will enact the bill. He argues that decentralized bill drafting practices allow greater consultation with interested parties, including those in Congress, providing the administration with feedback on proposals and the opportunity to negotiate and amend the bill before sending it to Congress. A more decentralized process not only may provide the administration with information about congressional reactions to the bill but also creates opportunities for the administration to attempt to influence members. Both Rudalevige's and my ideas concern aspects of the modern office. Neither of us argues that modernity per se leads to success or influence, but we do causally connect routinized practices associated with the modern presidency to the legislative policy-making process.

A second issue with simply classifying presidents as premodern versus modern is that it does not tell us when to date the transition from one epoch to the other. Most accounts view Franklin Roosevelt as the first modern; hence, 1933 might be a convenient date to mark the arrival of the modern office. Even so, with regard to legislative influence, and again referring to my central clearance hypothesis (Cohen 2012), it was the late 1940s before the president's program and the central clearance process were introduced, and it was not until perhaps the early Eisenhower years that they were institutionalized.[11] Theory should be used to generate hypotheses that mark when aspects of the modern presidency would have implications for presidential success in Congress.

Third, and closely related to the last point, should we conceive of the evolution to presidential modernity as a process of development or as an abrupt break or departure in the operation of the office? As these questions suggest, there is much we do not yet know about how the modern office affects presidential influence in Congress.

PRESIDENTIAL INFLUENCE IN THE POLICY-MAKING PROCESS

This study has shown that presidents have a measurable amount of influence with Congress, enough to carry the day on a significant proportion of roll calls, and this may have consequences for the production of public policy. Results presented here provide support for Bond and Fleisher's (1990, 2) conjecture that "presidential influence may increase success."

The question of presidential influence in Congress raises a larger question of the role of the president in the policy-making process. There is an assumption in the popular culture that presidents not only are (or can be) influential but are in fact the central actors in the policy-making process. Without presidential participation in policy making, the thinking goes, important policy will not be made.

For instance, during the 2017 debates over the repeal of the Affordable Care Act (Obamacare), critics charged that President Donald Trump not only was underinformed about policy details but also did not use his position effectively in support of Republican proposals. The *Washington Post* reported that "some allies of President Trump question whether he has effectively used the bully pulpit afforded by his office" and that "he has made relatively little effort to detail for the public why Republican replacement plans . . . would improve on the former president's signature initiative" (Wagner 2017). Implicit in such criticisms is the assumption that presidents are important to the passage of major legislation. Even if they are inept in dealing with members of Congress, they may still be able to build public support and thereby put public pressure on Congress when making policy.

Given the results of this study, just how important are presidents to the production of public policy? How do presidents compare with others in the legislative policy-making process? There is a surprising paucity of research on these questions. In fact, there are few studies of the relative impact of various actors on the production of public policy.

There are two important recent studies that suggest that presidents may be comparatively important to the enactment of major legislation: Baumgartner et al. (2009) and Grossmann (2012). In *Lobbying and Policy Change*, Baumgartner et al. (2009), though primarily concerned with the role of interest group lobbying in the production of major policy change, record the relative importance of other actors, including the president. Although their main message is about the difficulty of producing new policies in the United States, they find statistically significant effects of presidential involvement on policy change (233–235). They estimate, using two models, the success of the two sides on an issue—to protect or to change the status quo. In estimations of the success of each side within two years of the proposal, they found that when presidents support changing the status quo, the success rate of status quo protectors declines, and when presidents oppose change, the success rate of the side wanting to alter the status quo also declines. The only other factors that affect outcomes are the relative resources of each side and the support of midlevel government employees, in the status quo protection estimation. Baumgartner et al.'s findings suggest that presidents rank as among the few actors who are important in determining outcomes of the policy-making process.

Matt Grossman (2012) takes a different approach, looking at the enactment of all major policies, irrespective of policy-making venue (legislative, executive, or judicial), from 1946 to 2004. Grossmann uses policy histories to record who the authors of each study cite as important. His study is not concerned with measuring who is most important but rather with recording all actors who are thought to have had some influence over policy making. He reports that presidents are mentioned as being important approximately 50% of the time. But presidential importance varies across policy-making venue. For instance, presidents are mentioned very frequently when policy is made in the executive branch. They rarely are mentioned in relation to policies made in the judiciary, about 3% of the time. But, of importance to the present study, presidents are mentioned as important in more than half (55%) of policies enacted by Congress.

Both of these studies suggest that presidents are consequential for the production of policy, especially when made in Congress. Although neither of these studies explicitly uses the term "influence," their results bear on the question of influence. They reinforce the message of this study, that presidents have a measurable degree of influence in Congress. Neither their results nor the results presented in this book should lead one to conclude that presidents are extraordinarily influential. Presidents cannot rally enough members to win on *all* roll calls. But neither are they impotent in the legislative arena.

Baumgartner et al. and Grossmann both emphasize the difficulty of overcoming the status quo bias in making policy in the United States. There is great truth in the cliché that policy making is hard. Presidents, however, seem somewhat important, at least as important as other actors, and may be more important than most on many occasions. There is more to presidential–congressional relations than dumb luck. Presidents can do something to improve the odds that their side will win. They possess influence.

NOTES

1. ON PRESIDENTIAL INFLUENCE IN CONGRESS

1. For instance, in his groundbreaking study on the impact of presidential approval on support for the president, "Presidential Influence in the House: Presidential Prestige as a Source of Presidential Power," Edwards (1976) intends to study presidential influence, which he defines as "the ability of the President to move congressmen to support him when they otherwise would not" (101, note 2). But his dependent variable is member support for the president, or the percentage of roll calls on which a member voted with the president, not whether members changed their votes because presidents tried to influence them. Support can be thought of as an individual-level analog to success. To be fair, Edwards is quite aware of this distinction (see, for example, 110), and the point here is not to criticize him but to illustrate the state of research prior to Bond and Fleisher (1990) distinguishing between success and influence.

2. Presidents may be influential without being successful if the number of changed votes is not enough to produce a legislative victory or if the president's side would have won anyway.

3. Beckmann (2010) also argues that attention should focus on explaining whether the president wins: "The president's ultimate objective: outcomes, not necessarily roll-call votes. . . . The White House wants to change the nation's laws, so the paramount metric of presidential success is the substantive result" (65).

4. This relationship has attained nearly law-like status. As Barrett and Eshbaugh-Soha (2007) state, "Party control in Congress is by far the most important factor affecting presidential success in the legislative arena" (102).

5. The famous psychologist Albert Bandura (2000) defines human agency this way: "People are partly the products of their environments, but by selecting, creating, and transforming their environmental circumstances they are producers of environments as well.

This agentic capability enables them to influence the course of events and take a hand in shaping their lives" (75). Human agency, the idea that an individual can have an effect on the environment and on others, differs from agency as used in principal–agent theory, where an individual is empowered to act for another. See, for instance, Waterman and Meier (1998) and, more recently, Mitnick (2015).

6. In critiquing personal-based perspectives of the presidency, Jacobs and King (2010) argue, for instance, "Personality is not a solid foundation for a persuasive explanation of presidential impact and the shortfalls or accomplishments of Obama's presidency. Modern presidents have brought divergent individual traits to their jobs and yet they have routinely failed to enact much of their agendas" (794).

7. Baumgartner et al. (2009) demonstrate the difficulty of enacting policy change, and the advantages of those whose aim is to protect and maintain the status quo.

8. In previous work, for example, I found that some premodern presidents were as legislatively successful at times, if not more so, as many modern presidents (Cohen 1982, 2012), which calls into question the usefulness of the modern presidency idea, at least for understanding this one aspect of executive behavior. However, I did not test for the relative influence of the two sets of presidents, only their comparative success rates.

9. As has been noted, many studies of strategic presidential behavior detect systematic and measurable levels of presidential influence. Still, the minimal influence perspective is the dominant view of most students of presidential–congressional relations.

10. For a review of different perspectives on this point, see Beckmann (2010).

11. There is very little research on why presidents take positions on roll calls. See Cumins (2008); Marshall and Prins (2007); Shull (2000); Shull and Shaw (2004).

12. On the complications of assessing member vote intentions prior to casting a roll call, see Boehmke (2006); Box-Steffensmeier, Arnold, and Zorn (1997); Caldeira and Zorn (2004); Huang and Theriault (2012); Krehbiel (1991). See Sullivan (1988, 1990a, 1990b, 1991) for an attempt to assess whether members change their vote intentions in accord with the president.

13. In other words, and developed in more detail later, members move in a liberal (or conservative) direction when the president takes a liberal (or conservative) position.

2. A THEORY OF PRESIDENTIAL INFLUENCE IN CONGRESS

1. As in past research, this study only looks at recorded teller roll calls, but Congress may enact legislation through unrecorded votes. Unrecorded votes do not document how each member voted but only which side won the vote. In the House, the Speaker judges who won, often through a voice vote of all members or by having members stand up. There is very little research on whether there are systematic differences between recorded and unrecorded votes. Lynch and Madonna (2013) suggest that there are such differences. It is unclear what the implications are for presidential influence and success if unrecorded votes are used instead of recorded votes. See Beckmann (2004) for an extensive discussion of the varieties of ways that presidents can lobby Congress.

2. It is also possible that a president will take a position on a roll call for multiple reasons, such as *both* to lobby Congress and to repay voters for their support in the past election.

3. Richard Neustadt published several editions of *Presidential Power* after the first one in 1960. The differences, other than changes in the subtitle, are either a new preface or an additional chapter, but the chapters retained from the 1960 edition are never changed. In his *Modern Political Analysis*, Dahl (1976) discusses what he calls "influence terms" (25), which includes "power," "influence," "force," "authority," "coercion," and "persuasion," but throughout his work he uses "power" and "influence" interchangeably. See also Stinebrickner (2015).

4. In earlier formulations, Edwards (1990, 1991a, 2006) distinguishes between presidents as directors versus facilitators of change. Directors are transformative leaders, who may restructure the political setting. Facilitators exploit the opportunities for change that exist.

5. Major studies of this strategic stripe with regard to presidential–congressional relations include Beckmann (2010); Cameron (2000); Cameron and Park (2011); Canes-Wrone (2006); Cohen (2012); Hassell and Kernell (2016); Howell et al. (2013); Marshall and Prins (2007); Sullivan (1990a).

6. This is an admittedly narrow, behavioral definition of influence, but as I will detail, it leads to useful and tractable empirical tests, including estimating how much influence presidents have with Congress.

7. For a useful review of the literature on lobbying influence, which has implications for this research, see Lowery (2013).

8. A complication is that members can take one of three postures on their expected vote and the roll call—*against* the president, *with* the president, and *undecided/not voting* (abstaining), whereas figure 2.1 presents only two postures: against or with the president. It facilitates the discussion to combine *undecided/abstain* and *against* into one set, which we can label "nonsupport." Movement from undecided to support of the president works to the president's advantage, at least as far as vote tallies go. Still, at times, presidents may try to prevent a member who might oppose the president from voting. Such instances are rare, as the overwhelming number of members vote on the vast majority of roll calls. Most research considers abstention to be random, but others argue that there are systematic reasons for abstention, including cross-pressures, such as if the party wants the member to vote one way but constituents hold a different policy preference. On rational vote abstention in Congress, see Powell (2015).

9. Presidents may be uncertain about a member's expected vote because the member refuses to reveal how she will vote, perhaps to extract additional considerations and/or benefits from the administration.

10. The law of anticipated reactions is credited to Carl J. Friedrich (1941); also see Simon (1953) and Bachrach and Baratz (1962, 1963) for extended conceptual discussions.

11. For one experimental study of the effect of anticipated rewards and punishments on behavior, see Ford and Zelditch (1988). Punishment (penalty) seems to have stronger effects than rewards. The president's credibility and reputation may affect member estimates of whether and how the president will act.

12. Charles Cameron and Jee-Kwang Park's (2011) negative sign between presidential going public and Senate voting may be due either to members moving away from the president or to presidents having no influence on member voting (that is, the member was opposed before the president went public and stays opposed after the president goes public). Since they do not have data on members' expected votes before the president went public, there is no way to distinguish these two accounts of the negative sign. This illustrates the difficulty of empirically measuring presidential influence.

13. Beckmann (2004, 21–26) identifies five broad categories of lobbying tactics: persuasion, going public, exchanges (such as vote trading), modification (amending or altering one's position), and subsidy.

14. There also may be spillover effects from private presidential lobbying of a member. The privately targeted member may lobby other members for the president. The president, in privately targeting a member, may request that the member engage in pro-administration lobbying of fellow members. Such a request may be the president's motivation for targeting the member. And in Congress, an institution known for leaking information and secrets, the privately targeted member may spill the beans to other members about the content of the lobbying and the arrangement made with the president. Members may blab about their private contacts with the administration for several reasons, including to raise their stature and prestige among colleagues by asserting that the president thinks them so important that the president contacted them personally and privately.

15. The methodology developed here for assessing the impact of presidential position taking can, with some effort, be applied to numerous subsets of members, to assess the relative effects of position taking on various types of members.

16. Again, with some (great) effort, is it possible, using the methodology presented in chapter 3, to incorporate some of the discrete lobbying tactics as well as to identify members specifically targeted.

17. It is highly unlikely that the president will be so important to a member's roll call decision that the member assigns a weight of 1 to the president, that is, that the president solely determines the member's vote and that the member does not consider any other factor, such as constituent preferences or partisanship.

18. For a study of the electoral costs of party loyalty in Congress, an example of conflict between reelection and helping the party, see Carson et al. (2010).

19. Bond and Fleisher (1990) do this when they distinguish between president-centered and Congress-centered explanations of member roll call voting.

20. On presidential vote buying, see Jenkins and Nokken (2008) and Taylor (2014).

21. If he privately supports passage of the bill, the president may be better off if he does not take a public stance on the bill.

22. There is little research on whether presidential position taking will have a short- or longer-term impact on the salience of the particular issue. Elsewhere (Cohen 1995, 99–101), I have suggested that presidential rhetoric has a lasting effect on public salience only for foreign policy, among the three policy areas I studied (the others are economic and civil rights). Still, even if the effect is short-lived, if presidents time their position taking strategically, doing so may improve the odds that the president's policy will be enacted.

23. Remember, merely by taking a position, the vote is transformed from a nonpresidential to a presidential roll call. The simple direct effect of position taking (P) in equation (2.4) cannot discriminate between this transformative effect of position taking and other forms of presidential lobbying, like vote buying, going public, bargaining, and so forth.

3. ESTIMATING PRESIDENTIAL INFLUENCE IN CONGRESS

1. Recall, undecideds, and abstainers are combined with opponents to form the set of nonsupporters.

2. Or, to be more precise, position taking increases the weight of the presidential consideration on members' voting.

3. Even Beckmann's (2010) earlygame theory considers presidential actions after taking a position.

4. Presidential position taking, as a form of legislative agenda setting, differs from Beckmann's (2010) earlygame lobbying notion. Position taking affects the substance or content associated with the president's legislative agenda, which in turn affects member agenda perceptions, as they categorize some roll calls as presidential and others as nonpresidential. Earlygame agenda setting, in Beckmann's account, affects the rules under which presidential proposals come to the floor, such as the type of amendments and alternatives that will be allowed. By restricting the alternatives on which members can vote, presidents are strategically advantaged and thus more likely to get from Congress the legislation that they seek.

5. Although Marshall and Prins (2007) and I (in Cohen 2012) argue that presidents have policy motivations when either submitting legislative proposals to Congress (Cohen) or taking roll call positions (Marshall and Prins), we still find that presidents are less likely to do either if they think that they will be defeated in Congress. The seminal discussion of credit claiming is found in Mayhew (1974).

6. Presidential influence may also affect other aspects of presidential–congressional relations, such as which bills make it to the floor for a roll call vote, vote and debate rules governing the bill, the timing of the roll call, and the like. See Beckmann (2010).

7. It is also possible to measure the success of the president at each decision stage of the legislative policy making process other than the floor vote. For instance, Edwards and Barrett (2000) and Lovett, Bevan, and Baumgartner (2015) investigate the ability of presidents to set the agenda of congressional committees.

8. The cross-Congress comparison would require controlling for all other relevant differences across Congresses, such as party control, presidential approval, and so on.

9. The literature on the two presidencies is vast. For recent studies, see Canes-Wrone, Howell, and Lewis (2008) and Howell, Jackman, and Rogowski (2013). Shull (1991) has collected in his edited volume most of the major studies of the two presidencies as of 1990.

10. More precisely, Sullivan (1991, 693) defines sway as the proportional number of members who shifted from nonsupport categories in the headcount to support on the roll call. (For other studies using headcount data, see Sullivan 1988, 1990a, 1990b; Collier and

Sullivan 1995; and Conley and Yon 2007.) When numerous members have not committed to the president on the headcount, presidents have a large number of members to target. But when there are fewer nonsupporting members, presidents can concentrate their lobbying efforts. It is not clear which situation is better for the president.

11. In other words, members may lie about their *true voting preferences* to extract something from the president, to improve their bargaining situation with the president.

12. There may be no good reason for counting heads if the vote looks like it will go against the president. Head counting consumes resources, which would be wasted on lost-cause votes. Plus, headcounts enter the historical record at some point, even if only years later, when such documentation is made public at a presidential library. Avoiding headcounts on such votes may mean that presidents think they cannot later be blamed for losing, since they did not care enough about the vote to count heads on it.

13. William Howell and his colleagues are careful to ensure that agenda composition differences are not the source of change in member voting.

14. There is related literature on war and state building, which argues that wars expand and centralize power in the state, especially that of the executive (Tilly 1975; Rasler and Thompson 1985, 2015; Karaman and Pamuk 2013).

15. Another limitation of the method used by Howell and his colleagues is the assumption that particular presidents favor liberal or conservative alternatives across votes. This is probably a safe, albeit blunt, measure of presidential preferences. Wood (2009), for example, finds that, rather than staking out the median position on domestic policies, presidents tend to be aligned with their parties, with Democratic presidents on the liberal side and Republicans toward the conservative pole. But some presidents have supported liberal alternatives on some issues and conservative ones on others. For example, Eisenhower preferred internationalism in foreign policy, which was associated with liberals in both parties, although he took traditional Republican and conservative positions on most domestic and economic issues (Cohen 1997, 102–121).

16. They also conduct analyses on a subset of important foreign policy votes, for both chambers, with the dependent variable being the individual member's vote.

17. The various methods for identifying member ideology appear to produce essentially the same results (Burden, Caldeira, and Groseclose 2000; Hill 2001).

18. To test whether members vote differently on presidential and nonpresidential roll calls, we need a scaling methodology that allows for the possibility of differences across the two types of roll calls. The DW-NOMINATE methodology does not. I am not arguing that members shift their voting in response to different factors or pressures, such as presidential pressure. It might be the case, empirically, that member voting patterns are highly stable, even as contextual factors change, as some contend (e.g., Poole and Rosenthal 1997), and thus that presidents have no influence over member voting. Not everyone agrees with Poole and Rosenthal that members exhibit stable voting patterns across their careers. In fact, theories of representation contend that members are concerned with the preferences of their constituents for reelection reasons. Thus, members should respond in their voting when the policy preferences of their constituents change. For instance, Kristina Miler, using adjusted Americans for Democratic Action scores in her analysis,

finds that members who move from the House to the Senate change their roll call voting behavior in response to differences in the policy preferences of these two constituencies. See Miler (2016) for an extensive review of the relevant literature and debate.

19. See Alexander, Berry, and Howell (2016) and Fowler and Hall (2017) for applications of the conservative vote probability (CVP)–derived estimates for studying member voting behavior.

20. For instance, assume a president is a Democrat and the House is Democratic. The president's CVP score might not be very large, since the median would be a Democrat. But if party control changes hands, the president's CVP score will increase because the median member will shift from being a Democrat to being a Republican.

21. Moreover, although the outcome variable is binary, as Fowler and Hall (2013, 4) explain, "Maximum likelihood methods that account for the constrained nature of the outcome variable, like probit and logit, are unnecessary (and indeed unsuited) for the present application. Interest is in estimating conditional means—the average voting behavior for each legislator across all bills. Indeed, if all legislators were present and voting for all bills, the quantities of interest could be calculated without even running a regression, simply by taking means."

22. This scoring merely flips the direction that Fowler and Hall use, where conservative votes are scored 1 and liberal votes are scored zero.

23. When the president does not take a roll call stance, the president is scored as missing data.

24. The president is no longer treated as a voting member, as in the first stage.

4. PRESIDENTIAL INFLUENCE IN THE HOUSE IN THE MODERN ERA

1. But recall from chapter 2 that if a member is already predisposed to support the president, then presidential position taking cannot alter the member's vote, no matter how strongly the presidential consideration weighs in the member's voting calculus.

2. Fleisher, Bond, and Wood (2008) do not find support for the hypothesis that reputedly skillful presidents are systematically more successful in their dealings with Congress. But success on roll calls may not be a suitable measure for testing the connection between personal reputation and influence. In contrast, using methods developed to assess the relative importance of players and managers in baseball, Teodoro and Bond (2017) found that presidents reputed to be more skillful, such as Reagan, appear to be more successful.

3. At the same time, they retain those few votes where the president lost by lopsided margins. For a comparison among using all roll calls, using nonunanimous (conflictual) roll calls, and using important roll calls (*Congressional Quarterly*'s "key votes"), see Edwards (1985, 1990, chap. 2). Edwards (1985) finds lower levels of presidential support (80% or less on the president's side) for nonunanimous votes than for all votes, an indication of the inflation effect discussed in chapter 3. But he also detects a strong correlation across the various support scales: "No matter how we compare the indices, it is clear that they have a great deal in common. . . . The differences among all four of the indices are typically small" (683). For a related critique of *CQ*'s key votes, see Shull and Vanderleeuw (1987).

4. Fractional regression is a type of bounded regression in which the values of the dependent variable can only vary within certain limits. In particular, fractional regression allows the dependent variables, measured as a proportion, to vary from zero to 1, allowing zero and 1 values. In ordinary least squares (OLS), the dependent variable can vary from negative infinity to positive infinity—there are no limits to the values the variable can take. Practically, however, there appear to be few differences in results between the OLS and the fractional regressions, although there are some necessary differences in the model to be estimated. For the OLS, I cluster by year to control for the varying number of votes and other unmeasured yearly effects. Fractional regression does not allow clustering; thus, to control for the unmeasured annual effects, the fractional regression includes dummy variables for all years, with 2012 set as the criterion year. To estimate the fractional regression, I used fracreg in Stata 14, using the logit estimator.

5. Since all roll calls are used and the number of roll calls is very large, significance tests are not necessary, although they are presented in table 4.1. Coefficients easily reach statistically significant levels at 0.05 or better in the direction that the presidential influence hypothesis predicts.

6. An exogenous shock, which changes voting alignment in Congress, is rare, but such events do occur. Such events probably have to be very deep and have to restructure the political environment to alter congressional sentiment toward the policy. For example, the House rejected the Emergency Economic Stabilization Act of 2008, a Treasury Department plan to buy up to $700 billion of mortgage-backed securities and hopefully inject liquidity into financial markets, by a vote of 203 for and 225 against, on September 29, 2008, leading to an 8% drop in the stock market, the largest single-day drop since Black Monday, October 19, 1987. In reaction to the stock market tumble, the bill was amended. The amended bill was sent first to the Senate, where it passed by a 74–25 vote on October 1, and then, on October 3, the House passed the amended bill by a strong 263–171 margin. For an empirical examination, see Cayton (2016).

7. Jenkins and Monroe (2016), in redefining rolls, specify whether the agenda setter took a yea or a nay position. By taking a yea position, the agenda setter is trying to positively affect the legislative agenda, that is, to get Congress to enact legislation. A nay position, in contrast, reflects negative agenda control, that is, it is keeping Congress from enacting legislation. For Jenkins and Monroe, a "roll" is when the agenda setter takes a yea position and is defeated, whereas they term taking a nay position and being defeated a "block." Similarly, a yea position with victory is termed a "success," but a yea position that is defeated is a "disappointment." Since my data set does not record whether the president's position was a yea or a nay, I use the term "roll" differently from Jenkins and Monroe. For me, a roll is when the president loses by a large, lopsided margin.

8. Votes receiving from 80% to 90% support are still highly popular among the vast majority of members and will necessarily include support from members of both parties. Of 26,909 roll calls, 10,452 (38.8%) are lopsided and 16,457 (61.2%) are not.

9. An interesting question for future research is why presidents take positions when they are eventually rolled. Most of the time, the president, like other observers in Washington,

will be able to predict that the vote is not going to be close. Thus, we cannot argue that lack of information accounts for such position-taking "mistakes." Probably, presidents make a calculation that the benefits of taking a position when they will be rolled is higher than the costs of being on the losing side. Detailing that calculation becomes a task for future research.

10. Beta regression is used instead of fractional regression here because the dependent variable, the liberal vote proportion, cannot have a zero or 1 value. The major difference between beta and fractional regression is that the former does not allow zero or 1 values but the latter does. I used the betafit command, a user-written module, in Stata 14 to estimate the beta regression because it allows clustering by year. The Stata command betareg, in contrast, does not allow clustering. Again, clustering is used primarily to control for the varying number of roll calls per year.

11. Specifically, Democrats took 157 conservative positions among their 1,525 total positions, while Republicans took 377 liberal positions out of 1,750 total positions.

12. The regression equation is Liberal Proportion = 0.54 Constant + 0.025 (0.005) Presidential Position Taking – 0.046 (0.017) Democratic President + 0.013 (0.008) {Presidential Position Taking × Democratic President}. The estimation clusters on year.

13. The literature on the importance of personal traits of presidents is much too vast to cite or review fully here. Erwin Hargrove (2016) offers an important recent overview.

14. On Johnson, see Beckmann, Chaturvedi, and Garcia (2017); Dallek (1998); Evans and Novak (1966); Zelizer (2015). On Reagan, see Dallek (1984); Hogan (1990); Jones (1988a); Rudalevige (2005), 419–420; Sloan (1996). On Carter, see Hargrove (1988); Jones (1988b).

15. Since the dependent variable is a proportion, the roll call–level coefficients can be read as the proportion of members who shift to the president's side. They are easily converted into percentages by multiplying by 100. Thus, 0.03 would equal 3%.

16. The Nixon averages include all roll calls from 1974, although Ford was president for a number of them. Eliminating 1974 from the Nixon averages hardly affects the results, with Nixon's influence score rising slightly, to 0.07.

17. The coefficient of variation (CV), defined as {(standard deviation/mean) × 100}, can also be used to compare the variation within presidencies. In some cases, the CV is quite large, as for Clinton at 300. For the ten presidents in this list for which we can calculate the CV (we cannot do so for Ford, whose mean is zero), five (Eisenhower, Kennedy, Clinton, Bush, and Obama) have CVs of 100 or greater, while the remaining five have CVs under 100. There is enough intra-administration variability to undercut the personal president perspective.

18. They also perform a standard one-stage analysis of presidential success and find weak effects of approval on success, consistent with the bulk of existing research.

19. One caution about using these techniques is that researchers might continue to modify the outcome and treatment equations to produce the desired treatment effect.

20. The matching process works best when variables selected strongly predict the outcome and the treatment, which is found to be the case, as reported in the appendix at the end of this chapter.

21. Balance tests for both estimations find that the treatment effects are balanced, with mean = 0 and variance = 1.

22. This assumes a majority vote rule on each roll call. There are times, however, when the House uses a supermajority voting rule, but such instances are rare, especially in the House. The most important of these is the requirement of a two-thirds vote to override a presidential veto. From 1953 to 2012, there were only thirty-nine successful overrides out of 4,395 total presidential positions, or 0.9% of presidential positions. Of course, unsuccessful overrides will add to the total of supermajority votes, but as far as I can determine, no one has constructed a comprehensive list of override attempts. Data on presidential vetoes and overrides comes from the official Senate list. See United States Senate, "Vetoes: Summary of Bills Vetoed, 1789–Present," http://www.senate.gov/reference/Legislation/Vetoes/vetoCounts.htm, accessed on May 21, 2016.

    While veto override rules are prescribed in the Constitution, the House may enact its own rules about requiring supermajority votes. Again, these rules almost never pertain to presidential positions on roll calls, except perhaps rule XXI, clause 5(b), which comes up very rarely, if ever. An official report prepared for the House lists these rules with supermajority voting provisions: rule XV, clause 1, requires a two-thirds vote to suspend the rules of the House; rule XV, clause 5, requires a two-thirds vote to dispense with the call of the Private Calendar on the first or third Tuesday of a month; rule XIII, clause 6(a), requires a two-thirds vote to consider a special rule on the same day that the Rules Committee reports it, except during the last three days of the session; rule XV, clause 7(a), requires a two-thirds vote to dispense with Calendar Wednesday proceedings; rule XIII, clause 6(c), also requires a two-thirds vote to agree to a special rule dispensing with Calendar Wednesday; rule XV, clause 7(c)(2), requires a two-thirds vote to continue considering a measure on a succeeding Calendar Wednesday; and rule XXI, clause 5(b), requires a three-fifths vote to approve a measure, amendment, or conference report carrying a federal income tax rate increase. See Congressional Research Reports, "Super-Majority Votes in the House," http://congressionalresearch.com/98-778/document.php?study=Super-Majority+Votes+in+the+House.

23. Remember, the dependent variable is scaled as the percentage voting liberal on the roll call, and the 50% cutoff is actually 50% plus one member, to avoid fifty-fifty tie votes from being listed in the victory column.

24. The annual influence coefficients for non-lopsided votes is estimated by regressing the presidential position variable on the member vote for each year separately.

25. Causally, influence has to come prior to success; presidents have to be able to influence members before members cast their roll call vote.

26. Simultaneous equation models, like two-stage least squares, is one possible approach to sorting out the causal effects of influence on success, but such techniques require an instrumental variable, a variable that predicts influence (the strength restriction) and that plausibly affects influence but not success (the exclusion restriction). I was unable to locate a variable that meets the requirements necessary for implementing two-stage least squares.

5. POLITICAL PARTIES AS A SOURCE OF PRESIDENTIAL INFLUENCE

1. The literature on the impact of parties on members is huge, and there is some contro-versy about whether parties as legislative organizations have an impact on members above and beyond mere membership in a party. Krehbiel (1998), for instance, argues that par-ties comprise members who share policy preferences. This similarity in preferences accounts for why members of opposing parties vote differently on roll call votes. In con-trast, two perspectives argue that parties as legislative organizations, under some condi-tions, can influence member behavior beyond member policy preferences. One, the con-ditional party government perspective, argues that when there is policy agreement among the members within the party and the difference between the policy positions of the par-ties is wide, members of the majority party will endow its legislative party leadership with enhanced power to ensure the passage of legislation that its members prefer and to block legislative proposals from the opposition (Aldrich and Rohde 2000a, 2000b). The second perspective argues that parties in Congress act as cartels, which stresses the power of the majority party to set the legislature's agenda through institutional controls. This legislative agenda-setting power—deciding which issues come up for a floor vote under what voting rules—determines the ability of the majority party to enact its policy agenda. Enacting that agenda is important for the reelection of majority party legislators, as the agenda establishes the party's reputation or brand among voters. See Cox and McCub-bins (2005). On party brands, see Butler and Powell (2014).

2. With such a large number of cases for analysis, almost any relationship will reach statis-tical significance levels. Consequently, it makes more sense to focus on the magnitude of the effect than on its statistical significance.

3. The t value for the interaction is 6.10, with a p value < 0.0001.

4. Majority presidents benefit whether they take liberal or conservative positions, with somewhat greater effects for conservative position taking. When majority presidents take a conservative position, the effect is 9.5% (about forty-one members), compared to 6.9% (about thirty members) for liberal position taking. These estimates are determined by converting the presidential position variable into two dummies, one for conservative posi-tions and the other for liberal positions, and interacting these dummies with a majority-party-control dummy. The full results of the estimation are b (SE): Y(Liberal %) = 0.52(0.01) Constant + 0.01(0.01) – Conservative Position –0.02(0.01) Liberal Position + 0.00(0.02) Majority Control + {–0.095(0.019) Conservative Position × Majority Control} + {0.069(0.016) Liberal Position × Majority Control}.

5. The public mood and macropartisanship data can be found at James Stimson's website, http://stimson.web.unc.edu/data. Elizabeth Coggins, Stimson's collaborator, has also posted the public mood data on her website, http://kelizabethcoggins.com/mood-policy -agendas.

6. And many of the control variables reach statistical significance.

7. As above, the outcome equation is modeled as a function of whether there was a Demo-cratic majority in the House (= 1), whether the vote was on foreign policy (= 1),

presidential approval during the month of the vote, party polarization in the House, and whether the president was a Democrat (= 1). The outcome equation did not include whether the president's party was the majority in the House (= 1), which was used in chapter 4. The treatment equation employs only two variables: whether the president was a Democrat (= 1) and the public mood.

8. Again, the coefficient is significant, with a t value of 8.12 and a p value < 0.0001.

9. The two are strongly and negatively correlated on the non-lopsided roll calls (Pearson's $r = -0.76$, $p < 0.0001$), which is what we would expect, as the parties tend to divide on contested votes. Also as expected, Democrats are more likely than Republicans to vote liberal. The mean Democratic liberal percentage is 81%, compared to 19% for the Republicans.

10. Unlike the results reported by Lee (2008, 2009), whose study investigated the Senate, these findings are for the House.

11. This totals only 432 seats, not 435, because of scattered third-party members and vacancies.

12. Franzese and Kam (2009) show that such an estimation is mathematically equivalent to using an interaction term.

13. When polarization is low (0.25), the probability that an opposition member will vote liberal is 0.85, compared to 0.06 when polarization is high (0.75), a staggering difference of 0.79. But the probability that a co-partisan will vote liberal only moves from 0.32 to 0.89 as polarization increases from low to high, a 0.57 difference, which is still substantial.

14. When polarization is low (0.25), the probability that an opposition member will vote liberal is 0.68, compared to 0.80 when polarization is high (0.75), a 0.12 difference. But the probability that a co-partisan will vote liberal only moves from 0.25 to 0.21 as polarization increases from low to high, a paltry 0.04 difference.

15. When polarization is low (0.25), the probability that an opposition member will vote liberal is 0.30, compared to 0.22 when polarization is high (0.75), a 0.08 difference. But the probability that a co-partisan will vote liberal moves from 0.69 to 0.87 as polarization increases from low to high, a 0.18 difference, which is still substantial.

16. When polarization is low (0.25), the probability that an opposition member will vote liberal is 0.15, compared to 0.84 when polarization is high (0.75), a massive 0.69 difference. But the probability that a co-partisan will vote liberal moves from 0.07 to 0.71 as polarization moves from high to low, still a monumental difference of 0.64.

6. THE TWO PRESIDENCIES AND PRESIDENTIAL INFLUENCE

1. Aaron Wildavsky (1966) coined the term the "two presidencies" in his seminal paper, but the idea that presidents have advantages in foreign compared to domestic policy can be found as early as Dahl (1950, 58). Shull (1991) has collected in his edited volume most of the work on the two presidencies as of 1990. Recent analyses include Canes-Wrone, Howell, and Lewis (2008); Mack, DeRouen, and Lanoue (2013).

2. Several studies use non–roll call data: Marshall and Pacelle (2005) analyze executive orders; Canes-Wrone, Howell, and Lewis (2008) budgets and agency designs; Lewis (1997) presidential rhetoric; and Middlemass and Grose (2002) congressional franks. Lindsay and Steger (1993) critique roll calls for testing the two presidencies hypothesis.

3. Not everyone agrees that an anticommunist foreign policy consensus existed in the pre–Vietnam War era; see McCormick and Wittkopf (1990).

4. This does not mean that foreign policy never plays a role in elections, only that domestic policy generally is more important to voters. For a review of the literature on foreign policy and elections, see Aldrich et al. (2006); Brooks, Dodson, and Hotchkiss (2010).

5. These include Wildavsky (1966, 1969); Peppers (1975); LeLoup and Shull (1979); Sigelman (1979, 1981); Lee (1980); Shull and LeLoup (1981); Zeidenstein (1981); Cohen (1982); Carter (1985, 1986); Edwards (1986); Fleisher and Bond (1988); Oldfield and Wildavsky (1989); Shull (1991); Sullivan (1991); Canes-Wrone, Howell, and Lewis (2008).

6. These include Peppers (1975); LeLoup and Shull (1979); Sigelman (1979); Fleisher and Bond (1988); McCormick and Wittkopf (1990); Howell and Pevehouse (2005, 2007); Kriner (2010); Howell (2011); Milner and Tingley (2015).

7. See the Comparative Agendas Project, https://www.comparativeagendas.net. Originally, the data collection on agendas was called the Policy Agendas Project (PAP), and it focused exclusively on the United States. The Comparative Agendas Project (CAP) expanded the Policy Agendas Project framework cross-nationally. The CAP/PAP major topic codes were revised in 2015. The CAP/PAP was unable to classify all the roll calls into major topic policy areas, presumably because they did not clearly relate to a policy area or may have concerned a nonpolicy topic. For the contested roll calls, therefore, the n drops slightly, from 16,457 used in chapter 5 to 16,448 for this analysis, a minuscule difference of nine roll calls.

8. These figures are for conflictual roll calls. Including lopsided roll calls, there are 5,403 (20.8%) foreign policy votes and 21,499 (79.9%) domestic policy votes. Foreign policy roll calls are slightly more common on lopsided than on conflictual votes (22.4% versus 18.6%).

9. Several factors may lead presidents to take foreign policy positions more frequently than domestic policy positions, such as their constitutional duties and/or their assessment of being able to influence members' voting. Of the 3,061 conflictual foreign policy votes, presidents took 975 positions. Of the 13,387 domestic policy votes, they took 2,297 positions. However, there is no difference in presidential position taking on foreign versus domestic policy on lopsided votes, with presidents taking positions on both types of policies 10.7% of the time (on domestic policy, 869 positions on 8,112 roll calls; on foreign policy, 250 positions on 2,092 roll calls).

10. This is similar to the process described in Howell, Jackman, and Rogowski (2013) and Howell and Rogowski (2013).

11. Calculated by this formula: 435 members × 0.045 regression coefficient.

12. In earlier work, for example, I found that minority presidents tend to moderate their position taking more than majority presidents do (Cohen 2011, 2012). However, I did not separate presidential positions by policy area and thus the analysis does not reveal whether the moderation effect is specific to foreign policy positions.

13. This does not mean that presidents lack influence in Congress but rather that patterns of influence for foreign policy in the post–Cold War era resemble voting patterns on domestic policy.

14. Conservative position taking is associated with the use of military force over diplomacy, other exertions of US power, and anticommunist moves in the international arena, that is, with containment policy or, in the postcommunist world, with policies that resemble the older containment policy and its aim to challenge US adversaries and to support a vibrant and capable US military.

15. During the sixty-year period, polarization as measured here ranged from 0.29 to 0.83.

16. A major debate in the literature on party polarization is not whether it exists at the elite level—all studies find that it does (see the reviews in Theriault 2008; Layman, Carsey, and Horowitz 2006; Hetherington 2009)—but whether the general public is similarly polarized. For example, compare Fiorina, Abrams, and Pope (2005), who argue that there is little public-level polarization, with Abramowitz (2010), who makes a case for polarization among the general public, at least among partisan identifiers. On the sorting of liberals and conservatives among the general public into the Democratic and Republican parties, see Levendusky (2009). Such sorting can occur while a large segment of the public remains moderate.

17. Clausen (1973) is a seminal work on differences across substantive policy areas. Also see Lapinski (2013); Bateman, Clinton, and Lapinski (2017).

18. The model does not explain much variance, with an R^2 of only 0.09, yet the overall equation is significant, with an equation F of 171.25, $p < 0.0001$.

19. On the Akaike information criterion and the Schwarz's Bayesian information criterion model selection tests, see Burnham and Anderson (2004).

20. According to Raftery (1995), an absolute value greater than 10 provides very strong evidence in support of one model over another.

21. Specifically, several variables are common to both models: Presidential Position, Foreign Policy, and their interaction. The Cold War model includes the Cold War dummy and three interactions: Cold War × Position, Cold War × Foreign Policy, and Position × Cold War × Foreign Policy. The polarization model includes the Polarization variable and three interactions: Polarization × Position, Polarization × Foreign Policy, and Position × Polarization × Foreign Policy. To estimate the nested regression, I use nestreg in Stata 14. However, nestreg cannot handle clustered or robust data unless they are in survey mode in Stata, so I set the data as survey data set on year: svyset year. Again, lopsided votes are not included.

7. PUBLIC OPINION AS A SOURCE OF PRESIDENTIAL INFLUENCE

1. Studies finding a strong association include Barrett and Eshbaugh-Soha (2007); Brace and Hinckley (1992); Canes-Wrone and Demarchi (2002); Edwards (1976, 1980, 1989, 1997); Lebo and O'Green (2011); Ostrom and Simon (1985); and Rivers and Rose (1985).

However, Bond and Fleisher (1980, 1984, 1990); Bond, Fleisher, and Northrup (1988); Borrelli and Simmons (1993); Cohen et al. (2000); and Collier and Sullivan (1995) report weak or no effect. One study, Lockerbie, Borrelli, and Hedger (1998), even reports a negative relationship.

2. Congressional responsiveness to the president's approval level is not policy representation per se, although it may have indirect implications for policy. Canes-Wrone (2004, 2006) offers an alternative interpretation for the lack of relationship between presidential approval and congressional success and suggests that presidential influence in Congress comes not from approval but from increasing the salience of public opinion on an issue.

3. There are surprisingly few studies of the impact of issue salience on presidential influence in Congress. In contrast, there is a large body of literature documenting the relevance of issue salience for representation in Congress (Burstein 2014; Gilens 2012; Lax and Phillips 2012; Monroe 1979, 1998; Murray 2006; Shapiro 2011; Soroka and Wlezien 2010; but see Warshaw 2012, who finds that salience does not improve representation). One limitation of salience studies is that the public is rarely polled on nonsalient issues. Thus, we cannot say with certainty that policy makers are more response on salient than on nonsalient issues (Burstein 2003, 2014; Shapiro 2011; Wlezien 2017).

4. A consensus appears to be emerging, which views approval as a statistically significant but marginal influence on presidential success and support in Congress (Cohen, Bond, and Fleisher 2013).

5. I used the -approval- package in Stata 14.0 to access these data from the American Presidency Project at the University of California, Santa Barbara, www.presidency.ucsb.edu.

6. Approval and Corrected Approval are highly correlated (Pearson's $r = 0.99$), but analyses found that the Corrected Approval coefficients were stronger than the simpler approval level, although the basic substantive findings remain the same no matter which is used.

7. Linear interpolation is basically the same as taking the average between two adjacent data points. This is a reasonable approach, because presidential approval generally tends to shift slowly, in short periods of time, and usually there are only one or two months in succession that lack a poll. Although this procedure will induce some measurement error, such error will be slight.

8. This is to avoid using the previous president's last approval to predict the influence of the current president during the first month in office. For the roll call–level analysis, this loses only 164 lost cases, or 0.01%.

9. This assumes that, when averaging across, say, two or three or more months, readings from past administrations are being used for more than the initial month of a new president's tenure. It is possible to create a variable that uses a three-month average, for example, and to use only approval ratings from the second and third months, but doing so also means that the averaging process across a president's term of office is not consistent, which raises other measurement and estimation issues.

10. Within presidencies from 1953 to 2012, the average monthly change in approval is 3%, with an average 4% shift over two months. Nearly two-thirds of monthly shifts in

approval are 3% or less, which is approximately the expected sampling error for samples ranging from 1,000 to 1,500, as is the case for most Gallup polls. Most studies of presidential approval only investigate mean change over time, but several have looked at short-term volatility in approval ratings (see Gronke and Brehm 2002; Kriner 2006; and Kriner and Schwartz 2009). Moreover, studies of presidential approval find that using lagged approval soaks up much of the temporal variation in approval. For a recent discussion of this issue, see Dickerson (2015).

11. Comparative Agendas Project, "United States," http://www.comparativeagendas.net/us, accessed June 22, 2016.

12. Actually, the Most Important Problem (MIP) coding is for the issue area of the roll call and not for the particular roll call. It is not clear that voters discriminate into issue sub-categories, such as unemployment versus inflation in the case of economic policy. On this point, see Cavari (2017).

13. Each coefficient indicates the impact of a shift of zero to 1 (or zero to 100%) of the independent variable on the dependent variable, the proportion voting liberal. The ranges for the opinion variables are 0.26 to 0.98 for approval, and the most important problem ranges from 0.0 to 0.79.

14. This restricts the analysis to cases with salience of 0.15 (15%) and less, about 87.5% of the cases. This restricted analysis still finds a significant effect of the interaction between position taking and issue salience. A second analysis performs a log transformation on the salience variable, producing a variable that much more closely resembles a normal distribution. Analysis of that variable also reports the interactive effect between position taking and issue salience. Details are provided in the chapter appendix. Because neither of these alternatives affects results, and because the log-transformed variable is harder to interpret intuitively, the main text relies on the untransformed and unrestricted issue salience variable.

15. For example, when presidents do not take a position, the liberal vote percentage is 52.5%, but this declines modestly, to 51.5%, when the president takes a conservative position and rises to 53.5% when the president takes a liberal position.

16. As expected, opposition members tend to vote conservative when the president takes a liberal position and vice versa.

17. Formally, the formula is $\{\log \text{normal} \times ((MIP \times 100) + 1)\}$. Since the log of zero is undefined, I use the standard approach of adding 1. The log of 1 is equal to zero. To do this requires rescaling the MIP salience variable from proportions to percentages.

8. PRESIDENTIAL LOBBYING EFFORT AND INFLUENCE

1. The slope does not need to be as steep as is portrayed on the figure, nor does there have to be a one-to-one relationship between effort and influence.

2. Beckmann (2010, 173) uses a three-point presidential involvement scale, with zero indicating no presidential involvement, that is, the president and/or the administration is not mentioned in the relevant *CQ Almanac* case description of the vote; 1 is when the

president endorsed a position, and 2 is when the president actively lobbied. Beckmann allows many lobbying modes to count as active lobbying.

3. The data come from Palazollo and Swinford (1994), who use news reports to trace contacts. Lobbying is thus a dichotomy for whether the member was contacted or not, with no further information on the content of the contact, such as, for instance, whether bargains were struck, votes were traded, the administration offered anything to the member, or something else.

4. Uslaner's (1998, 352) contact measure is a dichotomy: whether the president contacted the member on NAFTA or not. Thus, it is not properly a measure of lobbying effort, of whether more intense lobbying of those contacted leads to a higher probability of support for the bill.

5. Other studies test the effectiveness of going public as a strategy for influencing Congress, but with mixed results. Barrett (2004), for instance, finds that the more a president publicly mentions an issue, the greater is his likelihood of floor success. Cummins (2010) finds that emphasis of a policy in the president's State of the Union Address (SUA) also improves prospects for success in Congress. In contrast, Powell and Schloyer (2003) do not find any floor effects from presidential activities of going public.

6. On this negative relationship, however, Cameron and Park (2011, 466) caution, "More complex estimation methods applied to the confirmation voting data, taking into account the endogeneity of going public, ought to show a positive relationship between confirmation votes and going public, controlling for the intensity of group opposition, nominee quality, and nominee ideology."

7. For instance, assume a weak opposition has one unit of lobbying effort to expend. A president may neutralize the weak opposition by expending one unit and beat the opposition by expending two units. For this illustrative roll call, the president has deployed two-thirds of the total lobbying resources to beat the opposition. Now assume a stronger opposition that has ten units of lobbying effort to expend. Here, the president will be able to neutralize the opposition by also expending ten units of lobbying effort and may realize some advantage over the opposition by expending an additional unit, for a total of eleven presidential lobbying units expended. Here, the president has expended only 52.4% (11/21) of the total deployed lobbying units, much less than the two-thirds in the first example. To match the vote outcome of the first example roll call, against a strong opponent, the president would have to expend a total of twenty units, which may be more than the president can afford or is willing to spend.

8. Beckmann (2016) is careful on this point. Although the Daily Diaries do not provide content on the meetings, they do classify activities. Beckmann reports that only 1.2% of presidential contacts with Senate leaders that lasted more than five minutes were classified as "leisure" (11).

9. These data are available at Comparative Agendas Project, "United States," http://www.comparativeagendas.net/us. The CAP now houses data from the original Policy Agendas Project. I omitted from these calculations SUAs delivered by outgoing presidents at the beginning of a year in which a new president takes office (Truman in 1953, Eisenhower in 1961, Johnson in 1969, Ford in 1977, and Carter in 1981). Since Nixon in 1969

and Carter in 1977 did not issue SUAs, there are no data for those years. In calculating the president's attention to an issue area, nonpolicy quasi sentences are excluded.

10. Using data from 1953 to 2000, Cummins (2010) finds that presidential policy emphasis in the SUA predicts position taking in economic and foreign policy but not in health and social welfare.

11. The degree of mobilization by presidential opponents, conversely, leads presidents to increase attention on the issue in the SUAs, as detailed in Cameron and Park (2011).

12. Figure 8.3 presents results on all members alone, not combined with those of same party and opposition party members, because the scale can be adjusted, making it easier to see the curvilinear pattern. One needs to keep in mind that effects, although statistically significant, are not large on member voting.

13. One direction for future research is to test whether presidents indeed lobby harder as they confront stronger opponents to their legislative initiatives, another prediction consistent with the conditional lobby theory proposed here. For instance, presidents may lobby harder when the public is split over an issue, assuming that a divided public reflects the amount of opposition to the president. Building on Canes-Wrone's (2006) theory, presidents may not go public or lobby Congress when the public strongly opposes their position, but when the public is more evenly divided, presidents may engage in an intense lobbying campaign.

14. Of course, as the president's majority grows in size, the president's side, through sheer increase in number, may be able to counterbalance the increasing tendency of opposition members to vote against the president.

15. Multicollinearity was too severe for stable estimation if the interactions between (1) position taking and public salience and (2) position taking and the foreign policy dummy are included. Public salience and foreign policy are very highly correlated with presidential position taking and/or presidential lobbying effort, as we would expect.

16. Recall that the conditional effect of presidential lobbying is not a function of the overall amount of polarization in Congress. As the results in table 8.3 in the appendix show, this conditional effect holds even when controlling for the overall level of polarization in the House.

9. MODERNITY AND PRESIDENTIAL INFLUENCE IN CONGRESS

1. It is illuminating to recall the titles of some early research in the modern presidency vein, such as, for instance, Erwin C. Hargrove's *The Power of the Modern Presidency* (1974) and Fred I. Greenstein's (1988) edited volume *Leadership in the Modern Presidency*. Among the first to review comprehensively the characteristics and implications of the modern presidency is Dorothy Buckton James's *The Contemporary Presidency* (1969). The front-cover blurb is telling: "A study of the structure, uses, and expansion of presidential power from Roosevelt to the present."

2. These frustrations in working with Congress often lead the president to make policy through unilateral means, such as by using executive orders (see Moe and Howell 1999; Howell 2003).

3. The early literature on the modern presidency appreciates the limits of presidential power that supposedly accreted to the office as a result of modernization (e.g., Seligman 1956; James 1969). Moreover, other factors may better account for presidential influence than modernization. Skowronek (1993) argues that the president's placement in political time, as opposed to linear or historical time, better explains the impact and accomplishments of presidents. The concept of political time, with its emphasis on the resources that ascendant parties offer to presidents, is a type of contextual factor.

4. I begin with 1877 because that is when the modern, two-party system of Democrats and Republicans emerged. Prior to that, the party system was quite fluid. Major parties, like the Whigs and the Republicans, arose, sometimes supplanting earlier parties or filling the void left by a weakened major party (such as the Federalists). Other research that looks at policy making in historical context also uses 1877 as the start date (Lapinski 2013). There have been a few attempts at longer historical comparisons, such as Ansolabehere, Palmer, and Schneer (2016, 2018) on the passage of significant legislation and my work on presidents' legislative requests and success with Congress (Cohen 2012). Only Chamberlain (1946) looks at the relative influence of the president and Congress on legislation across the premodern–modern divide, for ninety major enactments from 1873 to 1940. His data suggest greater presidential influence during Franklin Roosevelt's presidency than earlier. Neither Lapinski (2013) nor Ansolabehere, Palmer, and Schneer (2016) assess the relative influence of the president in their studies.

5. Although Patterson (1976) agrees that presidential power increased with Roosevelt, he cites factors besides those outlined by Greenstein (1988) to account for this change, such as the rise of the United States in international affairs, especially after the Second World War; the rise of labor unions and interest groups, which aided presidents in their elections and "added pressures on presidents to act decisively"; and intellectuals, who put their faith in "the Theodore Roosevelt–Wilsonian model of leadership" (56).

6. Edwards and Barrett (2000) find that Congress holds hearings on almost all major presidential policy proposals, although I have reported that only a small fraction of the president's legislative proposals reach the floor of either chamber for a roll call vote (Cohen 2012). Also see Lovett, Bevan, and Baumgartner (2015), who find that presidential approval increases the impact of presidential policy priorities on congressional committee attention to those issues.

7. A historical analog to public visibility is "presidential coattails." To my knowledge, there is only one major study of presidential coattails with a long historical viewpoint, Ferejohn and Calvert (1984), who investigate coattails from 1868 through 1980. They find that coattail effects appeared strongest during the premodern era. This presents a curious puzzle concerning the effects of the presidency on congressional behavior. But it is not clear that coattail voting has the same meaning for voters across the long sweep of US history. Coattail voting in the modern era may have much to do with the personalized, publicly visible president, but in earlier times it may have had more to do with partisan attachments.

8. It is commonplace to argue that presidents set the policy and public agendas. See Baumgartner and Jones (2010); Kingdon (1984); Light (1999).

9. I know of no research on executive order threats, akin to veto threats, in shaping legislation.

10. Moe and Teel (1970) update Chamberlain (1946) through 1967 and find that Congress has a larger role in policy making in the post–Franklin Roosevelt years than Chamberlain finds for the Roosevelt years.

11. The Reed Rules extended beyond quorum counts and included allowing the Speaker to deny recognition to members who sought to propose dilatory motions, reducing the quorum requirement in the Committee of the Whole to one hundred members, allowing the Speaker discretion to refer legislation to committees without debate, and enhancing the majority's ability to control the agenda in the House by increasing the Rules Committee's procedural authority and allowing the Committee of the Whole greater flexibility in choosing bills on the calendars, out of order (Jenkins and Stewart 2013, 270).

12. The strong speakership emerged for several reasons, some internal to Congress, such as the growing factional divisions within both parties (DiSalvo 2012; Jenkins and Stewart 2013). But the weakness of the presidency also may have contributed, with the strong speakership filling a leadership vacuum that resulted from the weak executive. Moreover, the growing strength of the speakership may have contributed to the decline of the presidency during the Gilded Age.

13. There is debate over when the modern presidency began to appear. Not everyone agrees that Franklin Roosevelt is the first modern president. Some point to aspects of presidential modernity appearing prior to Roosevelt, albeit not during the Gilded Age, and thus variously call William McKinley, Theodore Roosevelt, or Woodrow Wilson the first modern president. Clearly there is some conceptual disagreement over what constitutes the modern presidency and how "modern" the office must be for it to be considered fully modern. It might be useful to view Gilded Age presidents as premodern, the period from McKinley through Hoover as a period of modernizing, and presidents from Franklin Roosevelt to the present as modern. On McKinley as a modern president, see Gould (1980, 1982); Ponder (1999); Klinghard (2005); Merry (2017). On Theodore Roosevelt, see Arnold (1996); Dalton (2017); Gould (1991); Randall (1997). On Woodrow Wilson, see Bimes and Skowronek (1996); Clements (1992). Much of the work on Wilson as a modern president focuses on his public communications and rhetoric (Ryfe 1999; Tulis 1987).

14. There is also Skowronek's (1993) critique, which argues that the president's place in *political time* is more important to understanding the political and policy consequences of a president than is the premodern–modern divide.

15. This bargain allowed Rutherford B. Hayes to assume the presidency, although Democratic opponent Samuel Tilden received more votes, if federal troops were withdrawn from southern states and if Reconstruction were formally ended by allowing readmission of all Confederate states back into the Union and granting them representation in Congress and local home rule (Calhoun 2009).

16. Ironically, Roscoe Conkling never again served in the US Congress, although Thomas Platt resumed his Senate seat in 1897, serving until 1909.

17. In the 2017 C-SPAN rankings, Rutherford B. Hayes was ranked number 30 and Chester Arthur was ranked number 29 in relations with Congress, out of forty-three ranked presidents. Overall, Hayes was ranked 32 and Arthur 35. James Garfield, because of his very short tenure, was not ranked. See C-SPAN, "Presidential Historians Survey 2017," https://www.c-span.org/presidentsurvey2017.

18. Hayes's battle with Congress over patronage was reviewed earlier. James K. Polk may be less important to this argument, as he styled himself after his political mentor, Andrew Jackson.

19. One reason for not pushing their data collection earlier was the 1916 passage of the Revenue Act, which implemented the permanent income tax, making tariffs less important to financing government. From the nineteenth century to the Revenue Act, the tariffs were a major source of partisan division. As a consequence, presidents would be less inclined to manipulate tariff schedules for their own particularistic ends.

20. That Hayes clearly signaled his policy stance before receiving the objectionable bills means that this case does not fit into Cameron's (2000) sequential veto bargaining model, in which uncertainty about the president's true position leads Congress to produce bills that the president vetoes. Still, a bargaining game ensued after Hayes's vetoes, due to the necessity of passing appropriations bills.

21. As was true of Grover Cleveland, most of Arthur's vetoes concerned pensions for individual Civil War veterans.

10. COMPARING THE INFLUENCE OF PREMODERN AND MODERN PRESIDENTS

1. The request, in that case, is the policy initiative, not the dollar amount.

2. See www.voteview.com. The Voteview data were used in the earlier chapters for analysis of the years 1953 to 2012. Voteview uses the *CQ* presidential position for these years.

3. Given the public reticence of premodern presidents, Treier (2010) and Edwards (2014a, 2014b) argue that, to identify a president's *preferences*, all bills that the president signed should be included. Preference, however, differs from influence. For our purposes, which is to measure presidential influence, preferences cast too broad a net by including votes on which the president did not take a position on the roll call. Presidents, in Edwards, signify their preference after the roll call is cast by, for instance, signing the legislation but otherwise doing nothing to shape the bill or how members would vote on it. Plus, premodern presidents may have signed legislation even if they objected to it, due to a Whig or "clerkship" understanding of their role as president.

4. The Swift et al. (2001) Request data file, Rollreq, identifies an average of 12.7 positions, whereas my supplemental procedure identifies, on average, another 6.6 roll call positions per Congress.

5. Regressing the percentage of roll call positions on a Congress counter for the 45th to 72nd Congresses (1877 to 1932) finds a 0.2% increase in position taking with each additional Congress ($b = 0.20$, $t = 2.56$, $p = 0.02$, $R^2 = 0.21$), or about a 5.6% increase in roll call positions across the premodern period.

6. Of 8,962 roll calls, presidents took liberal positions on 414 (4.6%) and conservative positions on 318 (3.6%), for a total of 732 positions.

7. Premodern presidents took 165 liberal and 288 conservative positions out of 7,064, or 6.4%. Franklin Roosevelt and Harry S. Truman took 249 liberal and 30 conservative positions out of a total of 1,898 votes, or 14.7%.

8. For the 45th through 82nd Congresses, 2,350 of 8,962 roll calls (26.2%) are lopsided votes. For the 45th through the 72nd Congresses, 1,844 of 7,064 (26.1%) are lopsided votes, and for the 73rd through the 82nd, 506 of 1,898 (26.7%) are lopsided.

9. House party polarization is measured as the absolute difference in the first dimension of the DW-NOMINATE score for the Democratic and Republican parties for each Congress.

10. If House polarization is kept in as a treatment predictor, however, the substantive results do not change.

11. Approval may not be an important resource for premodern presidents, although not including it in the estimation may lead to model misspecification for the modern period. But there is no way to incorporate approval prior to the advent of modern polling. Thus, the analysis excludes approval, noting this estimation issue. In addition, although it is theoretically possible to categorize each roll call from 1877 to 1952 by policy area, as those from 1953 to 2012 are categorized, doing so would require a massive data coding effort. Again, lacking policy area information may affect estimation. Thus, we must be cautious when interpreting the results of pooling all years (1877 to 2012).

12. For instance, from 1877 to 1952 there are a total of 8,962 roll calls, compared to 26,909 from 1953 to 2012. Roll calls from 1877 to 1952 represent about 25% of all roll calls until 2012. Roll calls from 1877 to 1952 make up 28.6% of contested roll calls (6,612 from 1877 to 1992, and 16,457 from 1953 to 2012).

13. This lack of effect is repeated if we collapse the modern periods into one, with a dummy for the 73rd through 112th Congresses ($b = 0.02$, $SE = 0.03$, $p = 0.37$, one-tailed).

14. Democrats held 313, 322, and 334 seats during the 73rd through 75th Congresses (1933 to 1939), and 262 and 267 seats during the 76th and 77th Congresses (1939 to 1943), but only 222, 242, and 188 seats for the 78th through 80th Congresses (1943 to 1949), rebounding to 263 for the 81st Congress (1949 to 1951) but falling to 234 for the 82nd Congress (1951 to 1953). Thus, for many of the Franklin Roosevelt–Truman years, Democratic seats held either surpassed or nearly hit the 270-seat threshold.

15. But Congress also produced less public policy in the premodern era, which would increase the proportion of public policy that premodern presidents affect. To assess the policy impact of premodern presidents, we should look at both the absolute number of policies and the proportion of policies affected.

11. CONCLUSIONS: PRESIDENTIAL INFLUENCE IN CONGRESS

1. Similar to the heroic conception is the "textbook presidency," a phrase Thomas Cronin (1975) coined to describe how American politics textbooks depict the office, noting that

they focus more on the individual than on the office, especially highlighting those presidents ranked as great, and that they portray presidents as having more power than is the case. The textbook description of the presidency is still the dominant approach in secondary school textbooks (Roberts and Butler 2012).

2. This assumes that each additional roll call victory leads to enactment, which is not the case, because the Senate must act too, and the two legislative branches do not always agree. But it is a useful, simplifying assumption to illustrate the potential consequences of presidential influence.

3. To somewhat overstate the case, using Bond and Fleisher's (1990) seminal conceptualization, if presidency-centered factors do not affect congressional voting on presidential roll call votes but only Congress-centered factors do, then why even study presidency-centered factors? Of course, Bond and Fleisher and others recognize that one presidency-centered factor, presidential approval, has a marginal yet statistically significant effect on congressional voting. Still, approval, from their perspective, is only a small and secondary part of the story of presidential success in Congress.

4. Dahl's (1957) perspective on power and influence, as well as on behavioral orientations, is not without its critics. A useful critique of various definitions of power can be found in Isaac (1987). For a more recent debate and critique of Dahl, see Lukes (2015) and Baldwin (2015).

5. Several studies compare presidential approval across specific issues, especially foreign versus domestic issues. Generally, these studies find that when approval is higher on one issue, it is higher on another. Moreover, some suggest that policy-specific approval is merely a reflection of overall approval. See Cohen (2002a, 2002b); McAvoy (2006); Nickelsburg and Norpoth (2000). To my knowledge, there is only one study that looks at the impact of policy-specific approval on congressional support for the president. Gelpi and Grieco (2015) find that presidents do better in Congress when the public positively assesses their handling of international events.

6. It may be more difficult for the president, or for anyone, to affect voting on salient as opposed to less salient issues. On salient issues, the president may have to compete with constituent opinions, important interest groups, the political parties, and sometimes the member's own beliefs to influence a member's vote. On less salient issues, these competing forces may have less impact on the member's voting decision, if they are even present. Hence, this study's finding that presidents can influence member voting is all the more impressive.

7. Little research exists on why presidents take roll call positions. See Cumins (2008); Marshall and Prins (2007); Shull (2000); Shull and Shaw (2004).

8. But see Beckmann (2010) for one exception, with his comparison of earlygame and endgame lobbying efforts.

9. There is now extensive literature on presidential use of executive orders, much of it finding that presidents use executive orders more when the opposition party controls Congress. Belco and Rottinghaus (2017) review that literature.

10. There is already a small amount of literature on gubernatorial success (Ferguson 2003), on gubernatorial influence with regard to state budgets (McGrath, Rogowski, and Ryan 2016), and on executives cross-nationally (Saiegh 2011).

11. Recall the now famous anecdote, related in Neustadt (1954), in which congressional Republicans chided Eisenhower for failing to transmit a presidential program for them to work on in 1953. Eisenhower followed through with such a legislative program in 1954. Every president thereafter has followed suit.

REFERENCES

Abramowitz, Alan I. 2010. *The Disappearing Center: Engaged Citizens, Polarization, and American Democracy.* New Haven, CT: Yale University Press.

Aldrich, John H., Christopher Gelpi, Peter Feaver, Jason Reifler, and Kristin Thompson Sharp. 2006. "Foreign Policy and the Electoral Connection." *Annual Review of Political Science* 9: 477–502.

Aldrich, John H., and David W. Rohde. 2000a. "The Consequences of Party Organization in the House: The Role of the Majority and Minority Parties in Conditional Party Government." In *Polarized Politics: Congress and the President in a Partisan Era*, edited by Jon Bond and Richard Fleischer, 31–72. Washington, DC: CQ Press.

———. 2000b. "The Republican Revolution and the House Appropriations Committee." *Journal of Politics* 62 (1): 1–33.

Alexander, Dan, Christopher R. Berry, and William G. Howell. 2016. "Distributive Politics and Legislator Ideology." *Journal of Politics* 78 (1): 214–231.

Alter, Jonathan. 2006. *The Defining Moment: FDR's Hundred Days and The Triumph of Hope.* New York: Simon and Schuster.

Anderson, Sarah, and Philip Habel. 2009. "Revisiting Adjusted ADA Scores for the US Congress, 1947–2007." *Political Analysis* 17 (1): 83–88.

Ansolabehere, Stephen, Maxwell Palmer, and Benjamin Schneer. 2016. "What Has Congress Done?" In *Governing in a Polarized Age: Elections, Parties, and Political Representation in America*, edited by Alan S. Gerber and Eric Schickler, 243–266. New York: Cambridge University Press.

———. 2018. "Divided Government and Significant Legislation: A History of Congress from 1789 to 2010." *Social Science History* 42 (1): 81–108.

Arnold, Peri E. 1996. "Policy Leadership in the Progressive Presidency: The Case of Theodore Roosevelt's Naval Policy and His Search for Strategic Resources." *Studies in American Political Development* 10 (2): 333–359.

Arnold, R. Douglas. 1992. *The Logic of Congressional Action*. New Haven, CT: Yale University Press.

Ashbee, Edward. 2012. "The Obama Administration, the Left and Narratives of Failure." *The Political Quarterly* 83 (3): 567–575.

Austin, Peter C. 2011. "An Introduction to Propensity Score Methods for Reducing the Effects of Confounding in Observational Studies." *Multivariate Behavioral Research* 46 (3): 399–424.

Austen-Smith, David, and John R. Wright. 1994. "Counteractive Lobbying." *American Journal of Political Science* 38 (1): 25–44.

Bachrach, Peter, and Morton S. Baratz. 1962. "Two Faces of Power." *American Political Science Review* 56 (4): 947–952.

———. 1963. "Decisions and Nondecisions: An Analytical Framework." *American Political Science Review* 57 (3): 632–642.

Bailey, Jeremy D. 2007. *Thomas Jefferson and Executive Power*. New York: Cambridge University Press.

Bailey, Michael E. 2002. "The Heroic Presidency in the Era of Divided Government." *Perspectives on Political Science* 31 (1): 35–45.

Baldwin, David A. 2015. "Misinterpreting Dahl on Power." *Journal of Political Power* 8 (2): 209–227.

Balla, Steven J., Eric D. Lawrence, Forrest Maltzman, and Lee Sigelman. 2002. "Partisanship, Blame Avoidance, and the Distribution of Legislative Pork." *American Journal of Political Science* 46 (3): 515–525.

Bandura, Albert. 2000. "Exercise of Human Agency Through Collective Efficacy." *Current Directions in Psychological Science* 9 (3): 75–78.

Barrett, Andrew W. 2004. "Gone Public: The Impact of Going Public on Presidential Legislative Success." *American Politics Research* 32 (3): 338–370.

Barrett, Andrew W., and Matthew Eshbaugh-Soha. 2007. "Presidential Success on the Substance of Legislation." *Political Research Quarterly* 60 (1): 100–112.

Bartels, Larry M., Joshua D. Clinton, and John G. Geer. 2013. "Representation." In *Oxford Handbook of American Political Development*, edited by Richard Valelly, Suzanne Mettler, and Robert Lieberman, 399–424. New York: Oxford University Press.

Bateman, David A., Joshua Clinton, and John Lapinski. 2017. "A House Divided? Roll Calls, Polarization, and Policy Differences in the US House, 1877–2011." *American Journal of Political Science* 61 (3): 698–714.

Baumgartner, Frank R., Jeffrey M. Berry, Marie Hojnacki, Beth L. Leech, and David C. Kimball. 2009. *Lobbying and Policy Change: Who Wins, Who Loses, and Why*. Chicago, IL: University of Chicago Press.

Baumgartner, Frank R., and Bryan D. Jones. 2010. *Agendas and Instability in American Politics*. 2nd ed. Chicago, IL: University of Chicago Press.

Baumgartner, Frank R., and Beth L. Leech. 1996. "The Multiple Ambiguities of 'Counteractive Lobbying.'" *American Journal of Political Science* 40 (2): 521–542.

Beckmann, Matthew N. 2004. "Presidential Lobbying: How the White House Promotes the President's Policies on Capitol Hill." PhD diss., University of Michigan.

———. 2008. "The President's Playbook: White House Strategies For Lobbying Congress." *Journal of Politics* 70 (2): 407–419.

———. 2010. *Pushing the Agenda: Presidential Leadership in US Lawmaking, 1953–2004.* New York: Cambridge University Press.

———. 2016. "Up the Hill and Across the Aisle: Discovering the Path to Bipartisanship in Washington." *Legislative Studies Quarterly* 41 (2): 269–295.

Beckmann, Matthew N., Neilan S. Chaturvedi, and Jennifer Rosa Garcia. 2017. "Targeting the Treatment: The Strategy Behind Lyndon Johnson's Lobbying." *Legislative Studies Quarterly* 42 (2): 211–234.

Beckmann, Matthew N., and Joseph Godfrey. 2007. "The Policy Opportunities in Presidential Honeymoons." *Political Research Quarterly* 60 (2): 250–262.

Belanger, Eric, and Bonnie M. Meguid. 2008. "Issue Salience, Issue Ownership, and Issue-Based Vote Choice." *Electoral Studies* 27 (3): 477–491.

Belco, Michelle, and Brandon Rottinghaus. 2017. *The Dual Executive: Unilateral Orders in a Separated and Shared Power System.* Stanford, CA: Stanford University Press.

Berry, Christopher R., Barry Burden, and William G. Howell. 2010. "The President and the Distribution of Federal Spending." *American Political Science Review* 104 (4): 783–799.

Bimes, Terri. 2009. "Understanding the Rhetorical Presidency." In *The Oxford Handbook of the American Presidency*, edited by George C. Edwards III and William G. Howell, 208–231. New York: Oxford University Press.

Bimes, Terri, and Stephen Skowronek. 1996. "Woodrow Wilson's Critique of Popular Leadership: Reassessing the Modern–Traditional Divide in Presidential History." *Polity* 29 (1): 27–63.

Binkley, Wilfred Ellsworth. (1947) 1962. *President and Congress.* New York: Vintage.

Boehmke, Frederick J. 2006. "The Influence of Unobservable Factors on Position Timing and Content in the NAFTA Vote." *Political Analysis* 14 (4):421–438.

Bond, Jon R., and Richard Fleisher. 1980. "The Limits of Presidential Popularity as a Source of Influence in the U.S. House." *Legislative Studies Quarterly* 5 (1): 69–78.

———. 1984. "Presidential Popularity and Congressional Voting: A Reexamination of Public Opinion as a Source of Influence in Congress." *Western Political Quarterly* 37 (2): 291–306.

———. 1990. *The President in the Legislative Arena.* Chicago, IL: University of Chicago Press.

Bond, Jon R., Richard Fleisher, and Jeffrey E. Cohen. 2015. "Presidential–Congressional Relations in an Era of Polarized Parties and a 60-Vote Senate." In *American Gridlock: The Sources, Character, and Impact of Political Polarization*, edited by James A. Thurber and Antoine Yoshinaka, 133–151. New York: Cambridge University Press.

Bond, Jon R., Richard Fleisher, and B. Dan Wood. 2003. "The Marginal and Time-Varying Effect of Public Approval on Presidential Success in Congress." *Journal of Politics* 65 (1): 92–110.

Bond, Jon R., and Michael Northrup. 1988. "Public Opinion and Presidential Support." *Annals of the American Academy of Political and Social Science* 499 (1): 47–63.

Borrelli, Stephen A., and Grace L. Simmons. 1993. "Congressional Responsiveness to Presidential Popularity: The Electoral Context." *Political Behavior* 15 (2): 93–112.

REFERENCES

Box-Steffensmeier, Janet M., Laura W. Arnold, and Christopher J. W. Zorn. 1997. "The Strategic Timing of Position Taking in Congress: A Study of the North American Free Trade Agreement." *American Political Science Review* 91 (2): 324–338.

Boykoff, Jules, and Eulalie Laschever. 2011. "The Tea Party Movement, Framing, and the US Media." *Social Movement Studies* 10 (4): 341–366.

Brace, Paul, and Barbara Hinckley. 1992. *Follow the Leader: Opinion Polls and the Modern Presidents.* New York: Basic Books.

Brambor, Thomas, William Roberts Clark, and Matt Golder. 2006. "Understanding Interaction Models: Improving Empirical Analyses." *Political Analysis* 14 (1): 63–82.

Brewer, John, and Albert Hunter. 1989. *Multimethod Research: A Synthesis of Styles.* Thousand Oaks, CA: Sage.

Brooks, Clem, Kyle Dodson, and Nikole Hotchkiss. 2010. "National Security Issues and US Presidential Elections, 1992–2008." *Social Science Research* 39 (4): 518–526.

Bryce, James. 1989. *The American Commonwealth.* New York: Macmillan.

Burden, Barry C., Gregory A. Caldeira, and Tim Groseclose. 2000. "Measuring the Ideologies of US Senators: The Song Remains the Same." *Legislative Studies Quarterly* 25 (2): 237–258.

Burnham, Kenneth P., and David R. Anderson. 2004. "Multimodel Inference: Understanding AIC and BIC in Model Selection." *Sociological Methods and Research* 33 (2): 261–304.

Burstein, Paul. 2003. "The Impact of Public Opinion on Public Policy: A Review and an Agenda." *Political Research Quarterly* 56 (1): 29–40.

———. 2014. *American Public Opinion, Advocacy, and Policy in Congress: What the Public Wants and What It Gets.* New York: Cambridge University Press.

Butler, Daniel M., and Eleanor Neff Powell. 2014. "Understanding the Party Brand: Experimental Evidence on the Role of Valence." *Journal of Politics* 76 (2): 492–505.

Caldeira, Gregory, and Christopher J. W. Zorn. 2004. "Strategic Timing, Position-Taking, and Impeachment in the House of Representatives." *Political Research Quarterly* 57 (4): 517–527.

Calhoun, Charles W. 2002. "Reimagining the 'Lost Men' of the Gilded Age: Perspectives on the Late Nineteenth Century Presidents." *Journal of the Gilded Age and Progressive Era* 1 (3): 225–257.

———. 2009. "Hayes, Tilden, and American Politics." *Reviews in American History* 37 (3): 407–412.

Cameron, Charles M. 2000. *Veto Bargaining: Presidents and the Politics of Negative Power.* New York: Cambridge University Press.

———. 2002. "Studying the Polarized Presidency." *Presidential Studies Quarterly* 32 (4): 647–663.

Cameron, Charles M., and Jee-Kwang Park. 2011. "Going Public When Opinion Is Contested: Evidence from Presidents' Campaigns for Supreme Court Nominees, 1930–2009." *Presidential Studies Quarterly* 41 (3): 442–470.

Canes-Wrone, Brandice. 2004. "The Public Presidency, Personal Approval Ratings, and Policy Making." *Presidential Studies Quarterly* 34 (3): 477–492.

———. 2006. *Who Leads Whom?: Presidents, Policy, and the Public.* Chicago, IL: University of Chicago Press.

——. 2015. "From Mass Preferences to Policy." *Annual Review of Political Science* 18 (1): 147–165.

Canes-Wrone, Brandice, David W. Brady, and John F. Cogan. 2002. "Out of Step, Out of Office: Electoral Accountability and House Members' Voting." *American Political Science Review* 96 (1): 127–140.

Canes-Wrone, Brandice, and Scott de Marchi. 2002. "Presidential Approval and Legislative Success." *Journal of Politics* 64 (2): 491–509.

Canes-Wrone, Brandice, William G. Howell, and David E. Lewis. 2008. "Toward a Broader Understanding of Presidential Power: A Reevaluation of the Two Presidencies Thesis." *Journal of Politics* 70 (1): 1–16.

Carpenter, Daniel P. 2000. "State Building Through Reputation Building: Policy Innovation and Coalitions of Esteem at the Post Office, 1883–1912." *Studies in American Political Development* 14 (2): 121–155.

Carroll, Royce, and Keith Poole. 2014. "Roll Call Analysis and the Study of Legislatures." In *The Oxford Handbook of Legislative Studies*, edited by Shane Martin, Thomas Saalfeld, and Kaare Strom, 103–124. New York: Oxford University Press.

Carson, Jamie L., Gregory Koger, Matthew J. Lebo, and Everett Young. 2010. "The Electoral Costs of Party Loyalty in Congress." *American Journal of Political Science* 54 (3): 598–616.

Cattaneo, Matias D. 2010. "Efficient Semiparametric Estimation of Multi-Valued Treatment Effects under Ignorability." *Journal of Econometrics* 155 (2): 138–154.

Cavari, Amnon. 2017. *The Party Politics of Presidential Rhetoric*. New York: Cambridge University Press.

Cayton, Adam F. 2016. "Consistency Versus Responsiveness: Do Members of Congress Change Positions on Specific Issues in Response to Their Districts?" *Political Research Quarterly* 70 (1): 3–18.

Ceaser, James W., Glen E. Thurow, Jeffrey Tulis, and Joseph M. Bessette. 1981. "The Rise of the Rhetorical Presidency." *Presidential Studies Quarterly* 11 (2): 158–171.

Chamberlain, Lawrence H. 1946. "The President, Congress, and Legislation." *Political Science Quarterly* 61 (1): 42–60.

Choi, Seung-Whan. 2009. "The Effect of Outliers on Regression Analysis: Regime Type and Foreign Direct Investment." *Quarterly Journal of Political Science* 4 (2): 153–165.

Clarke, Andrew, and Kenneth Lowande. 2015. "The Vote-Buying President." Presented at the annual meeting of the American Political Science Association, September 3–6, 2015, San Francisco, CA.

Clausen, Aage R. 1973. *How Congressmen Decide: A Policy Focus*. New York: St. Martin's.

Clements, Kendrick A. 1992. *The Presidency of Woodrow Wilson*. Lawrence: University Press of Kansas.

Clinton, Joshua D., David E. Lewis, Stephanie Riegg Cellini, and Barry R. Weingast. 2004. "Strategically Speaking: A New Analysis of Presidents Going Public." http://papers.ssrn.com/sol3/papers.cfm?abstract_id=1153516.

Cohen, Jeffrey E. 1982. "The Impact of the Modern Presidency on Presidential Success in the US Congress." *Legislative Studies Quarterly* 7 (4): 515–532.

———. 1995. "Presidential Rhetoric and the Public Agenda." *American Journal of Political Science* 39 (1): 87–107.

———. 1997. *Presidential Responsiveness and Public Policy-Making: The Public and the Policies that Presidents Choose.* Ann Arbor: University of Michigan Press.

———. 2002a. "'The Polls': Policy-Specific Presidential Approval, Part 1." *Presidential Studies Quarterly* 32 (3): 600–609.

———. 2002b. "'The Polls': Policy-Specific Presidential Approval, Part 2." *Presidential Studies Quarterly* 32 (4): 779–788.

———. 2010. *Going Local: Presidential Leadership in the Post-Broadcast Age.* New York: Cambridge University Press.

———. 2011. "Presidents, Polarization, and Divided Government." *Presidential Studies Quarterly* 41 (3): 504–520.

———. 2012. *The President's Legislative Policy Agenda, 1789–2002.* New York: Cambridge University Press.

———. 2013. "Everybody Loves a Winner: On the Mutual Causality of Presidential Approval and Success in Congress." *Congress and the Presidency* 40 (3): 285–307.

———. 2015. "Presidential Leadership of Public Opinion: An Embedded Survey Experiment." *Political Communication* 32 (3): 345–355.

Cohen, Jeffrey E., Jon R. Bond, and Richard Fleisher. 2013. "Placing Presidential-Congressional Relations in Context: A Comparison of Barack Obama and His Predecessors." *Polity* 45 (1): 105–126.

———. 2014. "The Implications of the 2012 Presidential Election for Presidential–Congressional Relations." In *The 2012 Presidential Election: Forecasts, Outcomes, and Consequences,* edited by Amnon Cavari, Richard Powell, and Kenneth Mayer, 151–172. Lanham, MD: Rowman and Littlefield.

Cohen, Jeffrey E., Jon R. Bond, Richard Fleisher, and John A. Hamman. 2000. "State-Level Presidential Approval and Senatorial Support." *Legislative Studies Quarterly* 25 (4): 577–590.

Cohen, Jeffrey E., Michael A. Krassa, and John A. Hamman. 1991. "The Impact of Presidential Campaigning on Midterm US Senate Elections." *American Political Science Review* 85 (1): 165–178.

Coleman, John J., and Paul Manna. 2007. "Above the Fray? The use of Party System References in Presidential Rhetoric." *Presidential Studies Quarterly* 37 (3): 399–426.

Collier, Kenneth E. 1997. *Between the Branches: The White House Office of Legislative Affairs.* Pittsburgh, PA: University of Pittsburgh Press.

Collier, Kenneth, and Terry Sullivan. 1995. "New Evidence Undercutting the Linkage of Approval with Presidential Support and Influence." *Journal of Politics* 57 (1): 197–209.

Conley, Richard S. 2003. "George Bush and the 102d Congress: The Impact of Public and 'Private' Veto Threats on Policy Outcomes." *Presidential Studies Quarterly* 33 (4): 730–750

Conley, Richard S., and Richard M. Yon. 2007. "Legislative Liaison, White House Roll-Call Predictions and Divided Government: The Eisenhower Experience, 83rd–84th Congresses." *Presidential Studies Quarterly* 37 (2): 291–311.

Copeland, Gary W. 1983. "When Congress and the President Collide: Why Presidents Veto Legislation." *Journal of Politics* 45 (3): 696–710.

CQ Almanac. 1961. "How CQ Measures Congress' Performance." http://library.cqpress.com /cqalmanac/document.php?id=cqal61-879-29198-1371004.

Covington, Cary R. 1986. "Congressional Support for the President: The View from the Kennedy/Johnson White House." *Journal of Politics* 48 (3): 717–728.

——. 1987. " 'Staying Private': Gaining Congressional Support for Unpublicized Presidential Preferences on Roll Call Votes." *Journal of Politics* 49 (3): 737–755.

——. 1988a. "Building Presidential Coalitions Among Cross-Pressured Members of Congress." *Western Political Quarterly* 41 (1): 47–62.

——. 1988b. " 'Guess Who's Coming to Dinner': The Distribution of White House Social Invitations and Their Effects on Congressional Support." *American Politics Research* 16 (3): 243–265.

Covington, Cary R., J. Mark Wrighton, and Rhonda Kinney. 1995. "A 'Presidency-Augmented' Model of Presidential Success on House Roll Call Votes." *American Journal of Political Science* 39 (4): 1001–1024.

Cox, Gary W., and Mathew D. McCubbins. 2005. *Setting the Agenda: Responsible Party Government in the US House of Representatives.* New York: Cambridge University Press.

Cronin, Thomas. 1975. *The State of the Presidency.* 1st ed. New York: St. Martin's.

Cummins, Jeff. 2008. "State of the Union Addresses and Presidential Position Taking: Do Presidents Back Their Rhetoric in the Legislative Arena?" *Social Science Journal* 45 (3): 365–381.

——. 2010. "State of the Union Addresses and the President's Legislative Success." *Congress and the Presidency* 37 (2): 176–199.

Dahl, Robert A. 1950. *Congress and Foreign Policy.* New York: Harcourt, Brace.

——. 1957. "The Concept of Power." *Behavioral Science* 2 (3): 201–215.

——. 1976. *Modern Political Analysis.* 3rd ed. Englewood Cliffs, NJ: Prentice-Hall.

Dallek, Robert. 1984. *Ronald Reagan: The Politics of Symbolism.* Cambridge, MA: Harvard University Press.

——. 1998. *Flawed Giant: Lyndon Johnson and his Times, 1961–1973.* New York: Oxford University Press.

Dalton, Kathleen. 2017. "Changing Interpretations of Theodore Roosevelt and the Progressive Era." In *A Companion to the Gilded Age and Progressive Era,* edited by Christopher M. Nichols and Nancy C. Unger, 296–307. Malden, MA: Wiley Blackwell.

Davis, Eric L. 1979. "Legislative Liaison in the Carter Administration." *Political Science Quarterly* 94 (2): 287–301.

DiSalvo, Daniel. 2012. *Engines of Change: Party Factions in American Politics, 1868–2010.* New York: Oxford University Press.

Doenecke, Justus D. 1981. *The Presidencies of James A. Garfield and Chester A. Arthur.* Lawrence: University Press of Kansas.

Dominguez, Casey Byrne Knudsen. "Is It a Honeymoon? An Empirical Investigation of the President's First Hundred Days." *Congress and the Presidency.* 32 (1): 63–78.

Druckman, James N. 2006. "Brandice Canes-Wrone. Who Leads Whom? Presidents, Policy, and the Public." *Public Opinion Quarterly* 70 (3): 405–409.

Druckman, James N., Jordan Fein, and Thomas J. Leeper. 2012. "A Source of Bias in Public Opinion Stability." *American Political Science Review* 106 (2): 430–454.

Dwyer, Caitlin E., and Sarah A. Treul. 2012. "Indirect Presidential Influence, State-Level Approval, and Voting in the US Senate." *American Politics Research* 40 (2): 355–379.

Dynes, Adam, and Gregory A. Huber. 2015. "Partisanship and the Allocation of Federal Spending: Do Same-Party Legislators or Voters Benefit from Shared Party Affiliation?" *American Political Science Review* 109 (1): 172–186.

Edwards, Barry Clayton. 2014a. *Spatial Models of Presidential Behavior.* PhD diss., University of Georgia.

———. 2014b. "Putting Hoover on the Map: Was the 31st President a Progressive?" *Congress and the Presidency* 41 (1): 49–83.

Edwards, George C., III. 1976. "Presidential Influence in the House: Presidential Prestige as a Source of Presidential Power." *American Political Science Review* 70 (1): 101–113.

———. 1980. *Presidential Influence in Congress.* San Francisco, CA: W. H. Freeman.

———. 1985. "Measuring Presidential Success in Congress: Alternative Approaches." *Journal of Politics* 47 (2): 667–685.

———. 1986. "The Two Presidencies: A Reevaluation." *American Politics Quarterly* 14 (3): 247–263.

———. 1990. *At the Margins: Presidential Leadership of Congress.* New Haven, CT: Yale University Press.

———. 1991a. "George Washington's Leadership of Congress: Director or Facilitator?" *Congress and the Presidency* 18 (2): 163–180.

———. 1991b. "Presidential Influence in Congress: If We Ask the Wrong Questions, We Get the Wrong Answers." *American Journal of Political Science* 35 (3): 724–729.

———. 1997. "Aligning Tests with Theory: Presidential Approval as a Source of Influence in Congress." *Congress and the Presidency* 24 (2): 113–130.

———. 2006. *On Deaf Ears: The Limits of the Bully Pulpit.* New Haven, CT: Yale University Press.

———. 2009a. "Presidential Approval as a Source of Influence in Congress." In *The Oxford Handbook of the American Presidency,* edited by George C. Edwards III and William C. Howell, 338–361. New York: Oxford University Press.

———. 2009b. *The Strategic President: Persuasion and Opportunity in Presidential Leadership.* Princeton, NJ: Princeton University Press.

———. 2012. *Overreach: Leadership in the Obama Presidency.* Princeton, NJ: Princeton University Press.

———. 2016. *Predicting the Presidency: The Potential of Persuasive Leadership.* Princeton, NJ: Princeton University Press.

Edwards, George C., III, and Andrew Barrett. 2000. "Presidential Agenda Setting in Congress." In *Polarized Politics: Congress and the President in a Partisan Era,* edited by Jon R. Bond and Richard Fleisher, 109–133. Washington, DC: CQ Press.

Egar, William T. 2016. "Tarnishing Opponents, Polarizing Congress: The House Minority Party and the Construction of the Roll-Call Record." *Legislative Studies Quarterly* 41 (4): 935–964.

Ellis, Richard J. 2008. *Presidential Travel: The Journey from George Washington to George W. Bush.* Lawrence: University Press of Kansas.

REFERENCES

Eshbaugh-Soha, Matthew. 2010. "How Policy Conditions the Impact of Presidential Speeches on Legislative Success." *Social Science Quarterly* 91 (2): 415–435.

Eshbaugh-Soha, Matthew, and Sean Nicholson-Crotty. 2009. "Presidential Campaigning in Midterm Elections." *American Review of Politics* 30 (1): 35–50.

Evans, Rowland, and Robert D. Novak. 1966. *Lyndon B. Johnson: The Exercise of Power.* New York: New American Library.

Ferejohn, John A., and Randall L. Calvert. 1984. "Presidential Coattails in Historical Perspective." *American Journal of Political Science* 28 (1): 127–146.

Ferguson, Margaret Robertson. 2003. "Chief Executive Success in the Legislative Arena." *State Politics and Policy Quarterly* 3 (2): 158–182.

Fett, Patrick J. 1992. "Truth in Advertising: The Revelation of Presidential Legislative Priorities." *Western Political Quarterly* 45 (4): 895–920.

———. 1994. "Presidential Legislative Priorities and Legislators' Voting Decisions: An Exploratory Analysis." *Journal of Politics* 56 (2): 502–512.

———. 1996. "Vote Visibility, Roll Call Participation, and Strategic Absenteeism in the US House." *Congress and the Presidency* 23 (2): 87–10.

Fiorina, Morris P., Samuel J. Abrams, and Jeremy Pope. 2005. *Culture War?* New York: Pearson Longman.

Fleisher, Richard, and Jon R. Bond. 1988. "Are There Two Presidencies? Yes, But Only for Republicans." *Journal of Politics* 50 (3): 746–767.

———. 2004. "The Shrinking Middle in the US Congress." *British Journal of Political Science* 34 (3): 429–451.

Fleisher, Richard, Jon R. Bond, Glen S. Krutz, and Stephen Hanna. 2000. "The Demise of the Two Presidencies." *American Politics Quarterly* 28 (1): 3–25.

Fleisher, Richard, Jon R. Bond, and B. Dan Wood. 2008. "Which Presidents Are Uncommonly Successful in Congress?." In *Presidential Leadership: The Vortex of Power,* edited by Bert A. Rockman and Richard W. Waterman, 191–214. New York: Oxford University Press.

Folke, Olle, Shigeo Hirano, and James M. Snyder. 2011. "Patronage and Elections in US States." *American Political Science Review* 105 (3): 567–585.

Ford, Joan Butler, and Morris Zelditch Jr. 1988. "A Test of the Law of Anticipated Reactions." *Social Psychology Quarterly* 51 (2): 164–171.

Fournier, Patrick, André Blais, Richard Nadeau, Elisabeth Gidengil, and Neil Nevitte. 2003. "Issue Importance and Performance Voting." *Political Behavior* 25 (1): 51–67.

Fowler, Anthony, and Andrew B. Hall. 2013. "Conservative Vote Probabilities: An Easier Method for the Analysis of Roll Call Data" (September 24). https://dx.doi.org/10.2139/ssrn.2120720.

———. 2017. "Long-Term Consequences of Election Results." *British Journal of Political Science* 47 (2): 351–372.

Franzese, Robert, and Cindy Kam. 2009. *Modeling and Interpreting Interactive Hypotheses in Regression Analysis.* Ann Arbor: University of Michigan Press.

Friedrich, Carl J. 1941. *Constitutional Government and Democracy.* Boston: Little, Brown and Company.

Friedrich, Robert J. 1982. "In Defense of Multiplicative Terms in Multiple Regression Equations." *American Journal of Political Science* 26 (4): 797–833.

Frendreis, John, Raymond Tatalovich, and Jon Schaff. 2001. "Predicting Legislative Output in the First One-Hundred Days, 1897–1995." *Political Research Quarterly* 54 (4): 853–870.

Galvin, Daniel, and Colleen Shogan. 2004. "Presidential Politicization and Centralization Across the Modern–Traditional Divide." *Polity* 36 (3): 477–504.

Galvin, Daniel J. 2013. "Presidential Partisanship Reconsidered: Eisenhower, Nixon, Ford, and the Rise of Polarized Politics." *Political Research Quarterly* 66 (1): 46–60.

———. 2014. "Presidents as Agents of Change." *Presidential Studies Quarterly* 44 (1): 95–119.

Gelpi, Christopher, and Joseph M. Grieco. 2015. "Competency Costs in Foreign Affairs: Presidential Performance in International Conflicts and Domestic Legislative Success, 1953–2001." *American Journal of Political Science* 59 (2): 440–456.

Genovese, Michael A., Todd L. Belt, and William W. Lammers. 2016. *Presidency and Domestic Policy: Comparing Leadership Styles, FDR to Obama*. New York: Routledge.

Gilens, Martin. 2012. *Affluence and Influence: Economic Inequality and Political Power in America*. Princeton, NJ: Princeton University Press.

Godwin, Erik K., and Nathan A. Ilderton. 2014. "Presidential Defense: Decisions and Strategies to Preserve the Status Quo." *Political Research Quarterly* 67 (4): 715–728

Gould, Lewis L. 1980. *The Presidency of William McKinley*. Lawrence: University Press of Kansas.

———. 1982. *The Spanish-American War and President McKinley*. Lawrence: University Press of Kansas.

———. 1991. *The Presidency of Theodore Roosevelt*. Lawrence: University Press of Kansas.

Green, Matthew N. 2015. *Underdog Politics: The Minority Party in the US House of Representatives*. New Haven, CT: Yale University Press.

Greenstein, Fred I. 1978. "Change and Continuity in the Modern Presidency." In *The New American Political System*, edited by Anthony King, 45–85. Washington, DC: American Enterprise Institute.

———, ed. 1988. *Leadership in the Modern Presidency*. Cambridge, MA: Harvard University Press.

———. 2004. *The Presidential Difference: Leadership Style from FDR to George W. Bush*. Princeton, NJ: Princeton University.

———. 2009. *Inventing the Job of President: Leadership Style from George Washington to Andrew Jackson*. Princeton, NJ: Princeton University Press.

Gronke, Paul, Jeffrey Koch, and J. Matthew Wilson. 2003. "Follow the Leader? Presidential Approval, Presidential Support, and Representatives' Electoral Fortunes." *Journal of Politics* 65 (3): 785–808.

Groseclose, Tim, Steven D. Levitt, and James M. Snyder. 1999. "Comparing Interest Group Scores Across Time and Chambers: Adjusted ADA Scores for the US Congress." *American Political Science Review* 93 (1): 33–50.

Grossmann, Matt. 2014. *Artists of the Possible: Governing Networks and American Policy Change Since 1945*. New York: Oxford University Press.

REFERENCES

Hacker, Jacob S. 2001. "Learning from Defeat? Political Analysis and the Failure of Health Care Reform in the United States." *British Journal of Political Science* 31 (1): 61–94.

Hamman, John A., and Jeffrey E. Cohen. 1997. "Reelection and Congressional Support: Presidential Motives in Distributive Politics." *American Politics Quarterly* 25 (1): 56–74.

Han, Hahrie, and David W. Brady. 2007. "A Delayed Return to Historical Norms: Congressional Party Polarization after the Second World War." *British Journal of Political Science* 37 (3): 505–531.

Hargrove, Erwin C. 1974. *The Power of the Modern Presidency.* Philadelphia: Temple University Press.

———. 1988. *Jimmy Carter as President: Leadership and the Politics of the Public Good.* Baton Rouge: Louisiana State University Press.

———. 2016. *Effective Presidency: Lessons on Leadership from John F. Kennedy to Barack Obama.* New York: Routledge.

Hart, John. 1981. "Congressional Reactions to White House Lobbying." *Presidential Studies Quarterly* 11 (1): 83–91.

———. 1983. "Staffing the Presidency: Kennedy and the Office of Congressional Relations." *Presidential Studies Quarterly* 13 (1): 101–110.

Hassell, Hans J. G., and Samuel Kernell. 2016. "Veto Rhetoric and Legislative Riders." *American Journal of Political Science* 60 (4): 845–859.

Heaphy, Maura E. 1975. "Executive Legislative Liaison." *Presidential Studies Quarterly* 5 (4): 42–46.

Heffington, Colton, Brandon Beomseob Park, and Laron K. Williams. 2017. "The 'Most Important Problem' Dataset (MIPD): A New Dataset on American Issue Importance." *Conflict Management and Peace Science* (March 31): 1–24. https://doi.org/10.1177%2F0738894217691463.

Herrnson, Paul S., and Irwin L. Morris. 2007. "Presidential Campaigning in the 2002 Congressional Elections." *Legislative Studies Quarterly* 32 (4): 629–648.

Herrnson, Paul S., Irwin L. Morris, and John McTague. 2011. "The Impact of Presidential Campaigning for Congress on Presidential Support in the US House of Representatives." *Legislative Studies Quarterly* 36 (1): 99–122.

Hetherington, Marc J. 2009. "Review Article: Putting Polarization in Perspective." *British Journal of Political Science* 39 (2): 413–448.

Hill, Kim Quaile. 1998. "The Policy Agendas of the President and the Mass Public: A Research Validation and Extension." *American Journal of Political Science* 42 (4): 1328–1334.

———. 2001. "Multiple-Method Measurement of Legislators' Ideologies." *Legislative Studies Quarterly* 26 (2): 263–274.

Hoddie, Matthew, and Stephen R. Routh. 2004. "Predicting the Presidential Presence: Explaining Presidential Midterm Elections Campaign Behavior." *Political Research Quarterly* 57 (2): 257–265.

Hofstadter, Richard. (1948) 1989. *The American Political Tradition and the Men Who Made It.* New York: Vintage.

Hogan, Joseph. 1990. *The Reagan Years: The Record in Presidential Leadership.* Manchester: Manchester University Press.

Hollibaugh, Gary E., Lawrence S. Rothenberg, and Kristin K. Rulison. 2013. "Does It Really Hurt to Be Out of Step?" *Political Research Quarterly* 66 (4): 856–867.

Holmes, Lisa M. 2007. "Presidential Strategy in the Judicial Appointment Process: 'Going Public' in Support of Nominees to the US Courts of Appeals." *American Politics Research* 35 (5): 567–594.

Holtzman, Abraham. 1970. *Legislative Liaison: Executive Leadership in Congress*. Chicago, IL: Rand McNally.

Hoogenboom, Ari A. 1988. *The Presidency of Rutherford B. Hayes*. Lawrence: University Press of Kansas.

———. 1995. *Rutherford B. Hayes: Warrior and President*. Lawrence: University of Press Kansas.

Howell, William G. 2003. *Power Without Persuasion: The Politics of Direct Presidential Action*. Princeton, NJ: Princeton University Press.

Howell, William G., Saul P. Jackman, and Jon C. Rogowski. 2013. *The Wartime President*. Chicago, IL: University of Chicago Press.

Howell, William G., and Jon C. Rogowski. 2013. "War, the Presidency, and Legislative Voting Behavior." *American Journal of Political Science* 57 (1): 150–166.

Huang, Taofang, and Sean M. Theriault. 2012. "The Strategic Timing Behind Position-Taking in the US Congress: A Study of the Comprehensive Immigration Reform Act." *Journal of Legislative Studies* 18 (1): 41–62.

Hudak, John. 2014. *Presidential Pork: White House Influence Over the Distribution of Federal Grants*. Washington, DC: Brookings Institution Press.

Huntington, Samuel P. 1965. "Congressional Responses to the Twentieth Century." In *The Congress and America's Future*, edited by David B. Truman, 5–31. Englewood Cliffs, NJ: Prentice Hall.

Imbens, Guido W., and Jeffrey M. Wooldridge. 2009. "Recent Developments in the Econometrics of Program Evaluation." *Journal of Economic Literature* 47 (1): 5–86.

Isaac, Jeffrey C. 1987. "Beyond the Three Faces of Power: A Realist Critique." *Polity* 20 (1): 4–31.

Jacobs, Lawrence R., and Desmond S. King. 2010. "Varieties of Obamaism: Structure, Agency, and the Obama Presidency." *Perspectives on Politics* 8 (3): 793–802.

Jacobson, Gary C., Samuel Kernell, and Jeffrey Lazarus. 2004. "Assessing the President's Role as Party Agent in Congressional Elections: The Case of Bill Clinton in 2000." *Legislative Studies Quarterly* 29 (2): 159–184.

James, Dorothy Buckton. 1969. *The Contemporary Presidency*. Indianapolis, IN: Pegasus.

Jenkins, Jeffery A., and Nathan W. Monroe. 2016. "On Measuring Legislative Agenda-Setting Power." *American Journal of Political Science* 60 (1): 158–174.

Jenkins, Jeffery A., and Timothy Nokken. 2008. "Presidential Vote Buying in Congress." Presented at the annual meeting of the American Political Science Association, Boston, MA. https://pdfs.semanticscholar.org/4393/9542634f74108c30892d6cc99b286bc08311.pdf.

Jenkins, Jeffery A., and Charles Stewart III. 2013. *Fighting for the Speakership: The House and the Rise of Party Government*. Princeton, NJ: Princeton University Press.

Jenkins-Smith, Hank C., Carol L. Silva, and Richard W. Waterman. 2005. "Micro- and Macrolevel Models of the Presidential Expectations Gap." *Journal of Politics* 67 (3): 690–715.

Jennings, Will, and Christopher Wlezien. 2011. "Distinguishing Between Most Important Problems and Issues." *Public Opinion Quarterly* 75 (3): 545–555.

Jochim, Ashley E., and Bryan D. Jones. 2013. "Issue Politics in a Polarized Congress." *Political Research Quarterly* 66 (2): 352–369.

Jones, Bryan D., and Frank R. Baumgartner. 2004. "Representation and Agenda Setting." *Policy Studies Journal* 32 (1): 1–24.

Jones, Bryan D., Heather Larsen-Price, and John Wilkerson. 2009. "Representation and American Governing Institutions." *Journal of Politics* 71 (1): 277–290.

Jones, Charles O. 1988a. *The Reagan Legacy: Promise and Performance.* Chatham, NJ: Chatham House.

———. 1988b. *The Trusteeship Presidency: Jimmy Carter and the United States Congress.* Baton Rouge: Louisiana State University Press.

———. 2000. *The Presidency in a Separated System.* 1st ed. Washington, DC: Brookings Institution Press.

Karaman, K. Kivanc, and Şevket Pamuk. 2013. "Different Paths to the Modern State in Europe: The Interaction Between Warfare, Economic Structure, and Political Regime." *American Political Science Review* 107 (3): 603–626.

Keller, Morton. 1977. *Affairs of State: Public Life in Late Nineteenth Century America.* Cambridge, MA: Harvard University Press.

Kellerman, Barbara. 1984. *The Political Presidency: Practice of Leadership.* New York: Oxford University Press.

Kennedy, David M. 1999. *Freedom from Fear: The American People in Depression and War, 1929–1945.* New York: Oxford University Press.

Kerbel, Matthew R. 1991. *Beyond Persuasion: Organizational Efficiency and Presidential Power.* Albany: SUNY Press.

———. 1993. "An Empirical Test of the Role of Persuasion in the Exercise of Presidential Power." *Presidential Studies Quarterly* 23 (2): 347–361.

Kernell, Samuel. 1986. *Going Public: New Strategies of Presidential Leadership.* 1st ed. CQ Press.

———. 2006. *Going Public: New Strategies of Presidential Leadership.* 4th ed. CQ Press.

Kernell, Samuel, and Michael P. McDonald. 1999. "Congress and America's Political Development: The Transformation of the Post Office from Patronage to Service." *American Journal of Political Science* 43 (3): 792–811.

Kiewiet, D. Roderick, and Mathew D. McCubbins. 1985. "Appropriations Decisions as a Bilateral Bargaining Game Between President and Congress." *Legislative Studies Quarterly* 10 (2): 181–201.

———. 1988. "Presidential Influence on Congressional Appropriations Decisions." *American Journal of Political Science* 32 (3): 713–736.

———. 1991. *The Logic of Delegation.* Chicago, IL: University of Chicago Press.

Kingdon, John W. 1967. "Politicians' Beliefs about Voters." *American Political Science Review* 61 (1): 137–145.

———. 1984. *Agendas, Alternatives, and Public Policies.* Boston: Little, Brown.

———. 1989. *Congressmen's Voting Decisions.* 3rd ed. Ann Arbor: University of Michigan Press.

Klinghard, Daniel P. 2005. "Grover Cleveland, William McKinley, and the Emergence of the President as Party Leader." *Presidential Studies Quarterly* 35 (4): 736–760.

Kravitz, Walter. 1990. "The Advent of the Modern Congress: The Legislative Reorganization Act of 1970." *Legislative Studies Quarterly* 15 (3): 375–399.

Krebs, Ronald R. 2015. "How Dominant Narratives Rise and Fall: Military Conflict, Politics, and the Cold War Consensus." *International Organization* 69 (4): 809–845.

Krehbiel, Keith. 1991. *Information and Legislative Organization.* Ann Arbor: University of Michigan Press.

——. 1998. *Pivotal Politics: A Theory of US Lawmaking.* Chicago, IL: University of Chicago Press.

Kriner, Douglas L., and Andrew Reeves. 2014. "Responsive Partisanship: Public Support for the Clinton and Obama Health Care Plans." *Journal of Health Politics, Policy and Law* 39 (4): 717–749.

——. 2015a. *The Particularistic President: Executive Branch Politics and Political Inequality.* New York: Cambridge University Press.

——. 2015b. "Presidential Particularism and Divide-the-Dollar Politics." *American Political Science Review* 109 (1): 155–171.

Krutz, Glen S. 2005 "Issues and Institutions: 'Winnowing' in the US Congress." *American Journal of Political Science* 49 (2): 313–326.

Kuklinski, James H. 1978. "Representativeness and Elections: A Policy Analysis." *American Political Science Review* 72 (1): 165–177.

Lang, Matthew, Brandon Rottinghaus, and Gerhard Peters. 2011. "Polls and Elections: Revisiting Midterm Visits: Why the Type of Visit Matters." *Presidential Studies Quarterly* 41 (4): 809–818.

Lapinski, John S. 2013. *The Substance of Representation: Congress, American Political Development, and Lawmaking.* Princeton, NJ: Princeton University Press.

Lax, Jeffrey R., and Justin H. Phillips. 2012. "The Democratic Deficit in the States." *American Journal of Political Science* 56 (1): 148–166.

Layman, Geoffrey C., Thomas M. Carsey, and Juliana Menasce Horowitz. 2006. "Party Polarization in American Politics: Characteristics, Causes, and Consequences." *Annual Review of Political Science* 9 (2): 83–110.

Lebo, Matthew J., and Andrew J. O'Geen. 2011. "The President's Role in the Partisan Congressional Arena." *Journal of Politics* 73 (3): 718–734.

Lee, Frances E. 2008. "Dividers, Not Uniters: Presidential Leadership and Senate Partisanship, 1981–2004." *Journal of Politics* 70 (4): 914–928.

——. 2009. *Beyond Ideology: Politics, Principles, and Partisanship in the US Senate.* Chicago, IL: University of Chicago Press.

Leech, Beth L., and Frank R. Baumgartner. 1998. "Lobbying Friends and Foes in Washington." In *Interest Group Politics*, 5th ed., edited by Allan J. Cigler and Burdette A. Loomis, 217–234. Washington, DC: CQ Press.

Leuchtenburg, William E. 2009. *In the Shadow of FDR: From Harry Truman to Barack Obama.* 4th ed. Ithaca, NY: Cornell University Press.

REFERENCES

Levendusky, Matthew. 2009. *The Partisan Sort: How Liberals Became Democrats and Conservatives Became Republicans.* Chicago, IL: University of Chicago Press.

Lewis, David. 1997 "The Two Rhetorical Presidencies: An Analysis of Televised Presidential Speeches, 1947–1991." *American Politics Quarterly* 25 (3): 380–395.

Light, Paul C. 1999. *The President's Agenda: Domestic Policy Choice from Kennedy to Clinton.* 3rd ed. Baltimore: Johns Hopkins University Press.

Lindsay, James M., and Wayne P. Steger. 1993. "The 'Two Presidencies' in Future Research: Moving Beyond Roll-Call Analysis." *Congress and the Presidency* 20 (2): 103–118.

Lockerbie, Brad, Stephen Borrelli, and Scott Hedger. 1998. "An Integrative Approach to Modeling Presidential Success in Congress." *Political Research Quarterly* 51 (1): 155–172.

Lovett, John, Shaun Bevan, and Frank R. Baumgartner. 2015. "Popular Presidents Can Affect Congressional Attention, For a Little While." *Policy Studies Journal* 43 (1): 22–43.

Lowande, Kenneth S., Jeffery A. Jenkins, and Andrew J. Clarke. 2018. "Presidential Particularism and US Trade Politics." *Political Science Research and Methods* 6 (2): 265–281.

Lowery, David. 2013. "Lobbying Influence: Meaning, Measurement and Missing." *Interest Groups and Advocacy* 2 (1): 1–26.

Lukes, Steven. 2015. "Robert Dahl on Power." *Journal of Political Power* 8 (2): 261–271.

Lynch, Michael S., and Anthony J. Madonna. 2013. "Viva Voce: Implications from the Disappearing Voice Vote, 1865–1996." *Social Science Quarterly* 94 (2): 530–550.

Mack, W. R., Karl DeRouen, and David Lanoue. 2013. "Foreign Policy Votes and Presidential Support in Congress." *Foreign Policy Analysis* 9 (1): 79–102.

Mak, Maxwell, and Andrew H. Sidman. 2014. "Get the Party Started: An Examination of the Influence of Presidential Approval on Party Unity in Congress." Presented at the annual meeting of the Midwest Political Science Association, Chicago, IL.

Manley, John F. 1978. "Presidential Power and White House Lobbying." *Political Science Quarterly* 93 (2): 255–275.

Marshall, Bryan W., and Richard L. Pacelle. 2005. "Revisiting the Two Presidencies: The Strategic Use of Executive Orders." *American Politics Research* 33 (1): 81–105.

Marshall, Bryan W., and Brandon C. Prins. 2002. "The Pendulum of Congressional Power: Agenda Change, Partisanship and the Demise of the Post–World War II Foreign Policy Consensus." *Congress and the Presidency* 29 (2): 195–215.

———. 2007. "Strategic Position Taking and Presidential Influence in Congress." *Legislative Studies Quarterly* 32 (2): 257–284.

Matthews, Steven A. 1989. "Veto Threats: Rhetoric in a Bargaining Game." *Quarterly Journal of Economics* 104 (2): 347–369.

Mayhew, David R. 1974. *Congress: The Electoral Connection.* New Haven, CT: Yale University Press.

McAvoy, Gregory E. 2006. "Stability and Change: The Time Varying Impact of Economic and Foreign Policy Evaluations on Presidential Approval." *Political Research Quarterly* 59 (1): 71–83.

McCarty, Nolan. 2009. "Presidential Vetoes in the Early Republic: Changing Constitutional Norms or Electoral Reform?" *Journal of Politics* 71 (2): 369–384.

McCormick, James M., and Eugene R. Wittkopf. 1990. "Bipartisanship, Partisanship, and Ideology in Congressional–Executive Foreign Policy Relations, 1947–1988." *Journal of Politics* 52 (4):1077–1100.

McElvaine, Robert S. 1984. *The Great Depression: America, 1929–1941*. New York: Times Books.

McGrath, Robert J., Jon C. Rogowski, and Josh M. Ryan. 2016. "Veto Override Requirements and Executive Success." *Political Science Research and Methods* 6 (1): 153–179.

McPherson, James M. 1992. *Abraham Lincoln and the Second American Revolution*. New York: Oxford University Press.

Meernik, James. 1993. "Presidential Support in Congress: Conflict and Consensus on Foreign and Defense Policy." *Journal of Politics* 55 (3): 569–587.

Meinke, Scott R. 2008. "Institutional Change and the Electoral Connection in the Senate: Revisiting the Effects of Direct Election." *Political Research Quarterly* 61 (3): 445–457.

Mellen, Rob, and Kathleen Searles. 2013a. "Midterm Mobilization: The President as Campaigner-in-Chief During Midterm House Elections, 1982–2006." *White House Studies* 13 (2): 187–199.

——. 2013b. "Predicting Presidential Appearances During Midterm Elections: The President and House Candidates, 1982–2010." *American Politics Research* 41 (2): 328–347.

Merry, Robert W. 2017. *President McKinley: Architect of the American Century*. New York: Simon and Schuster.

Mervin, David. 1987. "The President and Congress." In *The Modern Presidency: From Roosevelt to Reagan*, edited by Malcolm Shaw, 83–118. New York: Harper and Row.

Middlemass, Keesha M., and Christian R. Grose. 2007. "The Three Presidencies? Legislative Position Taking in Support of the President on Domestic, Foreign, and Homeland Security Policies in the 107th Congress (2001–02)." *Congress and the Presidency* 34 (2): 57–80.

Miler, Kristina C. 2010. *Constituency Representation in Congress: The View from Capitol Hill*. New York: Cambridge University Press.

——. 2016. "Legislative Responsiveness to Constituency Change." *American Politics Research* 44 (5): 816–843.

Milkis, Sidney M., and Michael Nelson. 2015. *The American Presidency: Origins and Development, 1776–2014*. Washington, DC: CQ Press.

Milner, Helen V., and Dustin Tingley. 2015. *Sailing the Water's Edge: The Domestic Politics of American Foreign Policy*. Princeton, NJ: Princeton University Press.

Mitnick, Barry M. 2015. "Agency Theory." *Wiley Encyclopedia of Management* (January 21). https://doi.org/10.1002/9781118785317.weom020097.

Moe, Ronald C., and Steven C. Teel. 1970. "Congress as Policy-Maker: A Necessary Reappraisal." *Political Science Quarterly* 85 (3): 443–470.

Moe, Terry. 1985. "The Politicized Presidency." In *The New Direction in American Politics*, edited by John E. Chubb and Paul E. Peterson, 235–271. Washington, DC: Brookings Institution Press.

Moe, Terry M. 2009. "The Revolution in Presidential Studies." *Presidential Studies Quarterly* 39 (4): 701–724.

Moe, Terry M., and William G. Howell. 1999. "Unilateral Action and Presidential Power: A Theory." *Presidential Studies Quarterly* 29 (4): 850–873.

Monroe, Alan D. 1979. "Consistency Between Constituency Preferences and National Policy Decisions." *American Politics Quarterly* 7 (1): 3–19.

———. 1998. "Public Opinion and Public Policy, 1980–1993." *Public Opinion Quarterly* 62 (1): 6–28.

Morgan, Stephen L., and David J. Harding. 2006. "Matching Estimators of Causal Effects: Prospects and Pitfalls in Theory and Practice." *Sociological Methods and Research* 35 (1): 3–60.

Mullen, William F. 1982. "Perceptions of Carter's Legislative Successes and Failures: Views from the Hill and the Liaison Staff." *Presidential Studies Quarterly* 12 (4): 522–533.

Murray, Shoon Kathleen. 2006. "Private Polls and Presidential Policymaking: Reagan as a Facilitator of Change." *Public Opinion Quarterly* 70 (4): 477–498.

Neustadt, Richard E. 1954. "Presidency and Legislation: The Growth of Central Clearance." *American Political Science Review* 48 (3): 641–671.

———. 1955. "Presidency and Legislation: Planning the President's Program." *American Political Science Review* 49 (4): 980–1021.

———. 1960. *Presidential Power.* New York: Macmillan.

———. 1991. *Presidential Power and the Modern Presidents: The Politics of Leadership from Roosevelt to Reagan.* New York: Simon and Schuster.

Nickelsburg, Michael, and Helmut Norpoth. 2000. "Commander-in-Chief or Chief Economist? The President in the Eye of the Public." *Electoral Studies* 19 (2): 313–332.

Ostrom, Charles W., and Dennis M. Simon. 1985. "Promise and Performance: A Dynamic Model of Presidential Popularity." *American Political Science Review* 79 (2): 334–358.

Palazollo, Daniel J., and Bill Swinford. 1994. " 'Remember in November?' Ross Perot, Presidential Power, and the NAFTA." Paper presented at the annual meeting of the American Political Science Association, New York.

Patterson, James T. 1976. "The Rise of Presidential Power Before World War II." *Law and Contemporary Problems* 40 (2): 39–57.

Paul, Ezra. 1998. "Congressional Relations and 'Public Relations' in the Administration of Rutherford B. Hayes (1877–81)." *Presidential Studies Quarterly* 28 (1): 68–87.

Pedhazur, Elazar J. 1997. *Multiple Regression in Behavioral Research: Explanation and Prediction.* 3rd ed. Belmont, CA: Wadsworth.

Perino, Michael. 2010. *The Hellhound of Wall Street: How Ferdinand Pecora's Investigation of the Great Crash Forever Changed American Finance.* New York: Penguin.

Ponder, Stephen. 1999. *Managing the Press: Origins of the Media Presidency, 1897–1933.* New York: Macmillan.

Poole, Keith T., and Howard Rosenthal. 1997. *Congress: A Political-Economic History of Roll Call Voting.* New York: Oxford University Press.

Powell, Eleanor Neff. 2015. "Pure Position-Taking in the US House of Representatives" (April 12). http://www.eleanorneffpowell.com/uploads/8/3/9/3/8393347/powell_-_expanded_roll_call_-_mpsa_2015.pdf.

Powell, Richard J., and Dean Schloyer. 2003. "Public Presidential Appeals and Congressional Floor Votes: Reassessing the Constitutional Threat." *Congress and the Presidency* 30 (2): 123–138.

Prins, Brandon C., and Bryan W. Marshall. 2001. "Congressional Support of the President: A Comparison of Foreign, Defense, and Domestic Policy Decision Making During and After the Cold War." *Presidential Studies Quarterly* 31 (4): 660–678.

Rabinowitz George, James W. Prothro, and William Jacoby. 1982. "Salience as a Factor in the Impact of Issues in Candidate Evaluation." *Journal of Politics* 44 (1): 41–63.

Raftery, Adrian E. 1995. "Bayesian Model Selection in Social Research." *Sociological Methodology* 25 (1): 111–163.

Rasler, Karen A., and William R. Thompson. 1985. "War Making and State Making: Governmental Expenditures, Tax Revenues, and Global Wars." *American Political Science Review* 79 (2): 491–507.

———. 2015. *The Great Powers and Global Struggle, 1490–1990.* Lexington: University Press of Kentucky.

Reeves, Thomas C. 1975. *Gentleman Boss: The Life of Chester Alan Arthur.* New York: Random House.

Rhodes, Jesse H. 2014. "Party Polarization and the Ascendance of Bipartisan Posturing as a Dominant Strategy in Presidential Rhetoric." *Presidential Studies Quarterly* 44 (1): 120–142.

Richardson, James D., ed. 1917. *A Compilation of Messages and Papers of the Presidents.* Online Books Page, http://onlinebooks.library.upenn.edu/webbin/metabook?id=mppresidents.

Rivers, Douglas, and Nancy Rose. 1985. "Passing the President's Program: Public Opinion and Presidential Influence in Congress." *American Journal of Political Science* 29 (1): 183–196.

Roberts, Jason M., Steven S. Smith, and Stephen R. Haptonstahl. 2016. "The Dimensionality of Congressional Voting Reconsidered." *American Politics Research* 44 (5): 794–815.

Roberts, Scott L., and Brandon M. Butler. 2012. "Idealizing and Localizing the Presidency: The President's Place in State History Textbooks." In *The New Politics of the Textbook: Critical Analysis in Core Content Areas*, edited by Heather Hickman and Brad J. Profilio, 287–303. Rotterdam: Sense Publishers.

Rogowski, Jon C. 2015. "Presidential Incentives, Bureaucratic Control, and Party Building in the Republican Era." *Presidential Studies Quarterly* 45 (4): 796–811

———. 2016. "Presidential Influence in an Era of Congressional Dominance." *American Political Science Review* 110 (2): 325–341.

———. 2017. "Bargaining Commitments and Executive Reputation: Legislative Response to Unilateral Action" (June 16). https://scholar.harvard.edu/files/rogowski/files/reputation.pdf.

Roper, Jon. 2004. "The Contemporary Presidency: George W. Bush and the Myth of Heroic Presidential Leadership." *Presidential Studies Quarterly* 34 (1): 132–142.

Rosenman, Samuel I., ed. 1938–1950. *The Public Papers and Addresses of Franklin D. Roosevelt.* New York: Russell and Russell.

Rubin, Donald B. 1973. "Matching to Remove Bias in Observational Studies." *Biometrics* 29 (1): 159–183.

Rudalevige, Andrew. 2002. *Managing the President's Program: Presidential Leadership and Legislative Policy Formulation.* Princeton, NJ: Princeton University Press.

———. 2005. "The Executive Branch and the Legislative Process." In *The Executive Branch*, edited by Joel D. Aberbach and Mark A. Peterson, 419–451. New York: Oxford University Press.

Rutledge, Paul E. 2009. *Agenda Setting and Presidential Power in the United States*. PhD diss., West Virginia University.

Ryfe, David Michael. 1999. " 'Betwixt and Between': Woodrow Wilson's Press Conferences and the Transition Toward the Modern Rhetorical Presidency." *Political Communication* 16 (1): 77–93.

Saiegh, Sebastian M. 2011. *Ruling by Statute: How Uncertainty and Vote Buying Shape Lawmaking*. New York: Cambridge University Press.

Savage, Sean J. 2012. "The First Hundred Days." In *The Obama Presidency: A Preliminary Assessment*, edited by Robert P. Watson, Jack Covarrubias, Tom Landsford, and Douglas M. Brattebo, 85–98. Albany: SUNY Press.

Schlesinger, Arthur M., Jr. 1958. *The Age of Roosevelt: The Coming of the New Deal*. Boston: Houghton Mifflin.

——. 1959. *The Coming of the New Deal*. Boston: Houghton Mifflin.

Seligman, Lester G. 1956. "Presidential Leadership: The Inner Circle and Institutionalization." *Journal of Politics* 18 (3): 410–426.

Sellers, Patrick J., and Laura M. Denton. 2006. "Presidential Visits and Midterm Senate Elections." *Presidential Studies Quarterly* 36 (3): 410–432.

Shapiro, Robert Y. 2011. "Public Opinion and American Democracy." *Public Opinion Quarterly* 75 (5): 982–1017.

Shapiro, Robert Y., Martha Joynt Kumar, and Lawrence R. Jacobs. 2000. *Presidential Power: Forging the Presidency for the Twenty-First Century*. New York: Columbia University Press.

Shull, Steven A., ed. 1991. *The Two Presidencies: A Quarter Century Assessment*. Chicago, IL: Nelson-Hall.

——. 2000. *Presidential–Congressional Relations: Policy and Time Approaches*. Ann Arbor: University of Michigan Press.

Shull, Steven A., and Lance T. LeLoup. 1981. "Reassessing the Reassessment: Comment on Sigelman's Note on the "Two Presidencies" Thesis." *Journal of Politics* 43 (2): 563–564.

Shull, Steven A., and Thomas C. Shaw. 2004. "Determinants of Presidential Position Taking in Congress, 1949–1995." *Social Science Journal* 41 (4): 587–604.

Shull, Steven A., and James M. Vanderleeuw. 1987. "What Do Key Votes Measure?" *Legislative Studies Quarterly* 12 (4): 573–582.

Sigelman, Lee. 1979. "A Reassessment of the Two Presidencies Thesis." *Journal of Politics* 41 (4): 1195–1205.

Simon, Herbert A. 1953. "Notes on the Observation and Measurement of Political Power." *Journal of Politics* 15 (4): 500–516.

Sinclair, Barbara. 2014. *Party Wars: Polarization and the Politics of National Policy Making*. Norman: University of Oklahoma Press.

Skocpol, Theda. 1997. *Boomerang: Health Care Reform and the Turn Against Government*. New York: W. W. Norton.

Skocpol, Theda, and Vanessa Williamson. 2012. *The Tea Party and the Remaking of Republican Conservatism*. New York: Oxford University Press.

Skowronek, Stephen. 1982. *Building a New American State: The Expansion of National Administrative Capacities, 1877–1920*. New York: Cambridge University Press.

———. 1993. *The Politics Presidents Make: Leadership from John Adams to Bill Clinton*. Cambridge, MA: Harvard University Press.

Sloan, John W. 1996. "Meeting the Leadership Challenges of the Modern Presidency: The Political Skills and Leadership of Ronald Reagan." *Presidential Studies Quarterly* 26 (3): 795–804.

Smith, Jean Edward. 2008. *FDR*. New York: Random House.

Sorauf, Frank J. 1959. "Patronage and Party." *Midwest Journal of Political Science* 3 (2): 115–126.

Soroka, Stuart, and Christopher Wlezien. 2010. *Degrees of Democracy: Politics, Public Opinion, and Policy*. New York: Cambridge University Press.

Spitzer, Robert J. 1988. *The Presidential Veto: Touchstone of the American Presidency*. Albany: SUNY Press.

Stanley, Harold W., and Richard G. Niemi. 2015. *Vital Statistics on American Politics 2015–2016*. Washington, DC: CQ Press.

Steger, Wayne P. 2005. "The President's Legislative Program: An Issue of Sincere Versus Strategic Behavior." *Politics and Policy* 33 (2): 312–329.

Stimson, James A. 1999. *Public Opinion in America: Moods, Cycles, and Swings*. 2nd ed. Boulder, CO: Westview.

Stinebrickner, Bruce. 2015. "Robert A. Dahl and the Essentials of Modern Political Analysis: Politics, Influence, Power, and Polyarchy." *Journal of Political Power* 8 (2): 189–207.

Sullivan, Terry. 1988. "Headcounts, Expectations, and Presidential Coalitions in Congress." *American Journal of Political Science* 32 (3): 567–589.

———. 1990a. "Bargaining with the President: A Simple Game and New Evidence." *American Political Science Review* 84 (4): 1167–1195.

———. 1990b. "Explaining Why Presidents Count: Signaling and Information." *Journal of Politics* 52 (3): 939–962.

———. 1991. "The Bank Account Presidency: A New Measure and Evidence on the Temporal Path of Presidential Influence." *American Journal of Political Science* 35 (3): 686–723.

Sullivan, Terry, and Scott de Marchi. 2011. "Congressional Bargaining in Presidential Time: Give and Take, Anticipation, and the Constitutional Rationalization of Dead Ducks." *Journal of Politics* 73 (3): 748–763.

Swift, Elaine K., Robert G. Brookshire, David T. Canon, Evelyn C. Fink, John R. Hibbing, Brian D. Humes, Michael J. Malbin, and Kenneth C. Martis. 2001. *Database of [United States] Congressional Historica Statistics, 1789–1989*. ICPSR 3371. Ann Arbor: Inter-university Consortium for Political and Social Research, University of Michigan.

Taylor, Andrew J. 2014. "Bill Passage Speed in the US House: A Test of a Vote Buying Model of the Legislative Process." *The Journal of Legislative Studies* 20 (3): 285–304.

Teodoro, Manuel P., and Jon R. Bond. 2017. "Presidents, Baseball, and Wins Above Expectations: What Can Sabermetrics Tell Us About Presidential Success?: Why Ronald Reagan Is Like Bobby Cox and Lyndon Johnson Is Like Joe Torre." *PS: Political Science and Politics* 50 (2): 339–346.

Theriault, Sean, Patrick Hickey, and Abby Blass. 2011. "Roll-Call Votes." In *The Oxford Handbook of the American Congress*, edited by Frances E. Lee and Eric Schickler, 575–597. New York: Oxford University Press.

Tilly, Charles. 1975. *The Formation of National States in Western Europe*. Princeton, NJ: Princeton University Press.

Treier, Shawn. 2010. "Where Does the President Stand? Measuring Presidential Ideology." *Political Analysis* 18 (1): 124–136.

Trumbore, Peter F., and David A. Dulio. 2013. "Running on Foreign Policy? Examining the Role of Foreign Policy Issues in the 2000, 2002, and 2004 Congressional Campaigns." *Foreign Policy Analysis* 9 (3): 267–286.

Tulis, Jeffrey. 1987. *The Rhetorical Presidency*. Princeton, NJ: Princeton University Press.

Uslaner, Eric M. 1998. "Let the Chits Fall Where They May? Executive and Constituency Influences on Congressional Voting on NAFTA." *Legislative Studies Quarterly* 23 (3): 347–371.

Vaughn, Justin S., and Jennifer R. Mercieca, eds. 2014. *The Rhetoric of Heroic Expectations: Establishing the Obama Presidency*. College Station: Texas A&M University Press.

Vazzano, Frank P. 1993. "President Hayes, Congress and the Appropriations Riders Vetoes." *Congress and the Presidency* 20 (1): 25–37.

———. 2006. "Rutherford B. Hayes and the Politics of Discord." *The Historian* 68 (3): 519–540.

Wagner, John. 2017. "President Largely Sidesteps the Bully Pulpit in Pushing Health-Care Bill." *Washington Post* (July 2). https://www.washingtonpost.com/politics/president-largely-sidesteps-the-bully-pulpit-in-pushing-health-care-bill/2017/07/02/4139245a-5c3a-11e7-a9f6-7c3296387341_story.html?utm_term=.9a92140972c6.

Warshaw, Christopher. 2012. "Are Legislators More Responsive to Public Opinion on Salient Issues?" Presented at the annual meeting of the American Political Science Association. http://ssrn.com/abstract=2107282.

Waterman, Richard W., and Kenneth J. Meier. 1998. "Principal–Agent Models: An Expansion?" *Journal of Public Administration Research and Theory* 8 (2): 173–202.

Waterman, Richard W., Hank C. Jenkins-Smith, and Carol L. Silva. 1999. "The Expectations Gap Thesis: Public Attitudes Toward an Incumbent President." *The Journal of Politics* 61 (4): 944–966.

Waterman, Richard W., Carol L. Silva, and Hank Jenkins-Smith. 2014. *The Presidential Expectations Gap: Public Attitudes Concerning the Presidency*. Ann Arbor: University of Michigan Press.

Watson, Richard. 1993. *Presidential Vetoes and Public Policy*. Lawrence: University of Kansas Press.

Wayne, Stephen J. 2009. "Legislative Skills." In *The Oxford Handbook of the American Presidency*, edited by George C. Edwards III and William G. Howell, 311–337. New York: Oxford University Press.

Weaver, R. Kent. 1986. "The Politics of Blame Avoidance." *Journal of Public Policy* 6 (4): 371–398.

West, Stephen G., Jeremy C. Biesanz, and Steven C. Pitts. 2000. "Causal Inference and Generalization in Field Settings: Experimental and Quasi-Experimental Designs." *Handbook of Research Methods in Social and Personality Psychology* 13 (1): 40–84.

Wildavsky, Aaron. 1966. "The Two Presidencies." *Trans-Action* 4 (December): 7–14.

Wilson, Rick K. 1986. "An Empirical Test of Preferences for the Political Pork Barrel: District Level Appropriations for River and Harbor Legislation, 1889–1913." *American Journal of Political Science* 30 (4): 729–754.

Wilson, Woodrow. (1885) 1981. *Congressional Government: A Study in American Politics*. Baltimore: Johns Hopkins University Press.

Wlezien, Christopher. 2005. "On the Salience of Political Issues: The Problem With 'Most Important Problem.'" *Electoral Studies* 24 (4): 555–579.

——. 2017. "Public Opinion and Policy Representation: On Conceptualization, Measurement, and Interpretation." *Policy Studies Journal* 45 (4): 561–582.

Wood, B. Dan. 2009. *The Myth of Presidential Representation*. New York: Cambridge University Press.

Yoo, John. 2007. "Andrew Jackson and Presidential Power." *Charleston Law Review* 2 (1): 521–583.

Zelizer, Julian E. 2015. *The Fierce Urgency of Now: Lyndon Johnson, Congress, and the Battle for the Great Society*. New York: Penguin.

INDEX